WHERE ARE YOU AFRICA?
Church and Society in the Mobile Phone Age

Castor M. Goliama

Langaa Research & Publishing CIG
Mankon, Bamenda

Publisher:
Langaa RPCIG
Langaa Research & Publishing Common Initiative Group
P.O. Box 902 Mankon
Bamenda
North West Region
Cameroon
Langaagrp@gmail.com
www.langaa-rpcig.net

Distributed outside N. America by African Books Collective
orders@africanbookscollective.com
www.africanbookcollective.com

Distributed in N. America by Michigan State University Press
msupress@msu.edu
www.msupress.msu.edu

ISBN: *9956-578-45-2*

© Castor M. Goliama 2011

DISCLAIMER
All views expressed in this publication are those of the author and do not necessarily reflect the views of Langaa RPCIG.

To my parents Michael (1925-2008) and Dafrosa Goliama

Table of Contents

List of Abbreviations.. ix

Introduction... xi
   The Mobile Phone and its Emergent Cultures........................ xii
   Quest for Mobile Phone Theology in Africa............................ xii
   Mobile Cultures, Corruption and the Church in Africa........... xvi
   Chapter Outline... xvii

Chapter One

Media or Social Communication in Pre-Mobile Africa................ 1
   Oral Media.. 1
   Visits... 3
   Meetings and Marketplaces.. 4
   Talking Drums.. 5
   Print and Electronic Media... 6
   Ecumenical and Interreligious Dialogue per Radio-call............ 7
   Gospel Music.. 12
   Political Manipulation of Gospel Music.................................. 15
   Gospel Music and HIV/AIDS... 16
   African Films with Religious Themes..................................... 18
   Hallelujah Films and Ecumenical /
   Interreligious Dialogue.. 19

Concluding Remarks.. 21

Chapter Two

Is the Mobile Phone Liberating Africa?.. 23
   The Mobile Phone as a Transformative Factor........................ 23
   Mobile Phones and Africa's Communication 'Revolution'....... 25
   Mobile Communication "Revolution" and the "Wealth Paradox"... 27
   Mobile Phones and Poverty Alleviation.................................. 30
   Optimistic Signs... 31
   Mobile Phones as Globalisation: Have the Rules Changed?.... 34
   Sacrifices of the Poor at the Altar of Modernity...................... 36
   Mobile Phone Mania.. 39
   Polarisation between the Rich and the Poor............................ 41

Online Beggars and Dependency Syndrome... 42
Feminisation of the Mobile Phone and African Women..................... 44
Amplifying the Voices of Women... 45
Which Mobiles are Suitable for African Women?................................ 47
Engaging Mobiles in Health Issues.. 48
Globalisation of African Traditional Healers....................................... 50
Mobiles and Democratisation of Africa.. 51
"Paparazzi-boom" and Empowerment of Whistleblowers................... 55
Spiritual Undertones of Mobile Communications............................... 57
Will the Rosary Survive?... 60
The Mobile Phone and the Idolatry of Work....................................... 60
Faith Communities and Negotiation of Mobile Technologies............ 61
Negotiation with Telephone by Amish Church.................................... 62
The 'Kosher' Cell-phone in Israel... 63

Concluding Remarks... 65

Chapter Three
Mobile Cultures and Ubuntu Paradigm of Solidarity....................... 71
   Anatomy of Mobile Cultures.. 71
   Ubuntu Philosophy of Life... 73
   Ubuntu-enhancing Mobile Cultures....................................... 73
   Solidarity in Sharing Mobile Handsets.................................. 74
   Crossing Social Divides and Interconnectedness.................. 75
   The Mobile Question "Where are you?"............................... 78
   Virtual versus Face-to-face Communication......................... 80
   Youth-empowering Mobile Cultures...................................... 83
   Subversion of Women Traditional Gender Roles................. 85
   Mobile Reinforcement of Social Integrity............................. 86
   Mutual Empowerment of Migrants and Home Folks.......... 87
   Anti-Ubuntu Mobile Cultures... 88
   When "Absent presence" Overshadows Neighbour.............. 89
   Intrusion of Public Order.. 89
   Serving Two Masters at a Time.. 91
   Youth now "hanging out" Digitally.. 92
   African Women: Digitally confined to the "Kitchen".......... 94
   Mobile Gossip and Intrusion of Private Life......................... 95

Mobile Addiction Tendencies... 96
Mobile Alibis and Denialist Attitude of African Leaders...................... 96
Uncritical Consumption of Mobile-mediated Products.......................... 99
Utilitarian Mobile Working Cultures... 100
Mobile Cultures and the Millstone of Migration................................. 102
"Absent Presence" and the Culture of Blame..................................... 104
Fragility of Ubuntu Solidarity in Current Africa................................. 106

Concluding Remarks... 108

Chapter Four
Mobile Cultures and Social Justice... 111
   Media as "Gifts of God"... 111
   The Concept of Social Justice... 113
   Mobile Cultures and the Demands of Contributive Justice............... 114
   "Digital Divides" and the Demands of Distributive Justice................ 115
   Mobile Work Ethic and Commutative Justice................................ 116
   Demands of Social Justice in Mobile Popular Narratives.................. 118
   Fighting Graft by Mobile Theological Discourses in Tanzania........... 119
   Social Justice as Basic Key to True Peace..................................... 124
   "Domestic Justice" in African Church:
   Charity does not begin Abroad... 126

Concluding Remarks... 127

Chapter Five
Reimagining Church Community in the Mobile Age......................... 131
The Mobile Phone and the Blurring of Religious Frontiers................. 131
Virtual Communications vis-à-vis Ecclesial Community...................... 132
"Do it yourself" Spirituality... 133
"Yes" to Jesus, "No" to the Church... 135
Virtual Internet Christian Communities... 135
High-tech Remote Participation in Worship.................................... 136
Virtual/Face-to-face Communication and Church as God's Family...... 138
Face-to-face Interaction in Ecclesial Communities............................ 141

Face-to-face Ecclesial Communities and Christian Witness................ 142
Face-to-face Ecclesial Communities
versus Dangers of Private Religion... 143
Church Pastors and the Quest for the Apostolate of Presence.................... 143
Mobile Cultures and Border-transcending Churches........................... 144
The Gospel of Prosperity and Church-going in Africa............ 146
Quest for Solid Church Structures in Africa............................ 147
Envisioning Church-less African Christianity........................ 149
Concluding Remarks.. 150

Chapter Six
Mobile Cultures and Pilgrim Status of the Church................... 155
    Mobile Cultures and Pastoral Care of Migrants....................... 155
    Face-to-face Ecclesial Communities and Integration of Migrants............. 158
    Endorsement of Migration and Reverse Flow of Mission.................... 160
    Migrants as Embodiment of the Pilgrim Church...................... 161
    Concluding Remarks.. 163

Chapter Seven
Biblical and Theological Insights into Mobile Cultures.................... 167
    Biblical Insights into Mobile Culture............................... 168
    A "Beep" to the Righteous Heavenly Father.......................... 168
    Psalmists versus African Victims of Corruption..................... 170
    The Passion Narrative of Jesus and Post-independence Africa................ 172
    Mountains for Mobile Technologies versus the
    Mountain of the Lord... 174
    Mountains as Symbol of Radical Transformation in Jesus Christ............... 176
    Quest for "Perpetual Contact" with God................................ 178
    Theological Insights into Mobile Cultures............................ 180
    What has Christianity to do with the Mobile Phone?................ 180
    The Holy Trinity as Paradigm of Human Relationships............ 182
    'Imago Dei' as Paradigm for Crossing Divides in Society.................... 183
    The Incarnation and the Crossing of the Divine-Human Divide............. 187
    The Incarnate Jesus Christ as the Border-crosser par Excellence............... 188
    The Incarnation and Social Mobility.. 190
    The Incarnation and the Quest for Integrative
    Church Communities... 190
    The "Visio Dei": Overcoming Parochialism and Provincialism.............. 191

Concluding Remarks.. 193

Chapter Eight
"Where Are You?" The Mobile Question and
Its Implications in Africa.. 195
    "Where are you?" as God's First Question to Humanity............... 195
    "Where are your?" as Challenge to Respect Human Dignity...........196
    "Where are you?" as a Call to Conversion.................................... 197
    "Where are you?" as Mandate for Environmental Stewardship................ 198
    "Where are you Africa?" and Africa's Enigmatic Christianity................... 200
    Against Compromising the Prophetic Voice.............................. 202

Chapter Nine
Looking towards the Future... 207
    Need for Meaningful Church-State Dialogue.......................... 211
    Dulles' Model of Dialogue with Christian Politicians.................213
    Quest for Listening Leaders... 214

Selected Bibliography... 221

List of Abbreviations

EIA	Ecclesia in Africa
GS	Gaudium et Spes
AMECEA	Association of Member Episcopal Conferences of Eastern Africa
Et al.	Et alii, et aliae, et alia, and others
HIV	Human Immunodeficiency Virus
ITC	International Theological Commission
AIDS	Acquired Immune Deficiency Syndrome
SCC	Small Christian Community
CSDC	Compendium of the Social Doctrine of the Church
TBS	Tanzania Bureau of Standards
ICT	Information and Communication Technologies
EN	Evangelii Nuntiandi

Introduction

The obtrusive spread of mobile technologies in contemporary Africa impacts lives and relationships. African citizens and foreigners coming to Africa testify that they enjoy a sense of social interconnectedness, accessibility and security of perpetual contact with their loved ones, co-workers, and others. At business and professional levels, in family and personal life, the mobile phone speeds the pace and efficiency of performance. Does the mobile culture of perpetual contact then send any message to the people with regard to their availability to God and to fellow human beings whom they are obliged to serve? What does the mobile culture of blurring social borders speak to Christians with respect to shaping relationships within their ecclesial communities, with Christians of other traditions and with non-Christians?

Mobile technologies have so pervasively spread in the African Continent that they have reached even the poorest communities hitherto known as "communications margins". Does this pose any challenge to African government leaders as regards the quest to safeguard the common good and to ensure that resources of their countries likewise benefit all citizens? But, conversely, do African leaders care that poor citizens become poorer on account of their appropriation of the mobile phone?

These are some of the issues we wrangle with in this work, *Where Are You Africa?* The study avers that the current proliferation of mobile phones in Africa constitutes a wake-up call for the Church and the society at large to promote relationships and conditions that are life-affirming to all categories of people. To arrive at this thesis, the subject of mobile proliferation in Africa is interwoven with two other strands, namely: an explosive multireligious landscape and a persistence of rampant corruption. The two features are also salient in the current African scenario.

The work focuses mainly on Tanzania, but it cites also some examples from other parts of Sub-Saharan Africa. And in the final analysis, this study mirrors the situation prevalent in many countries of this part of Africa.

The Mobile Phone and its Emergent Cultures

Telecommunications technology has brought enormous changes in human society. It is worth to recall how the telephone initiated such changes. When the telephone was invented in 1876 it was possible for the first time in history to have a real-time conversational interaction at a distance.[1] Its communication power had then amazed people. Reportedly, many had become awe-struck, while others thought the telephone was mere legerdemain (Katz 2002: 2).

Today, however, the telephone does not seem as mysterious as it was at its first launching in the 19th century. And as far as the developed countries are concerned, landline telephone has become for billions of people in the twenty-first century literally a fixture of everyday life. People in these countries are surprised when the telephone is absent at home or in a certain office, but not by its presence.

The telephone has become even more commonplace with the inception of its latest mobile version and now it has come to occupy a unique place in the history of humanity's development. This evolvement in telecommunications is briefly depicted thus:

> In the history of human imagination the power of real-time interaction oral communication over great distances had been a power so great that even most divine beings were considered incapable of it: Zeus, king of the Greek gods, and the rest of the pantheon, had to rely on messenger-boy Mercury. Today a good many messenger boys have their own mobile phones (Katz 2002: 2).

Contemporary Africa witnesses a tremendous and unprecedented development in telecommunications subsequent to the pervasive proliferation of mobile telephony. Much research and a plethora of books and articles dealing with the impact of the mobile phone in Africa have been published. A work published by Langaa: Mobile Phones: The New Talking Drums of Everyday Africa (de Bruijn et al.eds.2009) is one of the most outstanding publications that explore whether and how the social appropriation of the mobile phone in Africa alters the society.

Many of these publications have reiterated the fact that the pervasive penetration of the mobile phone in Africa has reached even the remotest corners of the continent, which traditionally have been known as "communication margins". As a result of this, the mobile phone has been overwhelmingly extolled as a social communication device that spearheads communication "revolution" in the Continent.

Apart from facilitating social communications, the mobile phone is optimistically cherished by many as a device that will help induce real positive changes in other sectors, including economy, education, women empowerment, health and democracy. Notably, these areas which constitute an integral part of human liberation are particularly underdeveloped in Africa.

Analysing the various mobile cultures uncovers many realities that may not be immediately obvious to most mobile providers and policy-makers. For example, it becomes evident in the analysis that in almost every aspect in which the mobile phone is positively appraised as an instrument of liberation and empowerment of the people, it is found to be enslaving at the same time. While some women, for instance, claim that they do their business better because they own mobile phones, others complain that mobile phones serve to perpetuate patriarchal gender roles that subjugate them.

This may lead us to deduce that the mobile phone in Africa is a device that can both promote people and conversely demote them; it can hire them, but also fire them. This in effect, portrays the great ambivalence embedded in mobile cultures and warns us against any generalisations when discussing the impact of this mobile technology.

Quest for Mobile Phone Theology in Africa

Theological discourses on the impact of the mobile phone in Africa are conspicuously missing. This perhaps validates the widely held view that theology in Africa is a marginalized discipline. However, a theological vision of any medium of social communications offers the possibility for that medium to become a tool that affords people's openness to God (Ecclesia in Africa, no.1). Thus, it is imperative to cast a theological view on the emergent mobile cultures in Africa. By viewing mobile cultures from a theological perspective, I underline the fact that the benefits of the mobile phone in Africa can be more comprehensive and go beyond mere anthropological aspects of life.

This theological aspect is the focal point of this book. It attempts to bridge the seemingly yawning theological vacuum. It ventures to investigate on the theological engagement of ordinary people with the mobile phone. It also proposes how the mobile phone can further be employed theologically as a tool for holistic liberation of Africans in their contemporary life situation. And subsequently, the book invites more researches on this subject.

By embarking in such a theological quest, moreover, the book seeks to locate the niche of the current explosion of African Christianity. The contemporary religious landscape in Africa depicts a situation of booming churches and mosques in their myriad forms, and an intensification of religious revivalism in both Christianity and Islam (Chesworth 2007: 125f). Being the major monotheistic belief systems in the continent, the two religions have become as competitive as multinational companies and are torn in an unprecedented scramble for the African spiritual market.

African Religion (AR), nevertheless, has not receded into the background as some may be taken to believe. Rather, it continues to maintain a strong foothold in African societies. Its influence is felt among believers in both Christianity and Islam where some syncretise its elements, clandestinely albeit. It is true, however, that AR is increasingly undermined by both Christianity and Islam.

As far as Christianity is concerned, several prominent features accompany its current explosion in Africa. For our purposes we shall mention two of them, namely, the growth of Bible readership and the increasing number of Christian pastors who assume high political positions in African governments. With regard to the Bible, it is notable that among African Christians the Bible occupies a central position in their life of faith and it is widely read. In their view the Bible is not just a collection of inspired Books that reflect the spirit of their authors or speakers (LenkaBula 2008: 294). On the contrary, the biblical text as well as the object of the Bible itself, are believed to have a spiritual power and hence can effectively be used to address their daily needs, problems and concerns, much in the same way their pre-Christian African Religions did. Thus, the Bible has the power to combat evil and sickness, and on this regard, it is cherished as a mighty symbol that can overwhelm all fetishes and pagan amulets, and it can be a tool for divination that replaces the arsenal of traditional oracles (Jenkins 2006: 35).

Many African Muslims, especially scholars, read the Bible too, since they need it particularly in their public preaching which privileges comparative religious approaches. This is clearly epitomised in open-air Christian-Muslim debates that often take place in city squares.

In the context of such a religious topography where the Bible occupies a central position in the daily lives of the people, a biblical and theological infusion in the analysis of culture (including mobile cultures) is quite plausible.

Another phenomenon to which this work draws attention is the increasing rate of African Christian pastors, particularly of the Pentecostal or charismatic traditions, who as partisans assume political roles in high government echelons. Whether these pastor-turned politicians will succeed to address the problem of corruption from within the political systems is something we wait to see.

It is this complex religious landscape that has contributed towards making this study a theological quest. The complex multireligious context which we experience in Africa calls for a critical analysis of the role of mobile technologies in shaping mutual relationships among believers of the different belief systems and traditions.

The quest is resonant with the mind of the Church in Africa which urges the promotion of both ecumenical and interreligious dialogue as well as the engagement of social communication media in evangelisation. For example, both the First and the Second African Synods of bishops held in Rome in 1994 and 2009 respectively, expressed the need for dioceses and religious institutions in Africa to employ old as well as modern media forms of social communications for evangelisation. And, although modern media have been increasingly used in evangelisation, researches on the theological import of the media of social communications in Africa are, nonetheless, still needed.

Mobile Cultures, Corruption and the Church in Africa

In order to resolve the conundrum, thus far unanswered, of lack of sustainable economic development despite the availability of rich natural and human resources, there are some aspects that ought to be learned or unlearned in Africa. Or in the language of mobile cultures which I propose in this study, Africa needs to cross many divides. And corruption is one of the major hurdles to be crossed. In fact the Second Special Assembly for Africa of the Synod of Bishops in 2009 expressed the same concern ("Courage! Get on your Feet, Continent of Africa", no.4 & 5). Scholars and commentators of African affairs also express their concern about the harm done by corruption in Africa. Robert Calderisi for instance, points out that Africans keep on blaming foreign agents for their difficulties, instead of acknowledging the deleterious impact of corrupt government systems that flourish within their own borders.[2]

A cell-phone ecclesiology that envisages the incorporation of mobile virtues into the life and praxis of the Church is hoped to challenge church communities to spearhead a dialogue with other stakeholders geared towards combating corruption and other malpractices that relegate most Africans into a perpetual state of misery.

What bolsters the assumption that the mobile phone can serve this ecclesiological task is the power of the mobile phone that produces manifold shaping effects, including new ways of relating among people. It is this power that has engendered some scholars to describe the mobile phone as a mind- and society- altering technology (Katz 2002:2). Its constitutive elements are made manifest when mobile users communicate, and they include the blurring of borders among various categories of people, interconnectedness or networking of people, accessibility and perpetual contact, a listening attitude among communication partners, and also on the part of those who are fond of eavesdropping. Moreover, the frequent question "where are you?" asked by mobile users implies that today people inquire more about other persons' location. Again, the mobile phone promotes dialogue among people even those who are unfamiliar to one another.

These elements constitute the power of the mobile phone which provides the point of departure for the construction of what we may call a Cell-phone Ecclesiology in Africa. Consequently, while reinforcing new approaches to human relationships, such elements of mobile cultures challenge those socially constructed divides that have traditionally dominated in societies and kept people apart.

Among the most common socially erected borders, as far as Africa is concerned, gravitate around the vices of tribalism, racism, gender-based discrimination of women, polarisation between the 'haves' and the 'have-nots', mistreatment of migrants and refugees, marginalisation of people with physical disability, religious bigotry, and the like.

Set against the backdrop of the Catholic social teaching, such an ecclesiology will seek to transform those dimensions of society that tend to diminish people's relationships with God, others, the environment, and themselves. Instead, it will promote those factors that enhance these relationships (Groody 2009: 93).

And from an ecclesiological point of view, this study is intended to articulate the fact that when these values of mobile cultures are deployed in the church for evangelization, it will be capable of responding better to its call and mission as an agent of God's Kingdom. And the Church will be more relevant to the current African landscape characterised by multi-religiosity and a host of life-afflicting challenges as mentioned previously.

Besides, the majority of African Christians are young people and the majority of mobile phone users are young people too. As such, a Cell-phone Ecclesiology is envisaged to help young people find their proper place in the Church and cultivate a sense of belonging to church communities.

As a theological work, furthermore, this study interprets mobile phone cultures in the light of the Bible and Christian mysteries. Admittedly, the virtues of mobile communication as explicated in the various chapters of this book can by themselves be incorporated into church praxis and have a tremendous benefit to ecclesial communities because they promote love and other positive human relationships. However, this work posits a biblical and theological transformation of the same mobile communication virtues in order to emphasise that it is not these values that ultimately constitute the measure of the Church in its life and praxis. The measure, instead, are the divine mysteries.

Such a biblical and theological infusion is of paramount importance in this work because it helps to strengthen a religious appeal in the quest for justice. As the section on the study case in Tanzania will demonstrate, appeals for God's intervention in difficult situations are often predominant in the discourses of poor people. And I contend that for many Africans, it is religion that largely accounts for their resilience in their confrontation with adversity in their daily lives. This explains why despite (or in spite of?) their abject poverty, people fill the churches and mosques, and from there they hope to obtain their solace. Hence, religion serves as a coping mechanism in their difficult socio-economic situations. So I don't think the resilience of Africans is merely on account of 'the simple human instinct for survival' as Calderisi claims (Calderisi 207: 230).

Chapter Outline

The chapters contained in this book are outlined as follows: Chapter One makes a cursory survey on the media means of social communications which were employed in Africa before the introduction of the mobile phone. It unveils the strengths and weaknesses of these social media and how some of them have been effectively employed in evangelization.

Chapter Two addresses the question whether the mobile phone is liberating Africa. The chapter establishes first of all, that for the majority of average Africans, particularly those living in rural areas, the cell-phone has been their first phone they have ever come to own in life. For this reason, it has become a novelty, a status symbol and an instrument of empowerment. The chapter then indicates how the people in Africa after appropriating the mobile phone are optimistic about improving their lives in terms of telecommunications, income generation and management of business, security, empowerment of women, and in health as well as politics. This chapter suggests that the wind of change currently blowing across Africa subsequent to the global connectivity, fluidities and flexibilities influenced by mobile communications can be read as a sign that Africa is not condemned to a state of primitivism and stagnation, but that change for improving the lives of the people is possible. However, this chapter exposes the ambivalence of mobile cultures. It points out that some elements of mobile cultures are liberating while others are enslaving.

The ambivalence of mobile cultures is evident as well in Chapter Three which identifies mobile cultures that foster the African Ubuntu philosophy of life and those that diminish it. We notice here the discrepancy between the tendency of mobile phone descriptors and the real experience of mobile consumers. The former tend to highlight only the positive side of the mobile phone and appraise it as a device that is liberating, freeing, helpful, and beneficial to the society and so on.

Mobile consumers themselves, nonetheless, may discover the risks and yet continue uncritically to subscribe to the mobile phone and its pertinent cultures. Thus, this chapter underlines the need to embrace mobile cultures cautiously and wisely. Moreover, it invites African societies, especially churches and other religious faith communities, to spearhead a hermeneutics of suspicion with regard to the proliferation of mobile cultures. It suggests, in turn, that should such cultures portend any elements inimical to Ubuntu solidarity, then a dialogue should be held with mobile phone providers and policy-makers purported to protect the society from harm. In addition, the chapter introduces the theory of virtual and face-to-face communications which is essential in the analysis of human relationships.

Chapter Four assesses mobile cultures in relation to social justice. It indicates that some mobile cultures rehearse some of the socio-economic and political concerns that have been identified in Christian social doctrine over the centuries. A section in this Chapter also demonstrates how ordinary citizens in Tanzania—not being resigned in their daily adversity—challenge their status quo theologically through mobile phone discourses.

Chapter Five discusses the aspect of being a church community in the mobile age. It suggests that some virtues of mobile communications can be of tremendous benefit to the church when incorporated in its theology and praxis.

The discussion about the church of the mobile age is continued in Chapter Six which attempts to demonstrate how mobile cultures, viewed in the light of human migrations, can lead us to understand the theology of the Church as a pilgrim community.

Chapter Seven explores mobile cultures from biblical and theological perspectives. It seeks to establish a metaphorical link between towers and mountains that are used in mobile technologies and the significance of mountains in the Bible. This analogical association leads to the thesis that the mobile technologies mounted on mountains should lead human souls to God and promote healthy relationships among people as did the biblical mountains.

But the chapter engages also a theological infusion in the interpretation of mobile cultures. It proposes that the Christian mysteries of the Trinity, imago Dei, the Incarnation, and the visio Dei can be employed to purify and transform mobile-prompted human relationships since these mysteries constitute the paradigm of all relationships based on love.

In their social implication the doctrinal teachings serve to promote love, unity and solidarity, justice and peace, altruism, respect for human dignity, option for the poor and the marginalised, reconciliation and forgiveness, concern for the common good, responsibility and many other life-affirming aspects. Arguably the perpetration of vices inimical to these values largely accounts for the problems facing Africa.

Chapter eight highlights one of the most frequently asked questions in mobile telecommunications: "Where are you?" It is recalled that this question was God's first question to humanity in the biblical creation story. It is pointed out that, theologically, this question may be applied to any person as a wake-up call to consider his or her relationship with God and others. For African leaders, in addition, this question is proposed here to be a corrective hermeneutic. It is intended to help them realize the situation in which their countries are relegated as a result of malpractices such as corruption, irresponsibility and embezzlement of public funds.

This chapter is followed by general conclusions and suggestions. It is expected that such challenges should contribute to the orthopraxis of African Christians and enhance the performance of African political leaders. Some of the areas in which attention is called for are: the promotion of dialogue, the attitude of listening to the narratives of ordinary people and revival of the African Ubuntu solidarity.

As for the method of the research, apart from library sources, I have used resources from various seminars and workshops that I was privileged to attend in Tanzania, at the Catholic University of Eastern Africa in Nairobi (Kenya), and in Vienna, Austria especially among African immigrants. The research has involved a two-year collection of SMS texts that circulated in Tanzania on special occasions such as anniversaries of national events and particularly when corruption scandals in high government echelons were exposed and spread countrywide.

I am aware, nevertheless, that mobile cultures are kaleidoscopic on account of the fast advancement of mobile technologies. As a result, some of the concerns raised now will probably be a matter of past history by the time of the publication of this book.

Several people supported me in writing this book. I am grateful to my Archbishop, Dr. Norbert W. Mtega of Songea, for availing me with the opportunity to pursue doctoral studies. Were it not for this opportunity, I would not have achieved this milestone. I thank him also for his insightful sharing about the current religious landscape in Tanzania. The collection of some of the mobile texts that bemoan corruption in Tanzania was done by Valentine Chotti Mbawala. I am greatly indebted to him. I thank Father Jordan Nyenyembe for his suggestions and unwavering encouragement in the task of bringing this work to fruition. Thanks are due to John Mbonde, Father Alcuin Nyirenda OSB, Father Nicholaus Rathan OCD, Father Cyril Villareal and Father Richard Kimbwi. Each of them has offered invaluable suggestions that have helped improve the manuscript. I appreciate the interest of Father Dr. Laurenti Magesa, Father Martin Mapunda and Father Clarence Chilewa which gave me moral support to continue with this study.

A few other individuals deserve special mention: Andreas and Edith Wehrstein, and Father Bruno Fess and the family of Peter Klein. I thank them for their unceasing encouragement and solidarity when I discussed with them the idea of writing this book. Last but not least, I appreciate the cooperation of Langaa Publishers that has helped widen the horizon of this work.

Notes

[1] It is said that technically there existed already a kind of telephone, which was the equivalent of two tin cans connected by a taut string. But this is not considered as a distance-spanning real-time conversational communication technology.

[2] Robert Calderisi, the author of the book The Trouble with Africa: Why Foreign Aid isn't working, was World Bank's international spokesperson on Africa from 1997 to 2000 and lived in Ivory Coast and Tanzania. In this book Calderisi labours to underscore what he thinks to be the main reasons behind Sub-Saharan Africa's failure to register sustainable development despite being a beneficiary of much foreign aid in the past forty years. In the first place, Calderisi admits that Africa's harsh environment: its climate, diseases, soils, and insects, and the lack of sufficient natural harbours and rivers navigable from the sea contribute to stunt human progress. But on the other hand, Calderisi lists Africa's rich natural resources as a great potential for economic development. He contends also that Africa's talents both within the continent and abroad, if given the chance to prosper, is another huge potential for the continent's imperative economic renaissance. Yet, Calderisi's thesis is that the major cause for Africa's failure is corruption, irresponsibility, and incompetence of African governments. Calderisi points out that Africans tend to appeal to historical and external factors such as slave trade, colonialism, world economic order and, world monetary organisation to explain the causality of their woes while ignoring the reality around them, namely, the harm done to them by their own African governments.

Chapter One
Media of Social Communications in Pre-Mobile phone Africa

In view of the current situation in which the mobile phone co-ordinates work, business enterprises, and life in general, it becomes puzzling to many in Africa how such activities could be managed in the past without the mobile phone. This chapter attempts to present an overview of the old and new means of social communications that have preceded the pervasive spread of the mobile phone in Africa. Chronologically, some of these media forms are almost concurrent with the mobile phone in the African social communications landscape. The particular salience of the mobile phone consists in that it has spread more rapidly and pervasively in Africa.

The designation "pre-mobile phone Africa" is here intended simply to demarcate the period before the mobile phone penetrated significantly in Africa. Such an overview of the media forms is intended to help us assess their contribution in shaping human relationships and their role in evangelisation in Africa.

The media of social communications that we shall focus on in this chapter are: oral media, visits, meetings and marketplaces, talking drums, print and electronic media in general, the radio-call, Gospel music and Religious films.

Oral Media

The major traditional form of communication and knowledge transmission in African societies has been orality. Ugboajah has used the term *oramedia* to refer to the various oral media. They include proverbs, wise sayings, idioms, riddles, stories, poems, drama, legends, myths, oral history and songs. Walter Ong who has written much on orality and literacy differentiates between "primary orality" and "secondary orality". By the former, he refers to the forms of oral expression in a culture that is totally untouched by any knowledge of writing or print whatsoever. While by the latter, he means 'present-day high-technology culture in which a new form of oral expression is sustained by telephone, radio, television, and other electronic devices that depend for their existence and functioning on writing and print'(Ong 1982:11). With regard to "primary orality" Ong notes that, they learn by apprenticeship—hunting with experienced hunters, for example—by discipleship, which is a kind of apprenticeship, by listening, by repeating what they hear, by mastering proverbs and ways of combining and recombining them, by assimilating other formulary materials, by participation in a kind of corporate retrospection—not by study in the strict sense (Ong 1982: 9).

He, however, points out that oral cultures encourage fluency, fulsomeness, volubility, conservation or repetition of conceptualized knowledge as well as interaction with contemporary audience. Oral cultures are close to human life-world as they are normally not divorced from human or quasi-human activity (Ong 1982: 40ff). The people in such cultures learn a great deal and possess and practise great wisdom.

A further strength of oral cultures for Ong consists in that they 'produce powerful and beautiful verbal performances of high artistic and human worth, which are no longer even possible once writing has taken possession of the psyche' (Ong 1982: 14). Ong contends, nevertheless, that without writing human consciousness can neither achieve its fuller potentials nor produce other beautiful and powerful creations. Another obvious liability of orally transmitted knowledge is that it may be easily lost in the course of time or some words may lose their original referential meanings.

However, oral expressions such as proverbs, riddles and other traditional media forms are not used simply to store knowledge, rather they are often used in order to stir people to action. An utterance of a proverb or a riddle, for example, may sometimes be meant as a challenge to hearers to engage in verbal or intellectual combat.

Thus, despite their evident liability when compared with literacy, oramedia continue to play a significant role in African social communications. In much of the African continent the shift from orality to literacy came mostly with Christianity (Jenkins 2006: 22). But as Ugboajah has pointed out, oramedia in Africa were the structure form which provided the basis for "mass communication" and that pioneer missionaries in Africa took advantage of them for their missionary work (Ugboajah 1985:23).

It is significant to note that the various oral expressions reveal a rich source of African religious spirituality and philosophy and constitute the point of departure for constructing a theology of enculturation. Theologian Joseph Healey, for example, constructs such a theology by reflecting African proverbs in catechetical, liturgical and ritual contexts (Healey 1999).

Visits

Africans prefer to visit persons and places physically. The freedom of mobility for them is a person's power and an important aspect in consolidating relationships. Notably, mutual visits especially in rural areas have been mostly accomplished by walking to a place, since transport systems are still underdeveloped. Sometimes one walked long distances in order to visit a relative or a friend while knowing only too well that the host might not be at home.

If death occurs in the family, for example, and relatives in distant villages need to be informed, a young man who is a good runner is charged to deliver the message to them. In some communities, such as among the Ngoni people of Songea, Tanzania, an elder of the extended family would emphasise the immediacy of the message by spitting saliva on a leaf blade. The young man would then be instructed to return from his errand before the saliva dried up. If he managed to run and beat the deadline then this was a proof of his prowess and trustworthiness. Such customs contribute to the moulding of marathoners in some parts of Africa since they foster the spirit of striving and other qualities of sportsmanship.

Going to places physically had also dominated the sphere of business transactions. Rural farmers, for example, had to visit the market in order to know the current crop prices and hence determine whether to sell their crops at the time or not. Likewise, communication between big city-dwellers and their families and relatives living in remote rural areas upcountry by far required mutual visits since fixed telephone infrastructure was generally bad and posts services were largely inefficient. Letters would hardly reach their destinations or they would be long overdue. Thus, going to a place physically remained the surest way of social communication.

In relation to the pastoral work of the church the story was similar. Christians from remote outstations would travel for hours to meet their parish-priest for urgent sick calls or other pastoral matters. It would happen quite often that he was not found at the presbytery. Moreover, the co-ordination of many pastoral programmes required a face-to-face encounter. This often resulted into unnecessary delays.

Since the problem of underdeveloped infrastructures still persists in many parts of Africa, the practice of walking long distances in order to accomplish important activities continues. As an official of MIVA-Austria[1] had once argued when stressing the need to promote mobility in poor countries: 'how many people in Africa, for example, are travelling only on foot throughout their lives, running over distances that are inconceivable to us? All these people, considered from our point of view, suffer in their lives from lack of mobility.'[2] It is quite logical, therefore, that when the mobile phone came to be introduced under such circumstances it was positively appraised as a device that economises time and energy since it helps many people reduce the strain of unnecessarily travelling and walking long distances.

Meetings and Marketplaces

Meetings and marketplaces too constituted important channels of communication in Africa. One characteristic of these traditional media is that they are interactive in nature and thus they offer avenues for immediate feedback. This, consequently, serves to create a space for communicators to seek on-the-spot clarification of issues. Public and private meetings of various kinds are principal channels for the expression of the interaction of the groups, subgroups and personalities that make them up. It is at meetings that people present their group interest and express their opinion and feelings, be it of joy or sorrow. Thus meetings are important avenues for popular participation in decision-making in a given community.

African marketplaces, as Nigerian author Uchendu notes, constitute important social centres with economic and noneconomic functions. They are important venues where news and gossips, ceremonials and parades take place. At marketplaces people meet to accomplish various social issues such as arranging marriages, negotiating a divorce, collecting one's debt, paying or collecting one's contribution, and having a drink with one's age mates, friends and in-laws (Uchendu 1965: 27f).

Ugboajah had similarly argued that marketplaces in Africa, in themselves, are veritable communication forums. They serve as natural infrastructure of news dissemination and exchange of opinions and rumours and they are important for the purpose of agitation. They are diffusion forums for important social interaction rather than just places where people go to buy or sell. From marketplaces, moreover, vogues are copied. For example, many young people learn from their fellow vendors and auctioneers the art of bargaining as well as cheating in business deals. Serious social matters are censured at marketplace in some communities. Cases of incest, for instance, are censured in some villages in the eastern part of Nigeria by parading the offender in the marketplace (Ugboajah 1985: 169).

Perhaps it is at marketplaces more than any other public place that one frequently encounters an exchange of abusive language and blows especially among young people. So too, other unbecoming attitudes such as indecent approaches to women and execution of "mob justice" on suspects of various offences such as pick pocketing or shoplifting are common scenes at market places.

On account of the tremendous amount of interaction they generate, today African marketplaces have become one of the most preferred venues of public religious preaching and interreligious exchanges, particularly between Christians and Muslims. For many Pentecostal and charismatic preachers, for example, marketplaces have become their *areopaghi*. Such face-to-face interreligious encounters at marketplaces are sometimes informative and edifying, but at times they become explosive and dangerous.

Talking Drums

Talking drums have been another mode of social communications in many parts of Africa since time immemorial. They are in vogue in countries such as Ghana, Nigeria, Congo DR and in some parts of East Africa. Talking drums communicate message among people who can decipher the codes that are typical to the sound of the drums. It is said that the ability to change the drum's pitch is analogous to the language tonality of some African languages. Listening to the talking drum one can identify whether it signifies good news or bad news, whether it summons people to come to an important event or other message.

The *adowa* music of Ghana, as Ugboajah points out, is an excellent example of this type of oramedia. The music is performed by organized female choruses, its songs and dance express feelings about death, sympathy for bereavement and achievements of past chiefs and elders. Through the drum language of the *atumpan* drummer texts are communicated. The drummer in following the speech tones and duration of the Twi Language (one of the languages in Ghana) is said to be capable of drumming poems, proverbs, and comments of sympathy, welcome, and other instructions to dancers (Ugboajah 1985:170).

Print and Electronic Media

Print media that are commonly in use in Africa include books, newspapers, magazines, newsletters, brochures, business cards, flyers, printed materials hung on billboards or glued on walls or trees by the roadside as well as letters. Even after the mobile phone has undergone a wide penetration, print media are still predominant in African social communications landscape. And many churches still make their pastoral co-ordination mainly by print media.

Electronic media technologies such as transistor radio, radio-call, computers, internet, email, websites, television, cable television, fixed telephones, audio and visual CDs and DVDs and film, have increasingly pervaded Africa's social communications scene. Some churches such as the Pentecostal and Charismatic denominations have particularly privileged the use of radio, television and electronic musical instruments for evangelisation. These churches had emerged later in the history of African Christianity, yet they had started to employ modern means of mass communications much earlier than the older or missionary churches. Ogbu Kalu notes that, 'while missionaries concentrated on oral communication, education, and charitable institutions, Evangelicals exploited magazines, tracts, and radio because of their mass exposure, simultaneous coverage, and penetrative power' (Kalu 2008: 106). Ties existing between African Pentecostals and their American counterparts played part in making Evangelicals adopt the modern media earlier.

Fixed landline phones have constituted the main type of telecommunication before the penetration of the mobile phone. These phones, however, had their liabilities. First, apart from being the preserve of urban people and discriminating against the majority of rural people, they were provided by monopoly providers and were not well resourced or energetic about connecting customers. Waiting lists for new subscribers were long and it could take many years till one got connected. Secondly, the system provided loopholes for corruption, since some telephone officers were accustomed to requiring illicit money to connect new subscribers and helped unfaithful business people to waiver their telephone bills. Many customers, including churches, had sometimes to foot high telephone bills for calls they had not made.

We can see therefore that before the mobile phone came to dominate the social communications field in Africa, the continent had various forms of social communication media, but it has been increasingly adopting more modern and more sophisticated forms. This has meant an improvement in social communications in the larger part of the continent.

From a religious and pastoral point of view, the more the varieties of media sources in Africa have become available, the more the possibilities to employ various media forms as instruments for evangelisation have been presented in the continent. The foreseen benefits of such a shift in social communications landscape include the availability of more efficient ways of communicating the Gospel. The Good News can now be spread to wider audiences including those living far from places of worship, those with busy schedules, and those for various reasons such as age, sickness and physical disability are hindered from attending church liturgies.

Again, these media help in the provision of social communications among people, which are essential for dialogue and for the building up of ecclesial community. The media forms serve to amplify the critical prophetic voice of the Church amid life-diminishing constructions in society, and so on. All these benefits indicate, as some have put it, that 'each form of media provides the Church with new language.' (Kalu 2008:107).

Generally, however, financial constraints, lack of electricity and technical experts, *inter alia,* impede many churches in Africa from employing the modern means of mass communications in their work of evangelisation.

Ecumenical and Interreligious Dialogue per Radio-call

The radio-call has played a particularly significant role in some parts of Africa. Hence, I find it worthwhile to describe it here in some more details with particular examples from Tanzania. The radio-call in Tanzania has been extensively used by churches such as the Catholic Church, Anglican Church, Lutheran Church and Moravian Church. Some Catholic dioceses and their institutions relied heavily on radio-calls for internal communications and for linking with the outside world, including their missionary partners in other continents such as Europe. Radio-callers were lay people, or religious sisters and brothers, or pastors and priests.

The strengths of the radio-call as compared to the traditional radio consist in that it is more personal and capable of sustaining live person-to-person communications. And one of its weaknesses is lack of spontaneity since communication hours between callers have to be pre-arranged. Moreover, since fewer people had radio-call receivers as compared to transistor radios, this constituted another liability of the radio-call, namely, its catchment area was much smaller than that of the traditional radio. Notwithstanding these liabilities, radio-calls, in the absence of telecommunications services in the country, have offered a wonderful service particularly in rural areas.

Notably, however, apart from facilitating social communications, the radio-call fostered pastoral coordination, mutual relationships among various pastoral agents as well as ecumenical and interreligious dialogue. Within local dioceses radio-calls served to co-ordinate pastoral activities by linking different parishes and church institutions with their respective administrative centres and among themselves. Radio-call services were provided gratis even to the local people surrounding the parishes or church institutions.

The people needed radio-call services to pass information to their relatives and friends especially in events related to sacramental celebrations such as Baptism, First Holy Communion, Confirmation, sacerdotal Ordination and Marriage. So too information about church functions such as Profession of Religious vows and various occasions of jubilees of institutions and individual clergy, religious and lay people would be often communicated to distant relatives per radio-call.

Similarly, information about ordinary social events like interviews for entrants into private schools and technical colleges, arrangements for sports and festival events among schools and various villages would as well be exchanged via radio-call communications. The radio-call was indeed a very convenient communication device in the event of sickness, death, funeral arrangements and similar sorrowful situations.

Consequently, such a broad spectrum of radio-call services portrayed that parishes and church institutions were veritable centres of communication for the people who were in need of exchanging messages of joy and sorrow. This partly contributed to make the Church seem relevant to the poor rural people who otherwise resided in communication margins of their country.

Again, radio-calls linked members of different dioceses, and hence created room for mutual relationships and exchange of pastoral experiences. In the frequency assigned to the Catholic Church, radio-call hours were dominated by exchanges of messages between different centres of Catholic dioceses across the country. A good example of inter-diocesan networking per radio-call was exhibited in the eight dioceses that form the Metropolitan of Songea in Southern Tanzania, namely, Iringa Diocese, Lindi Diocese, Mbeya Diocese, Mbinga Diocese, Mtwara Diocese, Njombe Diocese, Tunduru-Masasi Diocese and the Archdiocese of Songea. Women and men religious congregations, seminaries, catechetical centres, hospitals and other church institutions within these dioceses also capitalised on the radio-call in coordinating their activities. Hence, the radio-call has significantly facilitated the sustenance of relationships among members of these dioceses. Most of these dioceses share a common history of being evangelised by pioneer missionaries from the Benedictine congregation of St. Ottilien, Germany. But apart from facilitating communication networking among the southern zone dioceses, the radio-call also linked these dioceses with other dioceses in the entire country and beyond.

The nature of messages exchanged ranged from regular official information to occasional news of joy and sorrow, and the sharing of pastoral experience as well as humour. Hence, radio-call hours were not merely tense moments dominated by serious exchange of messages, rather they were occasions of recreation for both radio-call attendants and their respective community members.

Due to frequent mutual communications radio-callers from one diocese could eventually become acquainted to their counterparts in distant dioceses, though they might not have met face-to-face. In my view, no other electronic media in Southern Tanzania for instance, has facilitated as effectively a real-time and person-to-person communication among various groups of agents of evangelisation as the radio-call.

Moreover, the churches in Tanzania had radio-call frequencies that were jointly accessible to various Christian institutions. This enabled mutual exchange of information among members of the various churches. For example, the Catholic Archdiocese of Songea and its institutions had frequent radio-call exchanges with the Anglican Diocese of Ruvuma which is located in the same political Region of Ruvuma.

In the interchurch radio-call exchanges it was the daily needs of the ordinary people that mostly dominated rather than typically church matters. Through the frequent mutual communications, the radio-call attendants and their communities came to develop good relationships, mutual assistance and trust. Significantly, it was clear that even where theologians may not have initiated any serious ecumenical dialogues, the ecumenical relationships built via radio-call exchanges filled this gap.

There was a similar experience with regard to the role of the radio-call in interreligious dialogue, particularly between Christianity and Islam. A good example was witnessed in the parishes of the Archdiocese of Songea such as Chengena, Kitanda, Ligera, Mkongo and Namtumbo that are located among predominantly Muslim populations. Parish radio-calls provided free services to all villagers surrounding these parishes irrespective of their creed. As such, it became possible even for Muslim neighbours to enjoy such services. Being located in a Ruvuma Region which is one of the 'communication margins' in Tanzania, these rural communities found the parish radio-call services tremendously helpful when they needed to pass urgent messages of joy and sorrow to their relatives and friends in far-flung regions.

The parish radio-call in these areas contributed towards fostering mutual Christian-Muslim relationships since it constituted one of the main reasons that brought Muslims to the precincts of the churches. Here Muslims would come into friendly interactions with the parishioners who attended to their services especially catechists, religious sisters and brothers, and priests. Mutual relationships that were fostered by such encounters would later be further strengthened through mutual invitations to respective religious feasts like Eid al-Fitr and Christmas celebrations.

Muslim-Christian relationships in this part of the Archdiocese of Songea are still good. For example, when the archbishop visits these parishes on occasions such as conferring the Sacrament of Confirmation, Muslims usually turn up in numbers with their gifts to salute him. And the bishop has on several occasions assisted in the renovation or construction of mosques in these areas by supplying building materials or cash. Christians and Muslims cooperate in various development activities, they dance together, bury their dead together and coexist peacefully.

This peaceful religious landscape is, nonetheless, occasionally marred by some radical religious preachers from both religions who, having been brainwashed in big cities like Dar es Salaam, come back to their villages and inseminate sentiments of religious bigotry.[3]

What is emphasised here is that the radio-call had contributed significantly towards sustaining interreligious relationships in this area. Scholars of interreligious dialogue refer to this kind of dialogue that is rooted in everyday encounters with people of different religious traditions as a dialogue of life. This is what the radio-call as a medium of social communications has helped these people to celebrate. And the dialogue of life is not an end in itself but it becomes a launching pad for a dialogue of action, which is a 'willingness to work together for justice based on common values' (Gaillardetz 2008:77).

Cardinal Francis Arinze has written elaborately on the quest for the dialogue of life in today's plural world (Arinze 1998: 17). There is a great quest for such a dialogue in Africa today since its religious landscape is becoming more and more plural and people in some African countries are already nursing wounds inflicted upon them as a result of religious intolerance.

Today on account of the pervasive penetration of the mobile phone, however, the parish radio-call is no longer a common denominator since many villagers own mobile phones and the radio-call has eventually become almost outdated. But this implies that the pastoral benefits and the instrumentality of the radio-call as an avenue of ecumenical and interreligious dialogue have now rather nostalgically paled into oblivion.

It is true, as this work will quite often emphasise, that mobile communications blur borders and connect people of various belief systems in a natural way. Yet the radio-call made a difference in being more effective as a tool of dialogue since it enabled many people to sustain a simultaneous, real-time and person-to-person conversation. It often involved a face-to-face communication between attendants and their customers, and above all, it offered free services to all people, thus benefitting the poor regardless of their religious allegiance. All these aspects which are unavailable in mobile-mediated communications had contributed significantly towards fostering ecumenical and interreligious dialogue. Arguably, the mobile phone is in this respect a poor substitute for the radio-call in those rural areas.

Gospel Music

Gospel Music has become one of the most effective media of popular expression in Africa today. Much of the music has been recorded electronically in visual and audiovisual CDs, DVDs and cassettes that make good sales. Gospel singers also perform on special occasions, for example, at popular open-air church gatherings known as "crusades".

The development of Gospel music is traceable along with the emergence and expansion of churches of various traditions in the continent. A series of Christian charismatic revivals had been witnessed in Africa. In East Africa, for example, the so-called East

African Revival had sent ripples across the region during the post-World War II period. It was a charismatic initiative of local African lay believers that started in Uganda and Rwanda. The revival movement came to be known as *Balokole*, in Luganda Language, meaning the "Saved Ones" (Kalu 2008: 94).

In the post-independence period, another cycle of Christian revivalism has emerged and continues to sweep throughout the continent, giving birth to countless numbers of churches and charismatic movements in the Continent. In its earlier phase, the post-independence revival manifested its strong impact for instance, in western and eastern Africa (Nigeria, Kenya, Uganda and Tanzania) in the years 1966-1986 (Kalu 2008: 88).

The ramifications of the post-independence wave of revival have been more far-reaching than those of its antecedent in the post-World War II period. One reason for this is that the euphoria of independence has been dominated by sentiments of decolonisation and the quest for African identity and indigenous expressions of Christianity. This was particularly salient during the early decades of the post-independence period. The general quest for African Christian expressions was reflected as well in Gospel music by composing hymns that corresponded to the African culture.

In general, therefore, Christian revivals have contributed towards shaping the African Gospel music by offering a form of genuine African piety and spirituality. Hence, in Tanzania, for instance, one notices that spiritual songs and church music have maintained a close affinity to the mentality and piety of the East African Revival even in some established churches (Veller 1993:42).

On the part of the Catholic Church, the general euphoria of the early post-independence decades coincided with the reverberations of the Vatican Council II (1962-1965), which spread far and wide in the continent. The Council's liturgical reforms stimulated Africanisation of church liturgies in the local dioceses in Africa. This was exemplified by the introduction of African rites such as the so-called the *Zairean rite*, the *Mass of the Lagunes*, the *Mass of the Savanna*, and others. These rites allowed the domination of African expressions in the liturgy, in terms of such aspects as language, rhythm, and happy participation (Sundkler et al. 2000: 1020).

Churches of Pentecostal and charismatic traditions seem to constitute a significant factor in the growth of Gospel music in Africa. One of the reasons that can be advanced to support this assertion is that these churches privilege the employment of modern mass media in evangelisation. Evidently their Gospel music can be recorded and spread far and wide through the use of these modern mass media.

Significantly, however, the particular salience of Gospel music in contemporary Africa does not consist merely in its role as a medium for spreading the Word of God. But more than that, Gospel music has become a mirror of prevailing socio-economic and political conditions endured by the people in everyday life. When the people languish in austere conditions of poverty and disease, and amid shattered political hopes, they tend to develop a strong yearning for the attainment of the joys of the heavenly glory (Veller 1993: 42). In fact, it is argued that even the flourishing of churches and religious movements in some parts of Africa can partly be attributed to the prevalence of socio-economic scourges experienced by the people (Lindhardt 2009: 44).

Under such difficult situations many spontaneous Gospel songs are improvised contrasting the people's current suffering on earth with the heavenly joys promised by Jesus Christ. A popular Swahili hymn that dominated the Christian waves in Tanzania between 1980s and 1990s, for example, had these words:

Natamani kwenda mbinguni (I am longing to go to heaven)

Njia ya mbinguni nyembamba (the way to heaven is narrow)

Ezra Chitando recounts a similar situation with regard to Gospel music in Zimbabwe. In 1990s, amid deteriorating economic conditions, there rose protest Gospel music as Christian composers released songs that dwelt on economic issues. They protested against such economic ills as the devaluation of the local currency, high inflation, unemployment, retrenchments, and high medical costs.[4] The people also expressed their disillusionment with the political leaders and called for divine intervention.

Political Manipulation of Gospel Music

On account of its popularity Gospel music has sometimes revealed a complex interaction of a malleable nature between religious and political discourses. To cite Zimbabwe again, as Chitando notes, some religious ideas were sometimes manipulated by shrewd politicians to suit their own agenda. The politicians would appropriate church hymns but replace the Christian message contained in them with a political motive. For example, a popular Christian hymn ran:
>I will never cry
>When Jesus is there
>To cry is cowardice.

This hymn was adopted by Mugabe's political Party ZANU PF Women's League, but Jesus' name was substituted by Mugabe's name, and the hymn now ran:
>I will never cry
>When Mr. Mugabe is there
>To cry is cowardice.

The opposition party in Zimbabwe, MDC, likewise, converted religious songs that addressed spiritual and material problems into commentaries on the current condition in the country. A good example was a Methodist choir hymn which ran:
>When the load is heavy
>Call upon Jesus
>He is the good leader.

The politicians changed its words for a political motive and it came to be:

>When the load is heavy
>Call upon the MDC
>They are the good leaders.[5]

A similar political exploitation of the popularity of Gospel music was witnessed in Tanzania's 2010 general election campaigns. Here it was a bit different in that some politicians would invite famous Gospel music singers to compose hymns that favoured their particular party-politics and to perform the songs at the stage along with the election campaigners. Many Christians in the country had expressed resentment over such a political manipulation of Gospel music.

Gospel Music and HIV/AIDS

In the period when there are high death rates attributable to HIV/ AIDS pandemic, many Gospel songs have been composed, which have a preoccupation with death. In Zimbabwe to quote Chitando again, hymns related to funerals convey different messages. Some are intended for the bereaved: to console them, to empower them to face the sting of death with courage, to remind them of the permanent and comforting presence of Jesus and to urge the mourners to take solace in Jesus. Other funeral hymns reaffirm Christian teaching on God's love and forgiveness and the future reunification of the living and the dead. Others, however, are addressed to those who are still living, to warn them against the danger of indulging in mundane affairs while forgetting God and life after death.[6]

In Tanzania, likewise, Gospel singers compose funeral songs that are mostly traceable to specific Christian denominations. But they focus also on creating awareness among the people about the HIV/AIDS pandemic, while other songs contain an invitation to the people to seek refuge in Jesus Christ by repentance and conversion as an antidote against the pandemic. Restituta Kayombo, for example, sings in her mother tongue *Kingoni,* a hymn in which she compares HIV/AIDS to a scary monster known in the mythologies of her people as *Namanjugulu.* This malevolent being *(likoko)* was reputed to be capable of swallowing whole cities with their inhabitants alive. Restituta then implores her listeners to seek refuge in Jesus Christ in order to overcome the lethal effects of this monster.

Leni lindu likoko, likoko wee limala vandu (This is a poisonous foe, it finishes people)

Livakomi viongozi, viongozi wee limalavandu (it has killed leaders, it finishes people)
Livakomi na vababa, wee limalavandu (it has killed fathers, it finishes people)
Livakomi na ve vavana, limalavandu (it has killed mothers, it finishes people)

Jumbalilayi kwa Yesu, kwa Yesu we yati upona (Take refuge in Jesus, you will be cured)
Jumbalilayi kwa Yesu kuna uzima (Take refuge in Jesus, there is life)

Ukimwi mwavalongovangu ... umalavandu (AIDS my brothers and sisters, finishes people)
Tujumbayi kwa Bwana Yesu ...kuna uzima (Let's take refuge in our Lord Jesus Christ, in Him there is life)

Tujumbayi mwavakinamama (Let's go mothers!)
Tujumbayi mwavasikana (Let's go girls!)
Tujumbayi mwavagosi (Let's go men!)

In the context of ordinary people such messages may often prove to be more appealing to the people than long academic speeches full of statistics on HIV/AIDS.

In summary, we can deduce that socio-economic and political conditions in a given society in Africa can be easily diagnosed by consulting its Gospel music, since it has proved to be an effective monitor and commentator of the real life conditions of the people. For leaders who usually care to listen to the discourses of the ordinary people, Gospel music may constitute the barometer of the mood prevailing in the society. Such leaders may find Gospel music to be a great boon for a better performance in their leadership. But, as it is often the case, some authorities tend to turn a deaf ear to the concerns of the people. Even under such circumstances Gospel music 'fills in the bureaucratic vacuum by becoming the "voice of the voiceless"' (Gwekwerere 2009: 353).

African Films with Religious Themes

Films constitute another medium that has occupied a significant position in the social communications landscape before the introduction of the mobile phone in Africa. And it continues to do so even during the mobile phone age. In this section I make a cursory survey on the impact of African films that deal with religious themes. I will base my assessment chiefly on the work of Jolyon Mitchell (Mitchell 2009: 151-155).

Historically films began to be produced in significant numbers by Africans in the 1950s and 1960s. Most of the famous films even among the early productions are said to depict religious practices and beliefs. Some of the films described religious tensions in a particular country as was the case of *Cairo Station* produced by the Egyptian film-maker, Youssef Chahine, in 1958. And others preoccupy themselves with the questioning of the religious traditions of Islam and Christianity. These religions are perceived in these films as being foreign imports to Africa and consequently, inevitably coming in conflict with African traditional cultures.

On account of such an orientation, such films are described by Mitchell as embodying a "decolonisation of the gaze". Examples of such films include: *Ceddo* (the people) produced by the Senegalese film-maker, Sembene Ousmane in 1977. In his film narrative Ousmane critiques what he perceives to be the dark side of religious traditions. Other film-makers, however, have engaged popular religious stories to make a critical reflection on the contemporary political situations in their own particular countries. The Malian film-maker Cheick Oumar Sissoko, for instance, presents cinematically in his production *Genese* of 1999, the biblical story of Jacob, Esau and Hamor found in the Book of Genesis. Sissoko is said to have been attracted by the Book of Genesis (especially chapters 23 to 37) since it belongs to all humanity and is the basis of three big religions, namely, Judaism, Christianity, and Islam. Hence, Sissoko re-interprets cinematically the well-known story of these biblical figures in a less familiar context in order to offer insights into some major challenges facing Africa in general and the 'fratricidal conflict' which his own country Mali had then experienced, in particular.

But in Nigeria and Ghana locally produced African films have gained popularity over films from Hollywood (USA) and Bollywood (India) which hitherto have dominated the screens and shelves of many cinemas and video shops in Africa. The Nigerian film industry, Nollywood, seems to dominate the cinematic scene in many African countries as its films with their religious themes seem to have great appeal even outside Nigeria. These religious films also known as *Hallelujah films* seem to conquer the hearts of many outside the African continent as well. These films are preoccupied with moral dilemmas and a wide range of concerns facing contemporary middle-class Africans; they include violence, religion, witchcraft, prostitution, HIV/AIDS, bribery, corruption as well as economic disparity and hardship (Highet 2009: 18). The films provoke discussions as people watch them on TV, and video player at home, video houses and even in churches.

Hallelujah Films and Ecumenical / Interreligious Dialogue

Hallelujah films feature the way various churches are responding to the problem of moral degeneracy in society (Highet 2009: 18). Apparently, most of these films are produced in the light of Pentecostal evangelism, and are intended to convey the Christian message of the superiority of divine powers over satanic powers. But one notices also the dominant tendency in them to portray the superiority of Pentecostal ministry over that of other Christian traditions, particularly the older mainline churches.

Mitchell gives an example of a Ghanaian film titled *Namisha* in which the portrayal of religious figures indicates clearly the tendency to undermine other Christian traditions. It is seen for example, that whereas ministers from the historic churches are regularly represented as being well intentioned but ultimately ineffectual and marginal to the outcome of a certain story, pastors from Pentecostal or Charismatic churches, on the contrary, are typically portrayed as being dynamic and spiritually powerful. These pastors are often depicted as using the accoutrements of power, such as mobile phones or computers, alongside a large black leather-covered Bible. Frequently, it is they, and not the ministers from mainline churches, who are shown as overcoming or at least helping to overcome the evil forces (Mitchell 2009:154).

Such portrayals often have the negative impact of antagonising Christians of different denominations since people often tend to hold what they watch in films as true. And since reportedly Nollywood films are currently the most watched in Africa, their impact can be far-reaching indeed. In Tanzania for example, a filmmaker translated into Kiswahili Language a Nollywood film with the title *Cross my Sin*, whose scenes clearly purported to undermine the virtue of sacerdotal celibacy practised in the Catholic Church. It provoked quite an uproar among Tanzanian Catholics.

Traditional African religious leaders are also frequently portrayed negatively in many of these films whereby they are said to be 'caricatured, stereotyped or even demonised' (Mitchell 2009:154).

But, while Mitchell attributes this attitude of Pentecostals vis-à-vis African Religion to Ghana's and Nigeria's colonial past, in which traditional religion was commonly portrayed in particularly negative terms, this seems to be only one side of the coin. The other side is that Pentecostalism in Africa generally encourages a complete break with African culture (Martin 2002: 144).

Some African scholars criticise the negative portrayal of African culture in the *Hallelujah films*. They suggest that these films should be more authentic in reflecting traditional culture and should seek to express how such cultures could interact with Christianity instead of condemning the culture and the people who embrace it (Mitchell 2009: 155).

David Martin, quoted from another context, maintains that African Pentecostals engage the power of the Spirit to stage a dramatic contest against the old African gods in satanic guise. They do it even by projecting the contest in stories and media presentations. With this evangelism approach Pentecostals have not only managed to build up an Africanisation from below, but also revived the healing practices of Christianity (Martin 2002: 142).

It is beyond the scope of this book to pursue further such debates that are currently part and parcel of the African Christian landscape. But it remains important to emphasise that portrayals of *Hallelujah films* such as those we have just discussed, may harm ecumenical and interreligious relationships and hamper any efforts towards the coveted ecumenical and interreligious dialogue.

Concluding Remarks

This chapter has attempted to present the numerous media forms that have dominated the social communications scene in Africa prior to the introduction and pervasive penetration of the mobile phone. As the analysis has demonstrated, some have exhibited a liberating potential in the African milieu. They have played a vital role in shaping human relationships and in exposing life-diminishing aspects that affect Africans. Others have portrayed a susceptibility of falling prey to political and religious manipulation which is inimical to the wellbeing of the people.

From a religious perspective, some of these media have played such a vital role in evangelisation that the mobile phone will probably never come to sufficiently substitute them. Notably, Christianity's centre of gravity is said to shift geographically and demographically from the global north to the global south, with Africa becoming one of the new prospective Christian heartlands. The shift of Christianity is partly attributed to the use of modern electronic media in the task of evangelisation. But one drawback in this religious topography is the dependence of many African churches on the global north for their media equipment. This dependence affects the structuring and theological articulation of the African churches (LenkaBula 2008: 302).

All in all, despite the presence of numerous media forms, the period before the mobile phone for many average Africans was generally characterised by the absence of instant and reliable communications, which eventually provided many excuses for things undone as well as gave little impetus for action.

Subsequent chapters will demonstrate how the mobile phone bridges that gap. This demonstration begins in Chapter Two which addresses the question whether the mobile phone is liberating Africa by exploring the perceived social, economic and political benefits of mobile phone use in Africa.

Notes

[1] MIVA-Austria is a Catholic aid agency that promotes human mobility through the provision of vehicles for mission, development projects, education and medical care in different countries of the world.

[2] Reflection from *MIVA-Christophorus Aktion 2009*, 26 July 2009.

[3] Interview with a Muslim leader at Chengena Village, 16 July 2010.

[4] Ezra Chitando, "'Down with the devil, Forward with Christ!' A Study of the interface between religious and political discourses in Zimbabwe," in: *African Sociological Review*, Vol.6, No.1(2002), URL: http://www.codesria.org/Links/Publications/asr6_1full/chitando.pdf (accessed 20th December, 2009).

[5] Ezra Chitando, "'Down with the devil, Forward with Christ!' A Study of the interface between religious and political discourses in Zimbabwe," in: *African Sociological Review*, Vol.6, No.1(2002), URL: http://www.codesria.org/Links/Publications/asr6_1full/chitando.pdf (accessed 20th December, 2009).

[6] Ezra Chitando, "'Down with the devil, Forward with Christ!' A Study of the interface between religious and political discourses in Zimbabwe," in: *African Sociological Review*, Vol.6, No.1(2002), URL: http://www.codesria.org/Links/Publications/asr6_1full/chitando.pdf (accessed 20th December, 2009).

Chapter Two
Is the Mobile Phone Liberating Africa?

The Mobile Phone as a Transformative Factor

The telephone as a medium of social communication is perceived to be both modern and old. Its modernity is seen in its being a medium of organisation that 'enables the real-time integration of highly complex organisations as well as a myriad coordination processes within cities that could not be realized on the basis of face-to-face interaction' (Geser 2005: 23). This has saved organisations from the trouble of moving messengers most of the time. Yet the mobile phone maintains continuity with the past, since it supports the oldest mode of verbal exchange namely, oral communication.

On account of this character, Geser describes the phone as "regressive". The advantage of this "regressive" character is that it helps minimise the usage of letter or written documents.[1] In addition, unlike written communication, verbal communication allows even illiterates to engage in trans-spatial communication. This makes telecommunications a more inclusive type of media of social communications than print media.

The merits of the phone have become even more ponderous today with the predominance of its mobile version. In Africa where literacy rate is generally low the mobile phone proves to be a convenient social communication device since even an analphabetic can use the mobile phone with relative ease. But the fact that the mobile phone preserves some old elements of social communications can be interpreted as a challenge for Africans not to relinquish from maintaining good elements of their culture. The tendency of young people in Africa in the current digital age is to adopt any elements of foreign culture, while undermining their own African culture.

Notably, even in the current mobile age, it is actually the radio which still dominates the African waves in terms of ubiquity. The radio has other merits that make it outstanding among other electronic media. As Ugboajah notes,

Radio in Africa is a more flexible medium and the content is more often locally produced or adapted to African styles of expression... "radio is the tribal voice...the announcer is local, the names in the news are more familiar, the people of the radio novella are old friends, the chanting is authentic, the tunes are singable..." (Ugboajah 1985:17).

Despite such merits, the radio is surpassed by the mobile phone in other qualities. For example, the mobile phone is handier[2] and more effective for person-to-person communications. Its other strengths include multi-functionality, convenience, immediacy, and the possibility of customization. Besides, the mobile phone is less prone to state censorship and it is free from editors' hands as compared to the radio (and Television and newspapers).

These qualities make the mobile phone a better medium for the expression of public opinion than the radio. Many ordinary Africans today require such a medium in order to challenge those conditions that diminish their well-being. Apparently, the quick appropriation and momentous pervasiveness of the mobile phone in Africa are partly attributable to these qualities.

Descriptors of the mobile phone perceive its high penetration in Africa as a transformative factor in the Continent. They consider the mobile phone as being potentially capable of stimulating real and comprehensive positive changes in the society. It is thought to be a tool for development that moves across population segments that earlier were least expected to be accessible by this technology.

One of the commentators is Len Waverman, an economics professor at London Business School. He observes that even in the more developed parts of Africa, where it was thought that the mobile phone would be perhaps just a toy of the urban rich, the situation has turned out to be different, since rich urban people too have engaged the mobile phone in productive activities. Africans use the mobile device with such creativity that the West has started to look to Africa for new ideas as to where to take the mobile technology next.[3] Other commentators go so far as to express their optimism that the mobile phone is apt to help Africans better to deal with their social, economic, and political challenges than any other agency (Kößmeier 2009: 434).

The question at stake, however, is: how far is the mobile phone a liberating factor in the African context? To address this question, the chapter undertakes to assess the perceived benefits of the mobile phone in Africa. The assessment focuses on the implications of the mobile phone in the spheres of social communications, poverty alleviation, empowerment of women, health, democracy and good governance, combat of corruption, and in spiritual life. Finally, the chapter expresses the quest for faith communities to negotiate with the mobile technology for the sake of safeguarding the moral integrity of the society and religious faith.

Mobile Phones and Africa's Communication "Revolution"

The history of the mobile phone in Sub-Saharan Africa is a recent one and for millions of Africans, who mostly live in rural areas, their encounter with the cell-phone is a unique experience. This is because telephones have not been a fixture of everyday life for most African households. In the late 1990s Manuel Castells had described Sub-Saharan Africa as a '"black hole of information capitalism"' (Carmody 2010: 110). Reportedly, at that time the city of Manhattan or Tokyo had more telephone landlines than the whole of Sub-Saharan Africa.

With the introduction of the cell-phone most Africans have come to own personal telephones for the first time in their lives. In this sense, a major technological leap in telecommunications has taken place in Africa. It is a leap from a situation of not having telecommunications system at all, to one of having the sophisticated and ubiquitous mobile telecommunications technology. Undeniably, this is one reason why in many African countries the "cell-phone mania" has taken millions by storm.

Initially, mobile phone companies were reluctant to invest in Africa since the Continent was perceived to have minimal potential for a successful business in mobile technology. Today, on account of the real uptake of mobile phones and prosperous business in mobile technology in Africa, such misperceptions are waning.

The number of mobile subscribers in thirty African countries, excluding South Africa, rose from zero in 1994 to more than 82 million in late 2004. And as Pádraig Carmody notes, 'from 2000 to

2007, Africa was the fastest-growing mobile phone market in the world as the number of subscribers rose from 10 million to 250 million, with a 66 percent growth rate in 2005 alone' (2010: 110).

Africa is generally characterised by poor infrastructure and communication systems. And since the penetration of fixed telephones was generally very minimal, the mobile phone appears to have come to the rescue of many. Those living in rural communities, for example, have been saved from the trouble of meeting high financial costs and time involved in travelling when they are confronted with a pressing need.

Countries that have been well served by solid landline infrastructures, in contrast, have experienced a relatively low uptake of mobile phones. Statistics for the year 2004, for instance, indicated that the United States had 62 mobile subscribers per 100 inhabitants, while Canada had 47. The uptake of mobile phones in these rich countries was low, although there was a high penetration of broadband (Goggin 2008: 42).

Across the African Continent mobile technology is gaining momentum all the time and users continue to confound researchers with their creativity in using mobile phones.[3] It is projected that by 2012 there will be 560 million mobile phone subscribers in Africa.

In Tanzania mobile phone ownership and usage which started in major cities in the mid 1990s has quickly spread in rural areas as well, wherever the network is available. In 2007 it was estimated that over 8.3 million Tanzanians owned mobile phones[4] whereas the mobile penetration rate was 21 per cent. Results of a survey conducted in 2008 revealed that 85 percent of people in Tanzania said they had greater contact and improved relationships with families and friends due to mobile phone use.[5]

Apart from the expanded mobile phone usage, there has been an increase in the number of mobile providers in Tanzania, from one in the late 1990s to five in 2010. They are: Tigo, Vodacom, Zain, Tanzania Telecommunication Company Limited (TTCL), and Zantel. There is a stiff competition among these network providers and this has resulted into reduction of tariff costs. But in my view, mobile phone tariffs are still very high as compared to the actual income of most Tanzanians.

Various motives account for the option of Tanzanians to own or use mobile phones. The following are generally the most commonly identified ones: communication with friends and family members, maintaining relationships, emergency situations, help in job search as well as business networking. However, it is well known that in Tanzania, as in many other parts of Africa, the number of mobile phone owners who use it for income-generating business is minimal indeed.

Some mobile phone consumers apparently came to the decision to own a mobile phone because they considered it as a status symbol. The rhetoric seems to be that in the age of Information and Communication Technologies (ICT) the mobile phone is a "must-have". However, as pointed out earlier, the previous environment of limited access to telecommunications among Tanzanians has played part too. Many people find it fascinating that today even an ordinary village dweller can own a telephone. As such, no one wants to be left in the "dark" again. Hence they strive to own mobile phones even if this entails living beyond their means.

Generally, much more development in the mobile telecommunications sector in Africa is in sight. Mobile phone manufacturers continue to improve the gadgets to suit consumer demands. For example, Nokia, the world's largest mobile phone manufacturer, had promised at the Mobile World Congress in Barcelona that by June 2009, it would expand the enterprise software it offers in its most affordable phones so that mobile users could now have access to the Internet and other services.[6] This is good news to mobile owners who have no computers.

The overwhelming perception is that the ongoing mobile technological advancement in Africa is a chance for the Continent to 'revolutionalise' its social communications systems. But what implications does this mobile revolution have upon Africa itself? The subsequent section examines this question.

Mobile Communication "Revolution" and the "Wealth Paradox"

The coveted social communication revolution in Africa has created growing demands for mobile phones. This section demonstrates the implication of the mobile demands on Africa. It reveals that the mobile revolution in Africa indeed redounds to Africa itself by being a source of other revolutions, violence as well as forced migrations (Carmody 2010: 114-116).

Africa has been linked to the global mobile phone industry as part of the globalisation process. In this industry many of the mobile phones are designed in the United States and Europe, while the assembling is carried out in China. Africa on its part provides raw materials, i.e. the precious metals coltan and diamonds, as well as the market for the mobile phones. Indeed, as the study reveals, high demand for the metals frequently contributes to the rehearsal of the well-known "wealth paradox" in Africa, namely: 'the richer in mineral resources an African country is, the more its local population is subjected to suffering and impoverishment' (Meienberg 2008: 73).

Coltan is an abbreviation for colombite-tantalite. From it are extracted the precious metals columbium and tantalum. Tantalum is very hard, has a high density and is extremely resistant to heat, rust and acid. It can also capture and release electric charge. It is therefore an important component in many modern electronic equipment, for example, capacitors for mobile phones and other modern gadgets for Information and Communications Technology (ICT).[7]

Tantalum was discovered in 1802 by a Swedish chemist named Eckberg. Researching the acid-resistant metal had proved to be so difficult that Eckberg almost despaired. Therefore, when he finally succeeded he named his discovery after the Greek god Tantalus, who is condemned in Hades to eternal suffering (Werner et al. 2001: 51). According to Greek mythology, Tantalus was punished because he had betrayed the trust of the gods. In his eternal condemnation in the Underworld he is portrayed as standing knee deep in water but he is unable to slake his thirst because whenever he bends down, the water vanishes. And a fruit hangs over his head, but whenever he reaches for it, it goes just beyond his reach. This is the story of the majority of Africans as far as mineral resources in their own countries are concerned. Although these people cannot be accused of having betrayed the trust of their ancestors, all the same the mineral wealth to the lot of them remains merely tantalizing. Only a few people in the particular countries reap the benefits.

The Democratic Republic of Congo (DRC) epitomises one of worst cases of this mineral "wealth paradox". The suffering of the

Greek god Tantalus is replicated by the Congolese people as it were. It is satirical that this country which owns eighty percent of the world's known reserves of tantalite is a chronic trouble-spot (Carmody 2010: 114). Resource conflicts and wars such as those which took place in 1998 to 2003 in eastern part of the country have been partly over the control of tantalite. Reportedly, in 1998 the new government of Laurent Kabila had attempted to nationalize the main coltan mining company. This move was met with an immediate rebellion to overthrow him which was supported by the directors of the company that was being expropriated. According to a UN report, coltan motivates the Rwandan army to continue its presence in DRC. The army protects the companies and individuals who mine the ore since it receives a share of the profits. Hence the army guarantees the necessary environment for further exploitation of the metal (Werner et al. 2001: 51).

The launching of the Sony PlayStation 2 console and Nintendo's "Gameboy" as well as the manufacture of new mobile handsets and the further development of computer market have all catapulted the prices of coltan. For example, between February 2000 and January 2001 the prices of tantalite spiked more than fivefold (from 180 to 950 Euros per kilogramme) (Werner et al. 2001: 50). When the prices dramatically fell in 2001 the war in Congo subsequently appeared to come to an end in 2003, since coltan was no longer paying much, and the rebels had now to solicit revenue from other sources. But when the price for tantalum ore rose again from 2007 to 2008, this resulted into renewed large-scale conflict in eastern DRC (Carmody 2010: 114f).

Other areas affected by the demand for coltan include environment and wildlife since, as Carmody observes, in eastern DRC much of the coltan mining is carried out in two World Heritage sites, namely, Kahuzi-Biega National Park and Okapi Wildlife Reverse. Hence, landslides, damage of agricultural land and the killing of endangered animals such as gorillas have accompanied the mining activities there.

Other minerals from Africa that are associated with the manufacture of the mobile phone are diamonds. These are used for encrusted luxury mobile phones that are sold to wealthy people in the rich countries (Carmody 2010: 115). Control over diamonds too has been part of the resource war in DRC and in other parts of Africa.

We notice, therefore, that the growing demand for mobile phones in Africa has far-reaching repercussions on Africa itself. The chronic conflicts in DRC are a case in point. Whenever such conflicts erupt hundreds of people lose their lives, hundreds of women become victims of rape and other sexual abuses, while hundreds of thousands of people flee their homes to become refugees and migrants. Neighbouring countries like Tanzania have often felt the pinch of the influx of refugees.

Even in the absence of conflicts, the conditions under which the artisanal and formal miners work are extremely dangerous since miners work with bare hands and simple tools. It is also highly exploitative as the miners are paid poverty wages. Child labour is also often employed in the mining sites. Referring to this fact, British member of Parliament Oona King had once remarked, "'kids in Congo are being sent down into mines to die so that kids in Europe and America can kill imaginary aliens in their living room'"(Carmody 2010: 115).

Moreover, the mobile phone revolution in Africa is implicated in environmental degradation and destruction of farming land and wildlife.

Mobile Phones and Poverty Alleviation

There is a general optimism in Africa that increased mobile accessibility in the Continent is boosting countries' economies. Some commentators compare its impact to that brought about in the West by the installation of fixed telephone lines back in the 1970s.[8] Hence some are confident that the mobile phone will liberate Africa economically.

However, we may pause and ask, does the mobile phone really serve to alleviate the poverty of the majority of Africans? Is the rapid adoption of mobile technology in Africa a transformative moment in Africa's economic history? Is it fundamentally altering Africa's existing dependent position?

In attempting to answer these questions I will first make a cursory survey on some of the perceived economic benefits of the mobile phone. Second, I will indicate that the rapid adoption of mobile technology in Africa is one facet of globalisation and that it reinforces Africa's dependency. And third, I will demonstrate how ordinary mobile users in Africa sacrifice a lot in order to maintain their mobile phones and how the mobile phone creates economic divides in the society.

Optimistic Signs

There is enough evidence to suggest that the mobile phone to some extent facilitates poverty alleviation in Africa. This can be viewed from different perspectives. One perspective is the promotion of foreign investment in Africa. Penetration by foreign companies in Africa is currently on the increase because of the increasing possibilities of telephone communications. This enables business people to remain tightly connected to their company bases and families at home and at the same time feel safer in Africa. Consequently, from the point of view of investors, accessing Africa has now become a more feasible and viable option (Pelckmans 2009: 28).

According to a survey, 62 percent of small businesses in South Africa and 59 percent in Egypt are deemed to have increased their profits following the use of mobile phones. Similarly in Tanzania, it was the communication sector that reportedly posted the highest growth rate in 2007, whereby mobile phone subscribers reached 8.3 million, thus making mobile phone providers significant contributors of revenue in the country. This was reflected in the 2008-09 national budget in which the excise duty on mobile phones was raised up to 10 percent.

The Government's perspective appears to be that for a country like Tanzania with many people outside the tax net, and where an increasing amount of consumer spending is on mobile phones, the taxes on mobile phone airtime (rather like taxes on fuel) are a pretty effective means of taxing the population at large.[9]

Besides government revenues, many small and big business in Tanzania rely solely on mobile phone for telecommunications. This is typified by business men and women in remote villages when they need information from their business partners in cities about current prices of agricultural products before embarking on transporting them to the markets. This helps them do their business profitably.

In the Sahel, pastoralists use Information and Communication Technology maps linked with mobile phones to communicate with other groups of livestock herders (e.g. the Maasai in Tanzania) about suitable pastures.

The same technology is used by conservationists, hunters and fishermen in some African countries such as Kenya, Botswana and Guinea for purposes such as tracking wildlife, game management as well as protecting fishing grounds from poachers. Equally important is the employment of technologies linked to the mobile phone in the so-called e-agriculture initiatives concerned with researches related to African soils and domestic animal genetics (Kabukuru 2009: 80).

Another important contribution of mobile phones in Africa's economic sector is the availability of employment opportunities. Business in airtime both in wholesales and retails is a preoccupation of many young people. From cities to remote villages one finds booths where airtime cards are sold. But equally significant is the petty business of street vendors popularly known in Tanzania as *machingas*. These ply the streets with huge loads of various items on their backs or fix themselves throughout the day at vantage angles at bus stations and other public places. For them, one of the most profit-making items is the mobile airtime or scratch cards (commonly known as vouchers).

Mobile Money and Banking is another significant contribution. Currently mobile phone providers in Zambia, Tanzania, South Africa, and Kenya for instance, have opened services to enable customers transfer money. This system known as *M-PESA* (Mobile money) allows cell-phone users to make person-to-person payments, money transfers and pre-paid purchases without needing a bank account (Kabukuru 2009: 78). In the past sending money home upcountry from the city involved the cost of someone physically travelling to and fro and risked car hijackings. But now no one carries cash anymore. It is hoped, moreover, that mobile phones could be about to make Africa a more liquid economy when such mobile money transfer systems go global because then the billions of remittance money sent by African migrants to their respective countries each year could start flowing this way.[10]

Engaging the mobile phone in money transfer transactions poses stiff competitions against banks since more and more of the customers prefer mobile financial system to the traditional bank systems. But the two systems often make joint ventures too. For instance, Zain, which is said to be the leading mobile telecommunications provider in Africa, is partnering with leading international and regional banks, including *Citigroup* and *Standard Chartered* to bring mobile banking to over 100 million people in Africa with the launch of its new service known as Zap.[11] This system will enable Zain customers to use their mobile phone to pay bills and good services, receive and send money to individuals and to bank accounts, withdraw cash, manage their bank accounts, top up their own airtime account or someone else's and other services.

Due to such economic possibilities presented by the mobile phone, many are optimistic that the mobile phone has the potential to induce real economic development in Africa. They hope that with the mobile phone the story will not resemble that of the mineral resources of oil, diamonds, copper, and others which historically have brought a considerable economic boom to some African countries, but nonetheless, have hardly benefitted ordinary Africans.

Their optimism is based on the experience from other poor people around the globe who have used the mobile phone in business and succeeded in alleviating their poverty. Some Africans even believe that the mobile phone has a greater potential to liberate Africa from its economic woes and to alleviate income poverty than any foreign development aid. One African with such views once observed: 'For all the talk about "making poverty history" through aid and debt relief at the G8 meeting in Scotland and among aging rock stars at Live8 concerts, perhaps the best tool for poverty alleviation on the Continent is the mobile phone.'[12]

It is contended that, unlike foreign aid, the mobile phone benefits households directly, not through the channels of African governments most of which are tainted with corruption. On account of this, the economic potential of the mobile phone to alleviate household poverty is comparable to that of remittances which African migrants send to their families back home.[13]

Mobile phone as Globalisation: Have the Rules Changed?

The question whether the mobile phone serves to alleviate poverty in Africa or not, can be approached from the perspective of the globalisation phenomenon. The rapid adoption of mobile technology in Africa is part and parcel of the ongoing process of globalisation. The characteristic features of globalisation in this context include interconnectedness between places and the creation of a global economy that is characterised by '"network trade", "deep integration" and information exchange' (Carmody 2010: 111).

As noted earlier, Africa is integrated into the global mobile phone industry as a supplier of the raw materials, the precious metals coltan and diamonds, and as a provider of market for the finished mobile products. Africa is a fast-growing market for mobiles many of which are counterfeit, while others are second-hand. By and large, the global mobile phone industry does not help Africa overcome its technological dependency. Much of the research and design of the mobile phones takes place in North America and Europe, not in Africa. China assemblies most of the phones designed in the West, besides manufacturing its own.

The little technological involvement of Africa in the manufacture of mobile phones is in connection with assembly operations now set up by China and other Asian countries. Rapid growth in demand for mobile phones in Africa has made these countries begin to assembly mobile phones in African countries such as Mozambique, Rwanda and Kenya (Carmody 2010: 113).

Another economic aspect that is important to reiterate, is that for most African subscribers the mobile phone is not used for coordinating income-generating projects, hence not for linking the people to the global economy, so to speak. For them the mobile phone is primarily used for maintaining family relationships and social networks. And as will be noted in the subsequent section, such mobile communications often extract money from budgets meant for poverty alleviation.

The global mobile phone industry thus perpetrates the long-standing dependent position of Africa as far as technology is concerned. Moreover, since Africa is not a producer of mobile phones, but merely a source of raw materials and a market, it has remained subservient to the same patterns of extractive globalisation that have characterised the relations of the Continent with other parts of the world for many centuries (Carmody 2010: 111).

There is also the overarching question of digital divide between Africa and the Western World. With the pervasive spread of the mobile phone scholars have come to believe that the mobile phone is helping in diminishing the divide. Earlier it was thought that the computer would do it.[14] However, an economic paradox still hinges around the proliferation of mobile phones in Africa. It is discernible that Africa, which is the poorest continent in the world, apparently pays among the highest mobile phone tariffs in the world. The huge tariff differences between Africa and Europe, for instance, are conspicuously noticeable. Whatever technical and economic arguments may be advanced to account for such differences, it remains true that African consumers sacrifice more to enjoy the mobile technology than their European counterparts.

Furthermore, while the poor are overwhelmingly enthusiastic about mobile phones, multilateral development agencies, in contrast, favour the Internet. For them it is to the Internet that any praise of Information and Communication Technologies (ICT) in business is directed, not the mobile phone (Molony 2009: 94). Since the most part of Africa has not adopted the Internet, the logical sequel is that multilateral development agencies will less likely direct their attention to those areas.

Today the attitude of avoiding remote areas replete with modern infrastructures such as the Internet holds true for church mission as well. Expatriate and African indigenous missionaries alike, increasingly seem to shun "communications margins" either by not considering to open mission stations there or by transferring their existing stations to urban areas. A young European nun once told me she could not do mission in Africa because there is no milk. Now the lack of Internet will certainly be another excuse. Ironically, the majority of Africans live in such 'margins'. Are the new media technologies then, not altering even our missionary priorities?

Back to the mobile phone in Africa, the insights provided in this section suggest, therefore, that the mobile phone does not fundamentally alter the previously existing power relations in world economics that have been exploitative to Africa. Nor does it often help in overcoming the perceived digital divides.

Sacrifices of the Poor at the Altar of Modernity

We now investigate whether the mobile phone helps individual users or households to alleviate poverty. This section underlines that for the majority of rural African communities the mobile phone does not alleviate poverty, on the contrary, it may aggravate their income poverty.

To elaborate on this point I present research findings focusing on the economic impact of the mobile phone on rural communities in Tanzania. The locale of the study is Tanzania's fertile Southern Highlands and it was conducted by researchers from Tumaini University in 2008.[15] The study revealed that most of the respondents had to pay much to maintain their mobile phones. The main running costs were in the area of purchase of airtime and recharging of batteries, since in Tanzania most households do not have electricity. In 2005, for example, 97 percent of the country had mobile phone network coverage, but only one in ten houses had electricity.[16] And even by 2010, only 14 percent of Tanzanians had access to electricity (*The Guardian* 24 August 2010). And in 2010 the Tanzanian Energy and Minerals Ministry projected that probably by 2033 that up to 75 percent of the country's population will have access to electricity, if there is greater innovation and financial investment in the sector (*The Guardian* 24 September 2010).

Under such circumstances most mobile phone owners in Tanzania have to pay a fee to other people for recharging their phones. And as this study in Southern Highlands revealed, most of the respondents (97.25 percent) lived far from where the electricity infrastructure was available. This meant an extra burden of walking several kilometres to obtain recharging services for their mobile phones. But while at the charging centres, they had still to wait up to three hours for the phones to be recharged. Eventually the maintenance of the mobile phone for these rural communities necessitated the postponement of other economical or business activities.

Furthermore, the sources of income for maintaining mobile phones, for most of the respondents (62 percent), was through their business or agribusiness. In the final analysis, this meant that the money that could help reduce household income poverty was now used for the maintenance of mobile phones. Other respondents (28 percent) said they got their airtime and recharge fees as gift, while fifteen percent said they could meet their mobile phone running costs through their salary. Interestingly, however, the majority of the respondents (66 percent) whose expenditure on mobile phones ranged between 15,000 and 30,000 Tanzania shillings per month, were those whose income ranged from 50,000 to 100, 000 Tanzania shillings. This is an average of 30 percent of their monthly income.[17]

Equally crucial was the fact that 48 percent of the respondents reported that in order to meet the maintenance costs of their mobile phones, they sometimes had to forgo important needs such as paying for education or decent food, clothes or other necessities for the upkeep of the family.

In summary, this study can lead us to the following deductions with regard to the impact of mobile phones in rural communities in Tanzania. First, for most rural people in Tanzania having a mobile phone does not reduce income poverty, on the contrary, it escalates it since the mobile phone drains money from other sources to cover its maintenance costs. Secondly, the costs of running a mobile phone are not comparable to its economic benefits. Thirdly, since most households in rural areas have no electricity, the maintenance of the mobile phone often requires owners to postpone other useful economic activities and travel to places where mobile phone recharge services are available. The impact of the mobile phone for them might have been different if the Tanzanian Government had put the issue of rural electrification into first consideration before extending mobile phone network coverage. Many in Tanzania wonder why the government is not following the example of the wide penetration of mobile phones and give as much precedence to the issue of electrification in the country (*The Guardian* 24 August 2010).

Fourthly, the maintenance costs of the mobile phone force poor people to forsake other essential needs such as education, decent meals and clothing. Thus, having a mobile phone entails big sacrifices for poor individuals and families.

Thus, it is quite understandable that Tanzanians have nicknamed the mobile phone *nyumba-ndogo* (lit. a small house, in Swahili Language). The terminology has rather sexist overtones and denotes a woman on whom a man squanders all his resources for an extra-marital affair, while leaving his wife and children in the lurch. It is intended to amplify how the mobile phone siphons out from the poor people even the meagre resources that would help them sustain their daily lives.

Interestingly, Thomas Molony had in 2003 carried out a research in the same Southern Highlands region of Tanzania. He sought to establish the significance of the mobile phone in the business of wholesalers and buyers of tomatoes and potatoes produced by farmers in this region. Molony came to the conclusion that some of these business people could operate successfully without using the mobile phone, since what seemed to matter most was the personal mobility of a businessperson and the maintenance of face-to-face relationships with business partners. And, contrary to the assumption that small farmers benefit drastically from their appropriation of mobile phones, Molony could establish that some of them found the running costs of the mobile phone so prohibitive that using them regularly was just not feasible (Molony 2009: 92-107).

For the sake of comparison, a similar research focusing on women was conducted in rural Uganda in 2007. It was intended to investigate on mobile phone use in households and what people were giving up in order to get mobile phones. It was found out that the women's income was about $ 1 a day which they got either from husbands or earned from small business. At the time of the research, 3 minutes off-peak talk time on the same network cost about 40 cent (Ugandan money) which was equal to about 40 percent of the daily household budget. Under such circumstances, in order to use mobile phones some households had to give up some store-bought food such as sugar, flour, oil, and so on. Those who had gardens had to resort to home produce to make ends meet, but those without gardens had actually to give up food.[18] It is curious how families are prepared to offer such sacrifice at the altar of this perceived symbol of modernity.

Mobile Phone Mania

The *mobile phone mania* in Africa indeed reveals a strange attitude of the people in that they seem to be so enamoured with this communication device that they simply cannot afford to shake it off, although it imposes a heavy economic burden on individuals and families. It is pointed out that today the redistribution of resources in families is not limited to food, transport and clothing, but increasingly it involves also the allocation of phone credit.

The people seem to be fully and inextricably wired by the mobile phone. Even those who have easy access to public telephone booths from which they could make cheaper calls, opt nonetheless to own mobile phones. But as experience shows, owning a mobile phone to a larger extent tempts one to make unnecessary calls. And unable to afford airtime tariffs some mobile phone owners end up merely beeping others in order to initiate conversations. The one being flashed is perceived to be better off and thus requested to phone back.

The seemingly irresistible attraction to the mobile phone echoes the Gospel parable in which the kingdom of God is likened to a treasure which a person, having discovered it, went and sold everything he had in order to buy the land where the treasure was hidden. To many in Africa the mobile phone has become a "treasure" in a similar fashion. Why is it so?

To resolve this puzzle, some propose the zeitgeist as the reason. As stated above, since this is an ICT age, no one, particularly those who have been in "communication margins", is prepared to stay behind again. It is notable that most mobile consumers languish in abject poverty. Tanzania itself is one of the poorest countries in the world and in Africa, yet it is one of the topmost countries in mobile phone ownership and usage in the Continent. Most of the people in rural and urban areas alike strive to save in order to buy a mobile phone. Curiously, most of these people who find it fashionable to own mobile phones, in fact, live on the equivalent of $ 1 a day. But when they eventually manage to buy a handset they often settle for the most current and hence the most expensive version.

Author Francis Nyamnjoh, referring to a similar attitude towards mobile phones, brands Africans who squander their money in this way as "beggars with the choices of kings". For him, it is amazing that Europeans who make the cell-phones and are relatively richer, are so frugal and crafty in their consumption of this device. Africans in contrast, despite being mere consumers of cell-phones and generally less affluent than Europeans, settle for kingly consumption of the mobiles, going 'for the latest, slickest and most expensive' (de Bruijn et al. 2009: 2). Perhaps the big lesson for Africans in this context is that saving and frugality, rather than prodigality are realistic pathways towards economic liberation, whether at individual level, household or national levels.

As pointed out above, it is even more curious how the poor people manage to meet the maintenance costs of their mobile phones under such an economic tightrope. Generally their desire to swim with the current of modernity necessitates high sacrifices that sometimes constitute imprudence and financial mismanagement.

But the second reason proposed in order to account for the mobile phone mania in Africa is on the basis that Africans cherish to sustain social networks, for example among family members, relations, and so on. This trait is consonant with the African Ubuntu philosophy of life. As Chapter Three will demonstrate, the mobile phone seems to be suitable for upholding Ubuntu solidarity.

In conclusion, such studies are helpful to avoid generalisations when assessing the impact of the mobile phone on society. The particular case studies from Tanzania and Uganda have revealed results that are at variance with the overwhelming assumption that the mobile phone helps alleviate poverty in poor rural communities in Africa.

Admittedly, some rural communities may actually benefit economically through the mobile phone. As some surveys testify, the mobile phone is used by some to inquire market prices for their farm products or to co-ordinate their business (Molony 2009: 92-107). But these are mostly a few prosperous farmers or business people. For the majority of the rural peasants this is not the case.

In Tanzania it is hard to expect that other regions benefit from the mobile phone in a significantly different way as compared to the Southern Highlands. In fact, most rural communities in the country live in similar environment characterised by high poverty levels, lack of electricity and modern social communication infrastructures and other problems.

Such observations should be an eye-opening insight to governments and policy-makers. Instead of merely celebrating the development reached in mobile phone coverage, they should as well analyse the economic impacts. This will enable them to realize the new economic challenges that are thrust upon poor rural communities, which use the mobile phone amid limited economic resources.

The economic burden of poor mobile users may not be quite obvious to the eyes of government officials and rich business people since they live in urban areas where generally electricity is available and most of them have enough resources to maintain their mobile phones comfortably.

Polarisation between the Rich and the Poor

The mobile phone boom in Africa constitutes a moment of truth. It unveils the prevalence of great economic disparities between the majority poor and the few rich people and, in fact, it reinforces them too. It is scandalous to note for example, that while poor families may survive on a meal a day, elite citizens on the other side of the divide may enjoy long hours of telephoning with their mobile phones without the slightest worry about cost implications. And the quality of the meal that the poor eat may be cheaper than the tariff for a two-minute mobile airtime. When using their mobile phones, poor people are forced to be always cost-conscious because of the high air-time tariffs. Any long conversations and endearments characteristic of African communications are to be curtailed. On this respect, the mobile phone diminishes among poor people the warmth of interpersonal relationships that is typical of Africans.

Moreover, while poor people seem to be further impoverished through ownership and use of mobile phones, rich people on the other hand, are normally well-placed to use this device for furthering their economic gains since they have more access to the resources of the country.

It would be interesting in this context to research on the amount of money allotted for mobile air-time as "office use" for government ministers and other high-ranking officials in Africa. It will most likely come up with shocking revelations for the sheer size of the budgets. But this will come as no surprise in those countries where normally expensive posh cars (nicknamed *"mashangingi"* in Tanzania) are purchased for government ministers and other high-ranking government figures while the poor ordinary people languish under poverty, lack of medical and school facilities, and so on.

Online Beggars and Dependency Syndrome

Some mobile users in Africa tend to "flash" or "beep" others as a way of requesting them to phone back so that a communication between them may be sustained. But in some parts of Africa, as Pelckmans notes, beeping can be likened to tapping someone's shoulder or winking at them as a way of confirming and reminding them that you are friends. This kind of flashing usually does not expect an answer from the other person (Pelckmans 2009: 29). Beeping may also serve as a type of code; two rings, for example, may mean "pick me up" (Carmody 2010: 118f).

Our concern here is not about these types of flashing. Of great concern is the type of flashing that reinforces economic power differences. It is a typical style of using mobile phones among people on low incomes where airtime tariffs are relatively high. Among poor mobile users flashing involves a clear and much discussed economic rationality, designed to win the fierce battle to keep a mobile in permanent operation' (Carmody 2010: 118f). It is not the case with mobile users in high income countries.

In this practice of flashing we notice at least two groups of flashers. There are those who practice flashing because they are in real need of mobile communication but genuinely lack the financial resources to sustain the communication. But there are flashers who only want to exploit others.

In the first category, flashers beep mobile users whom they consider to be richer than themselves as a way of requesting them to call back so that a conversation between them may be sustained. Flashing practices in this case create social hierarchies in which the poor are becoming more and more dependent on the rich. This eventually influences and (re) produces power relations among people. These are the typical power relations that persist in human society between the "haves" and the "have nots". As Molony rightly observes, many poor people in developing countries are embedded in such intricate systems of power, but unfortunately much of the pro-ICT community seems to be less concerned about it (Molony 2009: 107).

We can visualise the poor (mobile flashers) in this relationship as beggars like any other beggars who station themselves in the street corners of many African cities. The only difference is that the flashers do their begging digitally; they are *virtual beggars*. But as far as human dignity is concerned, what fundamental difference does it make whether one begs online or physically? In fact, even the virtual beggars may be subjected to social exploitation and rejection just like the *face-to-face beggars*. If they are women, for example, their begging for airtime may render them susceptible to sexual exploitation by men just as their counterparts who beg for alms in the streets.

In addition, just as the rich usually try to avoid and even stigmatise persistent beggars in the streets, rich mobile phone owners too, devise various strategies to avoid and stigmatise persistent flashers. Their strategies may include: changing their phone numbers regularly, giving a person a wrong number, or having several numbers from different mobile phone providers (Pelckmans 2009: 29).

The second category of flashers consists of mobile users who tend to run their mobile phones without willing to dig deep into their pockets. Some have dubbed them *mobile promoters*. Normally they can afford to run their mobile phones, but they are not willing to incur the costs. They put someone they consider to have more money at his disposal in the position of the "credit caretaker".

It is a habit that can be interpreted as an indication of a growing mindset that prizes "reaping without sowing". Ironically, 'if everyone fails to pay for communication, then this doesn't occur and no one enjoys the rewards of communication' (Balliet 2010: 49). This attitude may in the long-run shape a culture that gives less value to thrift and enterprise and instead promotes habits of admiration for unearned success.

Feminisation of the Mobile Phone and African Women

Domestication of the mobile phone is the act of incorporating the device into the day-to-day patterns of the users, for example, among members of a family within the framework of the household. It is observed that the mobile phone as an artefact is indeed 'situated instrumentally as a facilitator of social communication, particularly for women' (Goggin 2008: 44) According to recent study by British mobile 'Phonepiggybank' experts, a woman makes more than 288,000 mobile phone calls in her entire life, which is equivalent to 42,000 hours or about 5 years of nonstop use of the mobile phone. In comparison, a man makes 277,000 calls, equivalent to 28,500 hours or about three years of nonstop use of mobile phone (*Heute*, 29 April 2009). Moreover, according to the telephone company, T-Mobile Austria, women are said to write more SMS text messages than men (*Heute*, 29 April 2009).

Researches illustrate that the mobile phone is becoming increasingly woman-oriented both in its design and its market. Mobile companies are keen to appeal to women and female teenagers, for whom trendy and impulsive consumption styles are usually regarded as their staff (Goggin 2008:43). Gender scripts, for instance, essentialise women and their uses of mobiles. Fashion trends dominate.

Teenagers 'are particularly aware of the fashion aspects of their mobiles, competing to acquire the latest, coolest models and to customize them in the latest coolest way... Customisation includes ringtones, sticking logos and graphics on the phone, or attaching jewellery and trinkets (Goggin 2008: 44).

One woman admitting of this trend, observed that the mobile phone is not just a functional thing, rather it has become an accessory, like shoes, bags, belts or jewellery. As such, it is promoted in society as an extension of one's personal style and essence. Subsequently, one has to look for a phone with a personality that one enjoys and that matches with her. Some models of mobile phone are regarded as feminine by their sheer look. For example, Nokia's 7280 was referred to as 'Lipstick Phone (and) was heralded for being small... eye-catching and cool' (Goggin 2008: 45).

Another area where women feature highly, is with regard to camera and videophones, text messaging, ringtones and email. These are built into mobiles and marketed for women in their roles as consumers and girlfriends. Thus, the mobile phone uses women for sociability, shopping and entertainment, and essentialises their bodily preoccupations.

We notice here once again, user's ambivalence of the mobile phone with respect to women. On the one hand, it is deemed as an artefact of emancipation for women, particularly since it provides women with effective telecommunications, employment opportunities, expression of their identity as well gender scripts that accentuate women liberating aspects. On the other hand, the mobile phone may also be conceived as less liberating to women especially when they are merely assigned the role of the market, entertainment, sociability and bodily preoccupations.

Amplifying the Voices of African Women

How does the mobile phone serve the interests of African women? It is worth noting in the first place, that women in Africa, as in many other parts of the world, are the majority in the society. Nevertheless, as one woman author sarcastically observed, this statistical analysis is utilised by the society only as a justification for polygamy rather than using it to determine the way society is organised in the political sphere and public life (Affiong 2009:11).

It is quite evident that women in Africa play a very vital role in the society. As regards production, they are the ones who produce most of Africa's food and cash crops. And they undertake the greatest part of care-giving (Jere-Malanda 2009:14). However, Africa being still largely a patriarchal continent, the position of women in most societies is still undermined. Issues pertaining to gender equality, empowerment of women and ending of violence against women, among others, by far still cry for action. Women are denied rightful ownership and control of land, food, housing and property in general as well as deprived of the right to literacy and education.

Glaring disparities exist between women and men in the areas of health, higher education, employment and empowerment whereby men are normally favoured against women. In the arena of politics and public life, the invisibility of women is blinding (Affiong 2009:11). They are less or completely not involved in decision-making processes. Apparently the standard mantra of the male chauvinist politicians in Africa is that women are inherently incapable of high offices such as the presidential post. Thus during election campaigns for instance, the role of women in most cases is limited to singing, dancing, mobilising other women and men, selling party merchandise, advocating, cooking, serving and clearing.

In other words, the role of women as far as politics is concerned, is just to add life, colour and body numbers to campaigns. A female political candidate will be less likely elected even by fellow women. This leaves men to determine all the major issues. Thus, while men articulate, women on their part have to provide. Likewise, men discuss the issues, while women entertain, and men lead the country, while women must only tag along (Affiong 2009:11-13). By and large, women experience exclusion also in religious institutions such as churches.

Apart from staggering under the weight of these multiple structurally constructed burdens, women and girls in Africa are often subjected to violence which includes coercion into sex, early marriages, early pregnancies, domestic violence, human trafficking and forced prostitution, to mention but a few. Political instability and ethnic conflicts that have wrecked havoc in some parts of Africa, for example, have had horrific impacts on women. Women (and children) rank high among the victims of inhuman treatment when conflicts ensue. It is said that one in three women is subjected to sexually-related abuses during her lifetime.

In some of the conflict areas in Africa, rape of women and girls is employed as a terrorising weapon or tactic of war (Jere-Malanda 2009:14ff). The attackers use rape as a method of ethnic humiliation and elimination.[19]

In recent years, too, the trafficking of African women to work as prostitutes or in the sex trade abroad has been an increasing problem. Organised bands of human traffickers promise women with the opportunity to work abroad. Then they transport them, usually illegally, to a destination country at an agreed fee which the women would be required to pay in instalments after they start working. But while abroad, the women are forced to work as prostitutes and virtually all their income is taken by the traffickers (Khoser 2007: 64).

Which Mobiles are Suitable for African Women?

Confronted with such challenges, African women would require more a type of mobile phone that would be instrumental in tackling the problems that diminish their dignity as human beings. Such a mobile phone would be more liberating to African women, perhaps more than merely a gadget that appeals most to their feminine taste.

So far mobile achievement in Africa is celebrated by women in areas such as social security, health, political well-being as well as income generation.[20] As regards social security, the mobile phone seems to have expanded the locales and times that women can go, since having the mobile phone with them, they feel safer and less dependent on male companions to accompany them while accomplishing their activities even after dusk. Thus the mobile phone serves to increase their freedom and mobility (Pelckmans 2009: 28). To empower women, an SMS platform has been initiated in some parts of Africa by which rural women are trained and equipped with free text messaging to report violence committed against them and their children.[21] This allows the women to anonymously report on gender-based violence without fear of reprisal.

Economically, some women's cooperative groups are said to benefit greatly from improved mobile communications particularly in terms of sustaining communications among members and selling airtime by SMS to generate their income. The advantage of the mobile phone is that even women who do not enjoy the privilege of former education are able to actively embrace the technology for their empowerment.

In some parts of Africa mobile phone use is reported to have helped improve the education opportunities for a girl-child. An example is cited from a Millennium village in northeast Kenya, where before the coming of cell-phones it was difficult for girls from pastoral nomadic communities to board at school away from their families. But now with the cell-phone, there was the possibility to sustain contact between the girls at school and their families and this helped convince families to allow their girls to go to school and remain stable in the school setting.[22]

Even on the aspect of culture, the general appraisal is that mobile phones continue to play a remarkable role in matters pertaining to the emancipation of African women. However, mobile ambivalence is here again evident since, according to some women researchers in Africa, mobile phones provide a new focal point for social conflict between spouses and can reinforce traditional gender power differences. This subject will be further discussed in Chapter Three in connection with Ubuntu solidarity.

What needs to be asked at this juncture is whether women, who are so widely inscribed in the marketing strategy of mobile phones, are as well adequately involved by the mobile phone industry in other aspects, like designing and manufacturing of the mobile products.

As a conclusion, we can emphasise the following with regard to African women and the mobile phone. First, African societies should consider the impact of mobile cultures in their discourses about gender-based subjugation of women. Secondly, for the mobile phone to play a really significant role in liberating African women, the mobile phone industry should be challenged to design mobile phones and provide airtime tariffs that are affordable to poor people, including African women.

Thirdly, policies should be put in place that will provide women-oriented mobile forums. Such forums should enable women in an easy and convenient manner to deter and report domestic violence, sexual assaults, killings of old women suspected of witchcraft, combating harmful customs like female genital mutilation and other myriad forms of violence that daily skirt around the lives of African women. Only such mobile service provision will have undertaken more realistic steps towards liberating the African woman.

Engaging Mobiles in Health Issues

Mobile technology has been found to have the potential to contribute greatly in the fight against HIV/AIDS. In the year 2007, for instance, a scheme geared towards harnessing mobile phones to fight this epidemic in Africa was announced with the backing of leading companies and the American Government. The project titled

"Phones-for-Health" was expected to 'use software loaded onto standard Motorola handset to allow care workers in the field to enter critical health information into a central database in real time.'[23]

South Africa and Kenya are examples of African countries where the mobile technology is already employed in addressing the AIDS pandemic. One area in which this works is with regard to implementation of drug programmes such as the antiretroviral drugs for AIDS patients. Patients living in remote areas may miss their appointments either due to limited access to transport or because they simply can't afford the fare. This has been exposing them to the danger of suffering from the side effects of the drugs. But now with the mobile technology things are changing:

Doctors and caregivers can manage in information database containing a patient's treatment history, from remote locations using SMS. Likewise, upon visiting a patient they are able to report on side effects, check pill counts against data from the pharmacy, and provide additional information such as conditions that interfere in the treatment program like the absence of food and extreme poverty...symptoms indicative of dangerous side effects can be dealt with straight away by sending an SMS to the clinic and arranging an appointment as quickly as possible.[24]

In this way the mobile technology helps in providing a lifeline for AIDS sufferers as well as their caretakers. And as women in most African households are the ones who normally bear the burden of taking care of AIDS patients, the mobile phone on this regard serves as an instrument of their liberation as well.

A second area in which the mobile technology comes into play is in the provision of the right information about the HIV/AIDS epidemic. In Kenya, for example, a company known as "One World" has launched a service through which people can text questions to a special number and receive information regarding HIV/AIDS. Besides, daily tips are sent out to subscribers detailing how to prevent and deal with infection. Here again the strength of the mobile phone is witnessed as text messaging is relatively cheaper, more popular, and people can have access to information which is anonymous. This is an important step in the fight against HIV/AIDS pandemic since stigmatisation of victims is still high in Africa.

All these advantages of the mobile phone testify to the fact that it is of utmost importance for policy makers and mobile companies to *glocalise* the mobile phone in Africa so it can help address challenges that face Africa in a particular way.

Globalisation of African Traditional Healers

The phenomenon of globalisation has clearly escalated international human migrations. Many people have become global nomads. Evidently, migrants would move with their clinical problems such as diseases to their new countries. But some churches in Africa emphasise that even demons have gone global.[25] Hence, they urge their followers who have migrated to other lands to continue sustaining links with their pastors back in Africa in order to obtain protection from malignant forces. It is the mobile phone that largely enables the sustenance of such contacts.

Some African traditional healers as well tap into this resource of the mobile phone. As van Beek in his study in North Cameroon attests, they carry out their apprenticeship remotely:

The patients describe their ailments, (the healer) asks where the pain or problem is, and they have to pay his fees by transferring money by telephone. After he has received the money, he sends the products (concoctions) to the post-office box indicated...Once the patient has received the parcel they call him...He tells them...how to use the products—in what order, at what time, with what drink or food...Once they are healed, they are expected to phone him again; if not, he checks up on them by phoning them, about every two weeks... (van Beek 2009: 129).

Thanks to the mobile phone, this particular medicine-man has reportedly built up a wide circle of patients not only across his home country Cameroon, but also among African immigrants living in distant countries like Norway and France (van Beek 2009: 30). In this way, the mobile phone has endowed African traditional healers with the potential to carry out transcontinental medication and enter the global market.[26]

Van Beek notes that apart from making the healing services accessible even to patients living in far-flung places, this remote traditional healing facilitated by the mobile phone affords the healer to stay away from any risk that might accompany physical contact with the patients, including contamination. In consideration of abuses widely practiced by African traditional healers on their female patients, this kind of remote healing per mobile phone will probably contribute towards reducing the rate of HIV/AIDS infection.[27]

It is noteworthy that the trade of traditional medicine-men is booming because many poor people who cannot afford the relatively higher costs of modern medication resort to traditional medicine. Another reason for avoiding hospitals, however, is that some patients become mistrustful of them when medical doctors and nurses fail to abide by medical ethics. It is said that in some African countries, particularly at this time when sexually related diseases and HIV/AIDS are prevalent, most youths have more faith in traditional medicine because of their high sense of confidentiality. Health officials and nurses on the other hand, are said to have an unreceptive attitude towards those suffering from sexually transmitted infections. They allegedly tend to ridicule the patients and accuse them of promiscuity.[28] As a result, many patients are scared away and in turn take refuge in the booths of traditional healers.

Now that the mobile phone can be used by traditional healers for distant consultation and dispensing of medicine, the apprenticeship of African traditional healing, may probably continue to boom. And this indeed, challenges the health sector in Africa today to appraise the therapeutic attitudes of doctors and nurses to their patients as well as reconsider the efficiency and costs of medical treatment with regard to the poor in the society.

Mobiles and Democratisation of Africa

At the inauguration of the US President Barack Obama on January 20, 2009, Rev Joseph Lowery had urged in his closing benediction with words that can be paraphrased: 'let tanks be beaten into tractors.'[29] These words articulate a profound message that is applicable to many places across the modern world, including Africa. It is a message to dictatorial governments, suppressors of democracy, perpetrators of corruption and ethnic differences and other marginalising constructs that lead to wars, ethnic conflicts, hunger, forced migrations, poverty, and many other woes.

Africa yearns for a culture of peace. It longs for that day when one ethnic group shall not lift up sword against another ethnic group, when tanks will be beaten into tractors for increasing agricultural productivity to feed millions of hungry people there. When will that day come, when justice in the various countries of the continent will roll down like waters and righteousness as a mighty stream?

Perhaps no other non-African leader could emphasize this point with greater audacity than the US President Barack Obama. While in Ghana in July 2009, at his first visit to sub-Saharan Africa ever since taking office as US President, Obama emphasized that forces of tyranny and corruption must yield if Africa is to achieve its promise:

We must first recognise a fundamental truth that you have given life to in Ghana: Development depends upon good governance. That is the ingredient which has been missing in far too many places, for far too long. That is the change that can unlock Africa's potential. No country is going to create wealth if its leaders exploit the economy to enrich themselves, or if police can be bought off by drug traffickers...No business wants to invest in a place where the government skims 20 percent off the top, or the head of the Port Authority is corrupt. No person wants to live in a society where the rule of law gives way to the rule of brutality and bribery. That is not democracy, that is tyranny, even if occasionally you sprinkle an election in there, ...and now is the time for that style of governance to end... Africa is not the crude caricature of a continent at perpetual war...[30]

The mobile phone may prove to be an effective tool for the realisation of this yearning. It has been observed that there is a correlation between mobile communications and the spread of democracy and promotion of national unity in a country. The Democratic Republic of Congo is a glaring example. It is a very vast country with a generally poor infrastructure. Politically it has known decades of dictatorship under the late Mobutu Sese Seko, who was ousted in 1997. Reportedly, during the dictatorial regime mobiles were the preserve of elite of barely 20,000 people, who paid up to $3 per minute for local calls. But with the current mobile technology boom, phones are more accessible to the masses and analysts have observed that this helps unite the country and may lead to greater democratic freedom.[31]

In fact, in many countries mobile phones prove to have the potential as instrument of advocacy for development and public mobilisation against corruption and other malicious tendencies in government circles and other echelons of society. For example, offences committed by police and government officials can now be photographed and casually spread.

In Kenya a mobile based service called *Bunge* SMS that combines the internet and mobile telephony has been provided to the public with the aim of empowering Kenyans to influence Local Governance in their constituencies. By this forum people can report corruption and environmental degradation; they can influence choices of developmental projects to be carried out in their constituency as well as monitor development activities in general. This is achievable through an SMS platform which allows a person to send a message to his/her Member of Parliament.[32]

In Zimbabwe mobile phones and SMS were said to play an important role during President Mugabe's regime in mobilising the people and encouraging their civic and political participation. Election results from all over the country could also be collected within a short period of time via SMS (Kößmeier 2009: 434). Similar use of the mobile phone in the political arena is reported in other parts of the world.

In the Philippines for example, people employed mobile phones to organize public pressure against President Joseph Estrada on account of personal corruption charges and they eventually managed to force him from office in 2001 (Katz et al.2002: 2).

However, mobile phones have also been employed to undermine democracy. During 2010 general election campaigns in Tanzania, according to the *Guardian,* the Registrar of Political Parties and the anti-corruption bureau had to launch investigations into allegations that some members of political parties were transferring bribe money clandestinely to potential voters through mobile phones. The Registrar, John Tendwa, and the anti-graft agency had confirmed receiving complaints about such practices from Arusha, Arumeru and Mwanza and had to enter into an agreement with mobile phone providers to investigate the matter (*The Guardian* 24 July 2010). The investigation may be facilitated by the fact that SIM-cards have been registered in Tanzania.

It is a common experience in other African countries as well, that mobile phones have been used as instruments of terror and intimidation with the aim of suppressing democracy and frustrating anti-corruption efforts. They have been used to eliminate whistleblowers, critics, subversives and political opponents. Some have used mobile phones to rig elections. But positively, on other occasions the mobile phone has facilitated enrolment of new political party members, payment of annual fees, and polling procedures.

Since corruption is present to some degree in every country, it is indeed a global issue. Yet, studies by some bodies such as the World Bank and Transparent International reveal that African countries tend to be at the peak of the so-called "corrupt societies." (Kolade: 79). The kind of corruption that is greatly inimical to African economy is what is referred to as high-level corruption that is, the 'abuse of an influential position for private gains' and the 'exploitation of a system for securing unmerited advantage (Kolade: 79). Corruption is blamed for the failure of the tremendous aid that has been poured into Africa to translate to integral human development in the countries and communities that receive aid (*Kontinente, das Missio-Magazin* September-October 2009). It is observed that as compared to other continents Africa has registered the least economic leap-forward despite being beneficiary to much foreign aid. Rampant corruption coupled with suppression of democracy and freedom of expression and other forms of human rights abuse result into a situation which makes some African countries experience conflict as a part of life, as constant as the sun.[33] There are wars over land and wars over resources.

Employment of mobile phones to express public opinion and especially to bemoan corruption and other evils in society has also been a growing phenomenon in many African countries. In this sense, the mobile phone has really become a "voice of the voiceless." Popular protest discourses are disseminated in the form of personal complaints, news stories, or advertisements, and even cartoons. Amid the anxiety of worsening economic conditions and escalating poverty the people resort to such discourses as a way to name the reality, to prescribe solutions and project a more promising future for the country.

Some leaders tend to dismiss such mobile phone discourses as mere chatter. However, rather than ignoring them outright, some social analysts suggest that the discourses should be regarded as serving an epideictic function. In the Aristotelian sense of the word, epideictic function means using a speech in order to prove whether a person and their possessions or actions are worthy of honour or censure. Hence, an epideictic discourse stands in contrast to a forensic discourse in that the latter is the use of a speech to determine what happened (Katz 2002: 2).

It is, therefore, unfortunate that leaders tend to simply ignore epideictic discourses that occur in everyday cultural expressions made by ordinary people. Most African leaders prefer direct revealed insights of topical forensic discourse of experts. The ignored folk views may, however, prove to be more abundant in observations and explanations than expert discourses exchanged in long and expensive seminars and workshops or even in parliamentary sessions.

"Paparazzi-boom" and Empowerment of Whistleblowers

In the fight against corruption, it happens sometimes that some government leaders are really committed to the cause of scraping it and seek to engage the ordinary people in this fight. Yet one of the most common fears is about the protection of the whistleblowers. A Chief Justice in Ghana had once blamed the attitude of Ghanaians to corruption, accusing them of merely complaining and whispering with one half of the mouth covered, instead of naming and shaming the perpetrators of graft. Such an attitude, she pointed out, had bogged down the Judiciary's determination to resolve the problem of corruption and improve public satisfaction in the judiciary.[34]

Admittedly, what the Chief Justice said is the appropriate approach to resolving social vices. As US President Abraham Lincoln had once said, to sin by silence when they should protest makes cowards of men. However, such an air of democracy is not enjoyed by the people in most African countries. The call to 'name the culprits in order to shame them' is in most cases easy only when applied to the small corruption offenders and not in cases of graft that implicate tycoons and government ministers. Quite realistically, to be a public whistleblower is to risk one's security since in most cases one's protection would not be guaranteed. But on the other side, experience shows that government ministers and high-ranking officials who are implicated in corruption scandals are seldom brought to justice. This is why most average citizens develop cold feet on this matter.

Today, owing to the mobile phone, there are more *paparazzi*[35] in the society than ever before. There is a "paparazzi-boom", so to speak. A *paparazzo is* a 'freelance photographer who doggedly pursues celebrities to take candid pictures for sale to magazines and newspapers'.[36] The instrumentality of the mobile phone as an object of interference into other people's private life is enhanced by the mobile camera phones. Camera phones have a commonality with other (traditional) cameras as instruments for photographing. Nevertheless, the camera phone has specific feature that differentiates it from the traditional camera. This feature is that the camera phone is located in a device that is connected to telecommunications grid and which is usually carried by people wherever they go (Goggin 2008: 135). Hence, the camera phone has increased the opportunity for taking photos and has thus brought an unprecedented influence in the society as far as the culture of photographing is concerned.

The growing intrusive trend in society tends to assume a corrective or disciplining role. Today incidents of good-reporting and ill-reporting via camera phones abound. Their consequences have been either constructive to the society or disruptive of social peace and harmony.

The "paparazzi-boom" is of particular relevance in relation to Africa's quest for democracy and good governance. Now that there is the mobile phone, perhaps Africans will be spared of the fear of naming and shaming perpetrators of corruption and other crimes. The merit of the mobile phone on this regard can be asserted since its quality of privacy may offer protection to authors who disseminate information about corrupt elements (although now SIM cards are registered). Moreover, the mobile phone's ubiquity, its connectivity, its camera utility, and its link with the internet add up to the strength of this device on this regard.

Spiritual Undertones of Mobile Communications

Mobile phone usage has pervaded religious circles. Indeed interaction of religious communities with communication technology does not begin with the age of mobile phones. After telegraph conversation was held for the first time, Samuel Morse had reportedly posed his famous question: 'What hath God wrought?' From that moment on communication technology is said to have been infused with spiritual undertones'(Goggin 2008: 53). People have been amazed by the sheer imagination of a disembodied voice speaking across time and space, and this echoes an otherworldly quality that remains in many reflections on this technology.

The embracing and adaptation of the features of the mobile phone for religious purposes are today becoming more and more a common phenomenon among numerous religious groups in the world. Much research has been conducted already on this subject. Pope John Paul II, for instance, was said to send out daily religious texts and prayers by SMS. Similarly, Hindus in Bombay were said to make their offering using mobiles by sending their prayers to Ganesh via SMS, thus avoiding quest at temples. In Britain, Muslims could pay a small fee to receive verses from the Koran and were enabled to fulfil their religious duties to give alms to the poor through a special mobile forum "TXT & Donate Islamic Prayer alert".

Religious groups are said to be a stimulus for mobile innovation and designing by having special phone features suitable for devotion. This can be witnessed from Muslims receiving handsets with a built in "Mecca Indicator" that reminds them of prayer times. Similarly, a handset designed in Taiwan is dedicated to the Chinese goddess Matsu. It features the hologram of the goddess, religious changing ring tones and special ritual blessing in the temple (Goggin 2008: 53).

In Africa, it is becoming common practice to see images that express the Christian faith such as the Sacred Heart of Jesus, the Blessed Virgin Mary or the Holy Father, being displayed as screensavers on mobile phones. Moslems likewise place images of personalities they consider as role models in their faith. Mobile ringtones too have gone religious. Instead of the traditional inbuilt pieces of western music, now instrumentals of famous church hymns are customized as ringtones by many mobile users. Interestingly, a ringtone may be customized by a mobile user in Tanzania and shared to other users living as far away as Kenya, and vice versa.

Some churches already employ the mobile phone for Bible studies whereby they facilitate the communication between the congregation and their pastor during church services. For example, text messages containing questions from the congregants would be sent to the pastor and the pastor would later give answers to the questions before the whole congregation.

As far as the co-ordination of pastoral work in the parishes is concerned, mobile phone usage has brought unprecedented impacts. Unlike in the past, mutual communication among parishioners has become easier and appointments with church leaders can now be more conveniently arranged. Pastors can be more easily located and summoned to emergency events such as sick calls and meetings. Moreover, there is now the possibility to make real pastoral counselling and consultations over phone. Generally, the mobile phone has facilitated the alleviation of cumbersome pastoral situations.

The mobile phone has sometimes been used hand in hand with the radio in the task of evangelisation. In the Archdiocese of Songea, Tanzania, for instance, the world-famous *Radio Maria* had local correspondents in many remote villages who covered pastoral and social events and conveyed their reports to the broadcasting station via mobile phones. Listeners likewise used mobile phones to have their prayers broadcast live from their local villages.

The mobile phone impacts religion negatively as well. Arguably, while religious users may attempt to shape media to their need, the same media may conversely 'reshape the religions, and even trivialize the content and create a religious counterculture' (Kalu 2008: 107). Probably this concurs to what C.S. Lewis once said in his remark on the impact of media on the society of his day: 'whereas Zacchaeus "could not see Jesus for the press", we today often cannot see Him for the Press with a capital P' (Lee 2004: 84). This holds true as well in our mobile age context since an uncritical adoption of mobile-mediated products may stifle a person's growth in religious faith.

There are already indications that some cherished religious values are at stake due to the proliferation of the mobile phone. In the Middle East, for example, a growing tendency has been observed in the Muslim society whereby during Ramadan people simply send SMS greetings to family and friends instead of visiting them as has been the tradition hitherto. This mobile phone culture has received public criticism (Goggin 2008:53).

Mobile phone cultures seem to impact Christian practices as well. The always-on environment of the mobile phone may often interfere with believers' privacy and peace to comfortably pray or read sacred books.

In the Philippines, Catholic Bishops had to publicly denounce wireless confessional services, accepting confession or offering absolution via SMS. Apparently, some priests were doing such practices (Goggin 2008:53).

Today at entrances to many houses of worship one finds posters reminding worshippers to switch off their mobiles. This expresses one negative aspect of the mobile phone in relation to worship, namely, causing disturbance during liturgical celebrations. Distraction of congregations due to phone ringing and SMS alert buzzes is a common feature during worship. Ironically, even officiating ministers themselves may sometimes forget to switch off their phones, and as a result receive awkward calls in the middle of the liturgical celebrations.

Mobile phones may hinder active participation in liturgy as worshippers may be subjected to divided attention. Nuptial liturgical celebrations are a case in point. It is a common occurrence during such celebrations that some members of steering committees may attend the ceremonies in the church while simultaneously keeping in touch with the preparations going on at the venue of the festal reception. In this case, they even defy the order to switch off their phones. They intentionally leave their phones on so that they may be reachable and regularly exit the church to attend to incoming calls. This sometimes becomes irksome to other worshippers. In some places such as Seoul (Korea), some churches are said to have installed cell site dampeners in order to discourage parishioners from using their phones during services (Bell 2005: 80). But photographing in places of worship has increased as well because of camera phones. Liturgical celebrants and congregations are often distracted by the photographers and sometimes preachers have to halt in the middle of their homilies and ask the photographers to stop.

Will the Rosary Survive?

The obtrusive spread of the mobile phone does not affect believers while in houses of worship alone but it poses a drawback to their daily efforts to sanctify their time. Some Christian believers, for example, sanctify the hours of the day by praying the rosary or reading the Bible. Today, however, many believers are denied the peace to pray or read their holy books because of the distractions caused by phone calls either through their own mobiles or their neighbours'. Will the holy practices then survive the onslaught of mobile technology?

Catholic priests, deacons and religious refer to the prayer book for the *Liturgy of the Hours* (the Breviary) as *vademecum*. The word comes from the Latin phrase *vade mecum*, meaning "go with me". The clergy and religious are supposed to carry the prayer book with them as a constant companion in order to fulfil their obligation to pray at various periods of the day. Today, nevertheless, many may be challenged to realise that the mobile phone has become a more constant companion, a more pervasive *vademecum* than the breviary. The mobile phone interferes with daily prayer times, and periods of spiritual recollections and retreats. The temptation to view missed calls or SMS texts or to read emails often defies the requirement to observe silence and meditation.

The Mobile Phone and the Idolatry of Work

As later chapters will further demonstrate, the easy accessibility prompted by the mobile phone creates an environment in which workers are forced to continue working even beyond working hours and outside workplaces. Such work intensification may lead workers to break the commandment to keep holy the Sabbath and to do no work. In other words, the perpetual contact enabled by mobile communications may lead workers into idolatry of work. Work becomes an idol and the meaning of one's life. But 'the Sabbath invites us beyond the idolatry of work to worship the true God in freedom' (Radcliffe 2005: 195).

Faith Communities and Negotiation of Mobile Technologies

Faith communities as conveyors of the faith of their respective belief systems are usually among the most outspoken appraisers of a technology in relation to their religious community and the society at large. Religious user communities can be regarded as a "family of users" who create a distinctive "moral economy" of social and religious meaning which guides their choices about the technology in question.

Since religious communities are in a special way the conscience of the society, they ought to assist communities of users to respond to the influence of the mobile technology by publicly assessing its impact in the society. Quite concretely, this means that choices should be made about the meaning and practice of the mobile technology within the religious and social sphere. Thus, churches and other faith communities should evaluate how their members come to terms with the emergent mobile phone cultures. Religious responses to such cultures may range from accepting them, altering them or rejecting them. But in generic terms it is the desire of religious communities that the mobile phone, like any other media forms, should be culturally instructed and negotiated such that it caters to the needs of the larger society without in anyway harming that society. This is one way to realize the potential of a technology as an instrument of liberation for the community of users. In other words, the response of religious communities to the mobile phone cultures is normally resonant with those values that safeguard human dignity as well as religious values.

One way to tap into the resources of the mobile phone is to effectively use it for Christian evangelisation. This is what this book tries to demonstrate in subsequent chapters. On the other hand, it is true that the mobile phone may carry harmful products with it. This fact should serve as a challenge on the part of the bearers of religious faiths in Africa. They should spearhead a hermeneutics of suspicion with regard to the use of the mobile phone and endeavour to rid the society of any potentially harmful mobile phone cultures. This may be achieved by engaging the efforts of a faith community itself. But for it to be effective, it may sometimes require entering into dialogue with mobile phone providers and policy-makers in order to solicit their collaboration.

The proposal that faith communities come to a roundtable with mobile providers may appear to be unrealistic. Since mobile providers are business-oriented people, it may seem that they would not entertain dialogue with faith communities for the sake of safeguarding the moral integrity of the society.

However, the following section presents two examples of faith communities that dared to negotiate with telephone technology and succeeded. One faith community, the Amish Church, did it unilaterally by resisting the telephone or reconstructing it, while the other, the Jewish *heredi* religious community, did the technological negotiation through dialogue with mobile providers.

Negotiation with Telephone by Amish Church

The Amish are a devout Christian faith dating to the 1500s. They have roots in Switzerland and southern Germany and their ancestors began arriving in eastern Pennsylvania (USA) around 1730. They marry within the community and generally eschew modern conveniences such as motorized vehicles, instead rely on horse-drawn carriages.

The Amish permit only limited use of telephones and electricity.[37] Thus, they are a church community that offers a typical example of religious negotiation with technology. It is their beliefs about communication and social life that determines their response to the telephone. Home is for them the centre of community life where most social interaction occurs, including Sunday services and weddings. It is a place where funerals take place (Goggin 2008: 55). Consequently, when the telephone was introduced into the home in early 1900s this community resisted to it since they perceived this new technology to be a challenge to the very core of their social patterns and values.

For the Amish, while the telephone provided access to current information and emergency services, nevertheless, it was deemed to promote individualism and to draw their members into private gossip. This was perceived to encourage disharmony among community members and to facilitate association with outsiders, which was opposed to their principle of separation from the world. After church elders had weighed the benefits and problems that accompanied the use of the telephone, it was decided that it was not necessary for the Amish members to own the telephone privately at home. It was feared that private telephone would spoil the natural rhythm of family life. Community telephones created in 'shanties' were permitted, however, as they were placed in such a way that they encouraged face-to-face contact and their use could be closely monitored.

Drawing from the Amish reaction towards the telephone, Zimmerman argues that,

If the technology is seen as valuable, but incompatible in its current form, reconstruction must take place...this involves making choices about what form of the technology will be acceptable, the context in which it should be used, how it should be utilized and if any aspect must be modified. So if a social group decides that it must resist certain aspects of a technology in order to maintain its social boundaries the technology must be reconstructed so it can be integrated into community life (Goggin 2008: 55f).

It is noted in this study that the Amish church community had raised even more cry of concern when the cell-phone was introduced. Since it is handy, i.e. wireless, portable and personal, the cell-phone was regarded as posing a special challenge to the Amish community since now they could not monitor who was using the phone or was connected to it. The mobile phone for them was, therefore, a device that should be discouraged since it undermined their community values by encouraging assimilation of values outside the community such as individuality and personal control over community responsibility (Goggin 2008: 56).

The 'Kosher' Cell-phone in Israel

The 'Kosher' cell phone in Israel is another example of the outcome of a religious negotiation with a technology. In 2005 a mobile phone designed specifically for an ultra-Orthodox Jewish community was launched, following concerns over the potential unaccepted content infiltrating the community through the use of mobile phones. The community which is also referred to as *heredi* (or *cheredi)* is a small conservative segment of the overall religious community of Israel. It is highly religious and characterised by its rejection of the values of modernity.[38] They distance themselves from TV and internet, for instance, since they regard them as symbols of modernity and secular values. In some of their objections to the mobile phone trends, they described cell phone providers as 'purveyors of secular culture and corrupting influences' (Goggin 2008: 63).

With regard to religious culturing of the mobile phone the *heredi* community underwent a process whereby the mobile technology was publicly evaluated and standard mobile phone technology was resisted. In the public discussions it was revealed that community members spent a lot of time on their cell-phones and that some families experienced financial strain due to their use of the mobile phone. It was noted with concern that the cell-phone posed a danger to the morality of the community and was a conduit for infiltrating unacceptable content into their community (Goggin 2008: 59). Consequently, based on such concerns and other needs, the community entered into negotiations with various major cell- phone companies in Israel and eventually managed to sign a contract with a company which demonstrated to a readiness to produce specially designed "kosher phones" which met the community's public demands.

To make it an artefact of communication without posing any danger to the community, the "kosher phone" was stripped of all content services, set a block on numbers for phone sex, dating services and other dubious secular offerings.

Admittedly, the religious negotiation processes with the mobile technology as exhibited by the Amish church and the *heredi* community represent cases of small religious groups with strict social boundaries and patterns. They, nevertheless, exemplify the negotiation of technology by a faith community for the sake of safeguarding community values and practices.

Concluding Remarks

This chapter has attempted to address the question whether the mobile phone is a liberating factor in contemporary Africa or not. It has emphasised that to some extent, the mobile phone contributes towards improving the lives of Africans in areas such as social communications, poverty alleviation, empowerment of women, health, democracy and good governance, fighting corruption, and in spiritual life. In most of these spheres the mobile phone has, nonetheless, demonstrated a user ambivalence since it has proved to be liberating and enslaving at the same time.

Generally, global assessment positively appraises the mobile phone for significantly facilitating communication "revolution" and poverty alleviation strategies in Africa. Such an assessment, however, does not seem to pay heed to the fact that for the majority of Africans, the mobile phone is primarily used for maintaining social links and not for business. Besides, many average mobile users sacrifice a lot in order to maintain their mobile phones.

Again, the rapid adoption of mobile phones in Africa is an integral part of the ongoing globalisation process that reinforces extractive global power relationships inimical to Africa. In the global mobile industry, Africa supplies raw materials and markets, but technologically remains remains dependent as ever before. This has been a characteristic feature of the relationship between Africa and other parts of the globe for many centuries.

Apart from that, the demand for mobile phones in Africa is a cause of repeated resource wars and conflicts, forced migrations, child-labour, environmental degradation and destruction of wildlife. This is epitomised by Congo DR.

The chapter has also noted how the mobile phone impacts spiritual life both positively and negatively. This makes it imperative for faith communities to negotiate with the mobile technology and mobile users so as to address the negative impacts of the mobile phone.

Christian communities in Africa should spearhead a hermeneutics of suspicion with regard to the proliferation of mobile phones. Indeed, many churches in Africa today preach the *Gospel of Prosperity* to their members as gateway to their liberation from poverty and disease. Church members are taught the skills of financial management and encouraged to adopt proper spendthrift by avoiding squandering money through alcohol, smoking and sexual promiscuity (Martin 2002: 140). These are realistic approaches to reduction of household poverty. One wonders, however, if the churches equally teach their members to be wary in their use of the mobile phone.

Next chapter examines the relationship between emergent mobile phone cultures and the cherished African philosophy of life known as *Ubuntu*.

Notes

[1] Admittedly, reduction of written documents has also a negative effect of having minimal written history of a family, a society, etc, which could be referred to by future generations.

[2] The German name for cell phone is *das Handy*; hence a common English mistake occurs among German speakers whereby the English adjective 'handy' is often confused with the German noun *(das) Handy*.

[3] 'Mobile phones boom in Tanzania', URL: http://news.bbc.co.uk/2/hi/programmes/click_online/4706437.stm (accessed 11August 2010).

[4] 'Mobile phones boom in Tanzania', URL: http://news.bbc.co.uk/2/hi/programmes/click_online/4706437.stm (accessed 11August 2010).

[5] 'Cell phones may help save Africa', URL: http://news.mongabay.com/2005/0712-rhett_butler.html (accessed 8February 2009).

[6] 'Nokia to provide enterprise software for low-end phones', URL:
http://computerworld.co.ke/articles/2009/02/24/nokia-provide-enterprise-software-low-end-phones (accessed 26 February 2009).

[7] http://www.tanb.org

[8] 'Mobile phones boom in Tanzania', URL: http://news.bbc.co.uk/2/hi/programmes/click_online/4706437.stm (accessed 11August 2010).

[9] See:
http://www.pwc.com/extweb/pwcpublications.nsf/dfeb71994ed9bd4d802571490030862f/c79144b731ac02618025746700011320/$FILE/Budget%202008_9_Summary.pdf (accessed 16 February 2009).

[10] 'Kenya in Crisis', URL: http://news.bbc.co.uk/2/hi/technology/6241603.stm (accessed 16 February 2009).

[11] 'Africa: Zain introduces Mobile Banking', URL:
http://allafrica.com/stories/200902250724.html (accessed 26 February 2009).

¹² 'Cell phones may help save Africa', URL: http://news.mongabay.com/2005/0712-rhett_butler.html (accessed 8 February 2009).

¹³This observation was made at a workshop in Vienna, Austria, in June 2009. Participants discussed about African migrants in Europe and the prospect of remittances they send home in uplifting economic conditions of individual families in their respective countries.

¹⁴ 'Mobile phones boom in Tanzania', URL: http://news.bbc.co.uk/2/hi/programmes/click_online/4706437.stm (accessed 11August 2010).

¹⁵ See, Hosea Mpogole, Hidaya Usanga, Matti Tedre, 'Mobile Phones and Poverty Alleviation: A Survey Study in Rural Tanzania', URL: ict4dblog.files.wordpress.com (accessed 10August 2010).

¹⁶ 'Mobile phones boom in Tanzania', URL: http://news.bbc.co.uk/2/hi/programmes/click_online/4706437.stm (accessed 11August 2010).

¹⁷ 1 USA Dollar at the time of the research was equivalent to 1, 212 Tanzania shillings.

¹⁸ 'International Women's Day: Women in Mobile and Mobile for Women', URL:

http://mobileactive.org/international-womens-day-women-mobile-and-mobile-women (accessed 12 March 2009).

¹⁹ 'U.N. Relief Official Condemns Use of Rape in African Wars', URL

http://query.nytimes.com/gst/fullpage.html?res=9D01E6DC10 3BF931A15755C0A9639C8B63 (accessed 10December 2009).

²⁰ 'International Women's Day: Women in Mobile and Mobile for Women', URL: http://mobileactive.org/international-women's-day-women-mobile-and-mobile-women (accessed on 12 March 2009).

²¹ 'Women in South Africa, Domestic Abuse, and Mobile Phones', URL:

http://mobileactive.org/taxonomy/term/1239 (accessed 12 March 2009).

²² 'Women in South Africa, Domestic Abuse, and Mobile Phones', URL:

http://mobileactive.org/taxonomy/term/1239 (accessed 12 March 2009).

[23] 'Cell phones mobilised to fight AIDS in Africa', URL: http://www.reuters.com/article/technologyNews/idUSL1269690620070213 (accessed 15 April 2009).

[24] 'HIV/AIDS and Mobile Technology: SMS saving Lives in Africa', URL: http://www.awid.org/eng/Issues-and-Analysis/Library/HIV-AIDS-and-mobile-technology-SMS-saving-lives-in-Africa (accessed 15 April 2009).

[25] Asamoah-Gyadu's 'Did Jesus Wear Designer Robes?', in: *Christianity Today* (November 2008), URL: http://www.christianitytoday.com/globalconversation/november2009/response3.html(accessed 10 January 2010).

[26] According to some informants in Europe witchcraft beliefs are rife among African immigrants, causing fear, mistrust and jealousy among them. With this possibility of distant medical healing, African migrants can now consult traditional medicine-men and diviners back home through mobile communications. Similarly some immigrants use the mobile phone to communicate with Christian pastors in their countries of origin for healing and exorcism.

[27] Traditional healers in Tanzania for instance are often blamed for demanding sexual favours from their female customers in exchange for their services or as part of the healing process. This is particularly true in cases pertaining to cure of bareness. This observation was made at a seminar on Women and HIV/AIDS Infection, Dar es Salaam, 6 July 2007.

[28] 'Myths hamper AIDS education programmes', URL: http://www.newsfromafrica.org/newsfromafrica/articles/art_801.html (accessed 6 July 2009).

[29] 'Rev. Lowery Inauguration Benediction Transcript', URL: http://blogs.suntimes.com/sweet/2009/01/rev_lowery_inauguration_benedi.html (accessed 12 March 2009).

[30] 'Obama declares to Africa: End tyranny, Corruption', URL:

http://news.yahoo.com/s/ap/20090711/ap_on_go_pr_wh/obama (accessed 11 July 2009).

[31] http://www.news24.com/News24/Africa/Features/0,,2-11-37_1185668,00.html (accessed 26 February 2009).

[32] 'Emerging DG Trends that have Alliance Potential', URL: http://www.usaid.gov/our_work/global_partnerships/gda/dem_guide/dem3.html (accessed 12 April 2010).

[33] 'Obama declares to Africa: End tyranny, Corruption', URL:

http://news.yahoo.com/s/ap/20090711/ap_on_go_pr_wh/obama (accessed 11 July 2009).

[34] See: http://www.newtimesonline.com/content/view/18607/132/ (accessed 27 February 2009).

[35] Paparazzi invade the privacy of people for example by taking photos of celebrities at moments when they themselves least expect to be photographed, such as when they shop, walk through a city or eat at a restaurant. It is unlike press photography, or photojournalism undertaken at press conferences, red carpet affairs and other events in which the prominent people may expect or even desire to be photographed. Paparazzi tend to be independent contractors without any affiliation to a mainstream media organization.

[36] 'Paparazzo', URL: http://www.thefreedictionary.com/paparazzi (accessed 25 March 2009).

[37] The Amish also believe in the literal interpretation as well as application of Scripture as the Word of God. Following some biblical texts, they separate themselves from the things of the world. Worldliness for them is something that is believed to keep their communities from being close to God, and can introduce influences destructive to their communities and to their way of life. See, URL: http://www.800padutch.com/amish.shtml (accessed 23 March 2009).

[38] The members of this ultra-Orthodox Jewish community are faithful adherents of kosher practices whereby separation of the sacred from the profane in all areas of life is upheld. Commitment to religious study and prayers coupled with the wearing of the dress and head coverings of their ancestors of 18th century Europe also constitute their characteristic mark (Goggin 2008:58).

Chapter Three
Mobile Cultures and Ubuntu Paradigm of Solidarity

This chapter explores human cultures that emerge as a result of social appropriation of the mobile phone in Africa and how these cultures impact the African philosophy of life known as *Ubuntu*. The chapter reveals that there are mobile cultures that enhance Ubuntu solidarity and those that diminish it. It suggests that a revamp of Ubuntu solidarity is imperative since it constitutes important African values. Many Africans today perceive that the collapse of African values is the root cause of vices such as corruption, impunity, irresponsibility and others (II Special Assembly for Africa, *Instrumentum Laboris*). The current African mobile age is thus viewed as a chance for effecting this revival of Ubuntu solidarity.

Anatomy of Mobile Cultures

Robert Schreiter, a renowned expert in the areas of enculturation and world mission of the Church, regards the concept of culture as being notoriously slippery, with no agreed upon definition. However, he points out three dimensions which constitute a semiotic definition of culture. The first dimension views culture as ideational, inasmuch as 'it provides systems or frameworks of meaning which serve both to interpret the world and provide guidance for living in the world' (Schreiter 1997: 29). Thus, beliefs, values, attitudes as well as rules for behaviour are integral components of culture in this dimension. The second dimension which defines culture is performance. Culture as performance includes rituals which bind members of a particular group together, enabling them in a participatory way to embody and enact their histories and values. In addition, all sorts of embodied behaviours that people portray are also encompassed in this dimension of culture. Third, culture is defined as material, namely, 'the artefacts and symbolisations that become a source for identity: language, food, clothing, music and the organisation of space' (Schreiter 1997: 29).

As such, in line with our subject matter, the mobile phone like other artefacts (including technologies, rituals, myths and stories) should be read as a visible manifestation of culture (Goggin 2008: 3).

In this work, therefore, the expression 'mobile phone cultures' or simply 'mobile cultures', will be used to refer to histories, values, technologies, rituals, myths, stories and all sorts of embodied behaviours that people portray in their association with the mobile phone. To put it simply, I will employ the expressions 'mobile phone cultures' and 'mobile cultures' to denote all the consequences of the social appropriation of the mobile phone. That being the case, any other designation of 'mobile cultures' with the connotation of spatial change of human cultures will be clearly stated.

Looking at the functionality of the mobile phone one gets the impression that its use has been extended beyond the original intention of the manufacturers. Presumably the original intention of mobile phone manufacturers was to facilitate telecommunications. However, the technologies that are bundled into it have facilitated diverse uses such that across cultures this device has become a form of popular media.

In other words, the mobile phone, having achieved great pervasiveness, has now become such an important aspect of a user's daily life that it has moved from being a mere "technological object" to a key "social object", since it empowers social networks. But some studies indicate that the mobile phone also supports 'tendencies towards closure rather than towards the opening up to new acquaintances' (Geser 2005: 25). Moreover, long-term trends toward planning, scheduling and temporal discipline apparently diminish, while spontaneous, ad-hoc coordination dictated by current whims and circumstances become the order of the day (Geser 2005:32).

Nevertheless, the convergent use of the mobile phone has not only spawned a new way of life in society, but that new cultures are emerging with it. This is because in the process of using the mobile technologies as a means of social change and development some aspects of the society are eventually altered. But in this process the society also conversely acts upon the mobile technologies. Thus, there is a dialectical relationship between society and mobile technologies.

And like other media, the mobile phone offers a place for the formation of conscience and awareness (II Special Assembly for Africa, *Instrumentum Laboris,* No.144), and it is an integral part of the new *areopaghi*[1] of this century. These qualities open a window of opportunity for the mobile phone to be engaged in the task of renewing Ubuntu solidarity in current Africa.

Ubuntu Philosophy of Life

Ubuntu is a word that originates from the Nguni languages. It expresses the very high value of human worth which is found within African societies, and conveys a concept of humanism rooted not in western individualism but in a communal context. It is a concept expressive of a culture that places emphasis on communality and on the interdependence of the members of a community; a concept which conveys the belief that each individual's humanity is truly expressed through his or her relationship with others and theirs in turn through a recognition of his or her humanity' (Paul 2009: 5).

Hence a person with Ubuntu is compassionate, welcoming, hospitable, warm and generous, willing to share, open, available as well as affirming of others. The philosophy ensures that there should be no deprived person in the community and even categories of people such as widows and orphans are not left alone since there will be always someone in the community to take care of them. Ubuntu offers a conceptual paradigm of solidarity of humans, and the catchword which expresses this solidarity is, '"a person is a person through other persons"' (Paul 2009: 6).

Ubuntu solidarity as a human practice is potent. For example, in the history of liberation of the South African people (1948-1994), it is the quality of Ubuntu which gave the people resilience and enabled them to survive and emerge still human albeit the horrors of apartheid. And as Samuel Paul notes, it is Ubuntu that gave the people the courage which culminated in amnesty and reconciliation and led them to strive for the promotion of 'a new narrative of solidarity that embraces diversity, community and inclusivity' in post-independence South Africa (Paul 2009: 7f).

Ubuntu-enhancing Mobile Cultures

Mobile phone usage in Africa uncovers some cultures that are in resonance with Ubuntu solidarity. They are discernible in the way mobile users share their handsets. Mutual mobile communications too promote Ubuntu solidarity since they foster the crossing of social divides and the maintenance of social networks. This functionality makes the mobile phone in Africa a convenient device for maintaining extended family relationships or managing "local embedded reciprocities" (Carmody 2010: 117). It is this social function, rather than maintaining business links, which is the main benefit of the mobile phone for most Africans. The attitude of many African mobile users leads one to deduce that for them the maintenance of social contacts is so highly prized that even the risk of financial vulnerability would not deter it. This fact partly serves to solve the riddle why many Africans, despite their meagre economic resources, want to own or use the mobile phone.

Another mobile culture that points to Ubuntu solidarity is the most frequently asked mobile question: "Where are you?" This question implies care and concern for the wellbeing of others, unless applied in the negative sense of monitoring and controlling others. Ubuntu solidarity is likewise reflected in the theory of virtual and face-to-face communications which is discussed in relation to mobile-mediated communications. Some emergent mobile cultures are deemed to be liberating to young people and women, and hence are considered as well to be in resonance with Ubuntu spirit. But since many use the mobile phone to expose social vices, it becomes a tool that fosters transparency and integrity in the society. Ubuntu solidarity is also relevantly expressed in the question of African migrations. Let us now make a cursory survey on these mobile cultures.

Solidarity in Sharing Mobile Handsets

The Ubuntu spirit features prominently in the sharing of the mobile device. Many mobile subscribers in Africa have no mobile phones of their own. That means, they buy only SIM cards and use them in other people's phones. In Botswana for example, over 60 percent of phone owners share phones with family members, while 44 percent share with friends, and 20 percent do so with neighbours. In all this sharing only 2 percent of mobile owners demand charges from those who request to use their mobile phones. On account of this spirit of sharing there are more mobile subscribers in Africa than there are phones (Carmody 2010: 117). As Carmody remarks, this way of using and sharing the mobile phone expresses an Ubuntu spirit of nonpecuniary utility.

Crossing Social Divides and Interconnectedness

In the world of today human isolationism is being frowned upon more and more and at the same time humanity is becoming increasingly interconnected. Human beings are more and more feeling that they are one family. The advancement in social communication technologies largely contributes to this interconnectedness of humanity. Joshua Meyrowitz observes that electronic technologies help the world speed up the crossing of traditional divides by extending the human reach across old divisions and borders. The information conveyed through the technologies seep through walls that have been separating human beings and leap across vast distances. The 'relatively segregated systems that once defined distinct roles, nations, industries, products, services and channels of communication have been leaking into each other' (Meyrowitz 2003: 97). Consequently, boundaries have become more porous and sometimes to the point of functionally disappearing.

This is what the mobile phone is perceived to effect wherever it proliferates. Unlike conventional mass media, which have 'primarily supported centralised, formalised organisations, households and other supra-individual systems', mobile phones 'increase the reach and capacity of decentralised, informal systems based on inter-individual interactions' (Geser 2005: 31).

On account of its shaping effects some scholars have come to describe the mobile phone as a *mind- and society- altering technology*:

The spread of mobile communication, most obtrusively as cell phones, but increasingly in other wireless devices, is affecting people's lives and relationships. Cell phones spread the pace and efficiency of life, but also allow more flexibility at business and professional levels as well as in family and personal life. They are a boon for those who feel they are not accomplishing enough...Mobile technology also affects the way people interact when face-to-face (Katz 2002: 2).

The mobile phone promotes human connectedness that transcends race, class, and gender divisions, and this is achieved without relying on the 'middleman', since the interactions can be initiated and maintained by direct interpersonal communication. By defying borders and in turn enhancing human connectedness and interdependence, mobile cultures reinforce the modern globalist rhetoric that no part of the world can live without others. The differences between peoples, races and ethnicity are more and more considered as accidental rather than essential. Bernice Reagon Johnson brings home this point thus, 'we have pretty much come to the end of a time when you can have a space that is "yours only" – just for people you want to be there… we've finished with that kind of isolating. There is nowhere you can go and only be with people who are like you. It's over. Give it up' (Sandercock 1998: 117). Furthermore, while undermining the traditional mechanisms that have secured segregation between different social systems, the mobile phone now offers the chance to each individual to regulate the boundaries between different social relationships, groupings, organisations or institutions (Geser 2005: 32).

This border-crossing functionality of the mobile phone as an artefact is due to its ubiquity, its quality of being always-on, its ability to sustain perpetual contact, its SMS and camera phone facilities, and on. And as Schreiter further observes, it now becomes possible to have 'a networking that increasingly eludes hierarchical control; network has replaced hierarchy as a social model of communication' (Schreiter 1997: 8).

Communications technologies converge with other phenomena such as global capitalism to create globalisation. One of the definitions of globalisation is 'the extension of the effects of modernity to the entire world, and the compression of time and space, all occurring at the same time' (Schreiter 1997:8). This is one aspect of mobile phone cultures that features out prominently. In relation to Ubuntu solidarity, it is of paramount importance to understand the social impact of mobile phone cultures that tear down walls of human separation. These cultures pose the challenge that all divides that diminish human dignity be they physical, social, cultural, economical, religious and similar divides need to be crossed.

Later sections of this book will argue that it is this potential of mobile phone cultures to cross various divides in society that constitutes the point of departure for doing a *Cell-phone Ecclesiology* that is truly African and authentically liberating to various categories of people in the continent. Geser rightly observes that 'given its affinity with informal, non-institutional social spheres, the cell-phone may be the most useful for more marginal population groups (e.g. children, adolescents, migrants, the jobless or retirees) not integrated into work roles or other stationary institutions' (Geser 2005: 24).

Geser privileges the mobile phone by comparing it to the so-called "one-to-many" media, such as the printing press, radio, TV and the fixed telephone. He regards the latter category of media as pawns of supra-individual institutions and contends that these types of media have one commonality, namely:

They invade the private sphere of individuals with propaganda, commercials or other messages that serve the interest of enterprises, governments, political parties or other collective entities that are not usually part of daily life. As a stationary device, the landline phone also supports supra-individual institutions by connecting locally fixed offices and by forcing individuals to be at a certain place and to use such institutionally provided intermediaries for entering into mutual communication (Geser 2005: 24).

In Geser's view the mobile phone challenges this long-standing trend of the "one-to-many" media because it empowers bilateral or inter-individual interaction. This empowerment as well as enlargement of the sphere of micro-social interactions, avails individuals with the freedom to reach each other at any time and place. And what seems to be liberating is that such an interaction is achieved without the need to conform to institutional norms that demand a presence in a specific place, and without requiring a relationship with others present at this same location.

Descriptions of the mobile phone and its functionality as an artefact, testify to its suitability for human communication and integration. This is testified by its following prominent features: **adaptability:** most mobile phone types can be operated easily by consumers by simply following instructions from their operation manuals. **Mobility:** 'there isn't a single other electronic gadget you have around 24 hours a day, every day a year' like the mobile phone

(Goggin 2008:48). **Flexibility:** with the mobile phone one can be reached at any time and if one is not personally present a message can be left behind by mailbox or through SMS. **Convenience:** being easily portable everywhere the cell phone is deemed a very convenient device. **Connectivity:** the mobile phone offers users the possibility of permanent accessibility because of its virtue of always-on immediacy and reliability. **Customisation:** with the cell phone it is possible for the user to personalise ringtones and screensavers to suite personal design. **Context sensitivity** is another merit: data of the mobile phone users are recorded and thus can be evaluated. It is possible, for instance, to identify a calling number, the date and time of calling, or of sending SMS.

In summary, therefore, the cell-phone is described as a ubiquitous device. It is as if mobile users try, with this device, 'to realize hidden unconscious desires of mankind to be ubiquitous, and thus to be like God. (That) everything must be available at the push of a button (a phenomenon that) psychologists call…"thumb syndrome"'(Glanz 2006: 43).

Africa, a continent replete with a plethora of marginalising socio-cultural and economic divides such as gender-based discrimination of women, tribalism, ethnocentrism, religious bigotry, and the like, stands in need of such mobile cultures. These cultures reflect the Ubuntu spirit and convey the message that African societies should as well transcend all life-diminishing divides for the sake of promoting true peace, justice, reconciliation and integral development.

The Mobile Question "Where are you?"

One of the most frequently asked questions in mobile phone communications is: "Where are you?" Mobile users ask this question to initiate a conversation. Today this question tends to substitute the traditional greeting form "How are you?" Most mobile conversations would now often begin straight by locating the other person by asking, "Where are you?" Among many African societies, however, it is commonly considered lack of concern and even rudeness to go straight to business matters without first greeting the conversation partner. And for conversation partners who are familiar to one another, it may even be important to inquire about the other person's family and loved ones. Hence the greeting form "How are you?" or a similar form is more suitable for opening a conversation since it expresses warmth in human relationships. Thus a typical African greeting among familiar people will involve such questions as: "How are you?" "How is your family?" "How is the sick person faring?" "How is the rain this season?" "How is the food situation?" and so on.

Nevertheless, airtime tariffs in Africa are so forbidding that one is normally forced to forsake the luxury of prolonged conversations. As such, people have to be always cost-conscious and instead of starting conversations with endearments and prolonged litanies of salutation, as the African culture would cherish it, they tend to go straight to the point. But another reason for skipping the question "How are you?", of course, is that the question is a more personal interrogation and it normally requires adequate time to answer it, whereas the question "Where are you?" can be answered with a clear-cut answer.

In mobile conversation the question "Where are you?" is logical since, unlike stationary phones, the mobile phone allows one to be located anywhere. It is the caller who normally explicitly asks where the called person is. But sometimes the called person himself or herself without further being asked by the caller declares his or her location. By asking another person "Where are you?" the caller may wish to know if the called person has a convenient environment for holding a talk at the time. Whether he or she will be disturbed or whether other people will overhear their conversation. But the caller may also intend to find out whether the called person is in a secure place or not, or to know what distance stretches between the two conversation partners.

Hence inquiring about someone else's location has become an integral part of mobile culture. Set in the context of Ubuntu, it means that the mobile phone has become a tool for promoting and nurturing Ubuntu solidarity. This is testified by the fact that most Africans, as stated in preceding sections, use the mobile phone primarily for maintaining social networks and not for business. This means, they use the mobile phone to express their concern and care for others, to safeguard the security of others and to express their acknowledgement that they are keepers of their brothers and sisters.

Some mobile users on the other hand make phone calls for the sole reason of locating and tracking others in order to control them. This makes some people perceive that the mobile phone enslaves them. Using the mobile phone in this manner undermines the Ubuntu spirit. In some spousal relationships, for example, the question "Where are you?" may make some feel they are being remotely monitored by their partners. This research has revealed numerous cases in which cheating husbands or wives had used the mobile phone to conceal their actual locations. Such incidents had often catastrophic consequences on the marriages upon the revelation of the truth.

As contemporary Africa is struggling to combat the HIV/AIDS pandemic, one of the highly recommended antidotes is faithfulness in marriage. In such a context, asking a spouse "Where are you?" should perhaps be less construed as a control mechanism. The question may simply imply: "are you located at a safe place? Are you not indulging in acts that have dismal consequences on our marriage and lives?"

Virtual versus Face-to-face Communication

This section examines briefly the difference between virtual communication, which the mobile phone privileges, and face-to-face communication, which is unavailable in mobile communications. Virtual and face-to-face modes of communication constitute an important theoretical development in social communications. The section proposes that both modes of communication can be brought to bear on Ubuntu solidarity and challenge Africans to be both locally-oriented but at the same time to be universally-oriented by getting out of the cocoon of isolationism based on ethnic or national identities.

Face-to-face communication has been found to increase cooperation than a virtual communication that is sustained by written messages via e-mail or mobile phone. In Africa, for example, despite the wide penetration of the mobile phone, personal contact remains very important because personal relationships are formed during meetings conducted in person. Some case studies have testified that even in dealing with government administration 'using a phone call or sending a letter rarely generates the desired response', rather it is personal encounter that matters most (Molony 2003: 107).

Several factors account for the strengths of face-to-face communication. First, face-to-face communication is more dynamic and fluid as compared to written message and the issues under discussion can be even more accurately and effectively handled through a live exchange of ideas (Balliet 2010: 48). The mere realization of the presence of the other partner in the dilemma increases cooperation.

Secondly, face-to-face communication has an advantage of employing other social cues such as eye gaze, sound, and touch. Notably, such cues foster cooperation between communication partners and are often unavailable in written or computer-mediated messages. The same holds true for mobile phone conversation, since apart from sound, the cues of eye gaze and touch are also missing. But the significance of such subtle cues cannot be underrated since they might communicate the discussion partner's commitments in the dilemma.

Thirdly, face-to-face discussion in comparison to written communication 'is more likely to activate the social norm of promise keeping, which would subsequently increase levels of cooperation' (Balliet 2010: 48). In fact, social norm, which is a rule that individuals use to direct their behaviour in specific situations, will only direct such behaviour if people expect others to cooperate in the dilemma.

One of the liabilities of a virtual online communication is that it lacks leadership. This weakness is also regarded as a factor that makes it difficult to evaluate the credibility of others' promises in a social dilemma discussion. In a common project such a leadership vacuum coupled with lack of face-to-face discussion might hamper the efforts of some particular members. This may in turn lead to the collapse of the efforts of other members as well.

However, face-to-face discussions have also their weak points. For example, they are costly, time-consuming, and, if international, people may be required to travel very long distances. This promotes pollution of environment; for example, through more extensive air travel (Balliet 2010: 49).

Through its virtual communication, however, the mobile phone helps people stay in steady contact with one another. This type of communication and interaction is reminiscent of pre-modernity whereby people never move far and live in small towns and villages near each other such that everybody knows where everybody else is, and so on. By being virtual mobile communication, nevertheless, is no longer bound to any single locality, as was the case in pre-modern times (Geser 2005: 25). This 'virtuality' makes the mobile phone ubiquitous and capable of compressing time and space. It demonstrates the mobile phone's power to defy borders and to be adaptable to all places, to various kinds and status of people and to all forms of culture. In this sense the mobile phone is inclusive, global and universal, but also local and particular.

By introducing virtual communications the mobile phone initiates new ways of relating among Africans. Hitherto the African people have been accustomed to mutual physical visits and face-to-face social encounters. It is evident among many Africans for example, that issues merely discussed over phone may not seem to have reached a definitive conclusion unless they are further confirmed at a face-to-face meeting.

The virtual mode of communication seems to diminish the warmth of human relationships since physical interpersonal encounters are reduced. However, thanks to such modes of communication that today one can make friends with people he or she has never encountered physically. The Internet for example, is creating virtual societies and new forms of society organizations (Carmody 2010: 111) whose members may have no chance of meeting face-to-face. Many relationships, some of which culminating into marriages, begin with such virtual communications.

Both face-to-face and virtual modes of social communications can be assessed in relation to Ubuntu solidarity. Arguably, while face-to-face communication serves to further the sense of community, interdependence, and warmth in relationships among people, virtual communication, on the other hand, promotes the blurring of social borders. This then underlines the challenge that for Ubuntu solidarity to be relevant to contemporary Africans it should not be confined to ethnical or national boundaries rather it should transcend those boundaries and incorporate other people.

Youth- empowering Mobile Cultures

Studies suggest that more young people own and use the mobile phone than their elderly contemporaries. In Tanzania, it was found out that the largest age group of mobile phone owners was the cohort of 18-25 years old, followed by the cohort of 26-35 years old.[2] This implies as far as the mobile phone is concerned, young people become digitally more knowledgeable than elderly people. If this trend continues, mobile technologies will possibly leave the elderly behind.

Another social impact is with respect to the status of African elders. Increasingly the proliferation of mobile technologies challenges the power of knowledge, authority and respect formerly accorded to elders. This is simply because the new technologies have made private knowledge formerly acquired mainly through years of existence to become public knowledge. In this sense mobile technologies seem to empower young people to an extent of usurping the place of elders in their particular communities.

We can mourn what seems to be lost with the proliferation of the mobile phone, but we should focus on what has been gained, since the mobile phone is generating new forms of interaction that crosses many social divides in African societies. For example, those African societies in which gerontocratic authority has traditionally dominated, mobile cultures now challenge them by infiltrating an egalitarian spirit into them. This serves to promote Ubuntu solidarity in the societies. Gerontocracy in Africa may have functioned well in some cases. But it has often proved to be less life-affirming to some members of society, particularly women and young people. Apart from maintaining exclusionary attitudes on decision-making, elders in some societies have implicated women with witchcraft, while young people have sometimes been subjected to humiliating traditional customs.[3]

Even in the life of the Church, gerontocracy has scared aware many young men and women from membership in some churches. Experience with Small Christian Communities (SCCs) in Tanzania, for instance, indicates that young people do not cherish the meetings of these communities because they are dominated by elders. David Martin notes with regard to African Pentecostalism that, many young people and women leave the older (mainline, missionary) churches because decision-making is dominated by elders, mostly men (Martin 2002: 140).

The mobile phone, particularly through its texting utility, is said to exert changes in the lives of young people. Young people all over the world are leapfrogging over the PC straight to the mobile phone as their "first screen" for entertainment, communications, news, and social interaction. The Commonwealth Consumer Affairs Advisory Council had in 2002 reported that mobile phones for young people today are probably ranked the most important product. For them a mobile phone symbolises freedom, growing up, excitement and having fun and a "must have" for teenagers wanting to achieve social acceptance.[4]

With the mobile phone the youth form a connected class; they use it mostly for chatting, SMS and text messaging and at a lesser degree in voice conversation. Consequently, the mobile is becoming for the youth an extension of themselves and a part of their identity. Furthermore, the mobile phone is allowing young people to work at their relationships more energetically than they might have done before. The use of SMS is for them a resource in achieving a sense of co-presence and intimacy. This is because the SMS as compared to voice call has the strengths of convenience, easiness of access most of the time, less disturbance and cheapness. According to some studies SMS 'affords a sense of closeness and intimacy' (Goggin 2008: 163). It helps arrange social gatherings and other appointments, helps form a strong binding force between the sender and the receiver such that existing relationships are sustained and strengthened.

According to the studies, moreover, new forms of intimacy between lovers are facilitated by SMS because not only a platform for transmission of "unsayable" and ordinary topics is provided by it, but also the exchange of various poetic quotes that people seldom mention in other situations is facilitated via SMS. Moreover, the mobile phone being a very personal device, provides a sense of privacy which is conducive to the expression of inner feelings between the sender and the receiver. It also provides the possibility of saving the exchanged SMS texts, photos, and so on.

Besides, in amorous feelings and romance SMS has been found to instil personal bravery among users, as some find it easier to express themselves by SMS message rather than by speech. Thus, girls prefer to text their complaints to a boyfriend because this would not result in a physical outburst from him. Similarly boys prefer to text their own concerns since the girls would not respond with tears and weeping. When they communicate with texts girls find themselves less weepy, while boys likewise find themselves less prone to violence (Harper 2005:109).

The cell phone, therefore, is regarded as an ideal communication space between lovers, whereby more site to explore their desires is provided as compared to traditional face-to-face communication (Goggin 2008: 163).

It has been noted in some studies that the mobile phone also serves to indicate the passage from teenage to adulthood. As teenagers age they more and more adopt the various socially accepted patterns of mobile phone use, such as how to address someone and what to say. Thus, after a certain age the inability to observe such mobile phone social rituals is viewed as a measure of immaturity.

These mobile cultures can be interpreted as factors that confer empowerment on young people and help them shape their identity in society. This is an important aspect for Ubuntu solidarity to be really inclusive. After all young people are the majority in Africa.

Women and Subversion of Traditional Gender Roles

The mobile phone promises to empower women in terms of freedom of speech and decision-making process. This is signified, for example, by the remarkable change brought about by the mobile phone which enables women to subvert traditional gender roles in courtship. It is observed that with SMS women can now take the liberty to court men (Goggin 2008: 164). In many African societies this is a significant change since traditionally a woman was not expected to initiate a romantic relationship with a man. If she tried, she normally risked being misconstrued as an immoral woman. Traditional gender roles required that she should be always passive and at the receiving end. The best she could do was perhaps to try indirectly to attract the attention of the man say with gestures and kind deeds, but never express it verbally.

But now with the mobile SMS facility, African women have been provided with a new avenue of self-expression and relationship-building. They can develop intimate relationship more easily, even venture into romantically taboo behaviour, through this pervasive but indirect contact. The rhetoric now is: 'if you are shy to tell them personally, you can tell it through text' (Nyiri 2003: 203). This is not to say that this is an exclusively women issue. Men too, are beneficiary to this freedom of expression promoted by the mobile culture. But for women this mobile empowerment seems to change what so far has been regarded as taboo in some cultures.

Admittedly, there can't be any genuine Ubuntu solidarity when women, who are the main producers in Africa, have no voice on issues pertaining to their welfare and that of the society. Thus, the communication breakthrough initiated by the mobile phone should be extended to other important areas such as the participation of women in decision-making process in the church communities and society at large.

Mobile Reinforcement of Social Integrity

Chapter Two has described the presence of "paparazzi-boom" and the growing intrusive trend in society on account of the current pervasive social penetration of the mobile phone. People increasingly use their mobile phones to interfere into other people's private lives because of the possibility to communicate information anytime and from any place, and because of the camera phone which has increased the opportunity for taking photos and sending them instantly.

When mobile users interfere into private lives in order to expose vices such as corruption and protect the society from harm, then this is promoting Ubuntu solidarity. As noted in Chapter Two, the mobile phone used in this way is perceived to enhance democracy and good governance in Africa. But, as a section below will show, this mobile functionality is sometimes abused, and consequently results into undermining Ubuntu solidarity.

Mutual Empowerment between Migrants and Home Folks

One area in which the mobile phone fosters the qualities of Ubuntu is in relation to the migration phenomenon. As noted in Chapter Two, mobile phones create many opportunities for economic engagement and employment in Africa. This enables young people to improve the quality of their lives and in effect deters them from longing for migration in search of purportedly greener pastures. And for those who migrate, the mobile phone helps sustain links between them and their families remaining behind through regular SMS text messages or calling. The mobile phone provides the so-called symbolic presence or "absent presence" and through it mutual love and care between the migrants and their families and friends back home can be maintained.

This has proved to be advantageous to both the families of the migrants staying behind and to the migrants themselves. Cecilia Uy-Tioco in her study about migrant Filipino women working in the USA, as nurses, domestic helpers and night-club entertainers, offers a good example of this symbiotic benefit created by mobile phone usage. Most of the migrant women in Uy-Tioco's study had left their children behind to be taken care for by their husbands and extended families.

Among the Filipinos family life is greatly valued. Filipino theologian, Francisco Claver, notes that for Filipinos family identity comes before everything else: 'It is our greatest strength as a people. It is also our greatest weakness (Claver 2008: 45f). Besides, in the Filipino cultural tradition, family responsibilities of emotional nurturing, value-formation as well as care for physical well-being of the children are all attributed to mothering. This entails being physically present, feeding, clothing and providing emotional support for the children. But, to quote Claver again, it is precisely this need to have the means to meet the necessities of life for the family (welfare and education of children) that constitutes the prime reason for millions Filipinos immigrating into other countries in search for employment. For this reason, migrating abroad and leaving the family behind is a sacrifice which, nonetheless, is worth it.

To maintain links with families back home the Filipino migrants practised the so-called "transnational mothering" which was achieved via mobiles phones. A woman could send as many as 20 text messages a day and call home many times a day to inquire how the children were faring, what food they had eaten, and to wish them goodnight, and so on (Goggin 2008: 120). In this way, the mobile phone empowered these migrant women in their traditional mothering role and at the same time it availed them with new ways of mothering their children across time and space (Goggin 2008: 111).

The foregoing account is to some extent the story of African migrants too, particularly women. Studies indicate that the majority of skilled Africans who leave the continent for greener pastures in the developed world are women.[5] They too, often carry out their family responsibilities back in Africa per mobile phone.

Another benefit of the mobile phone on this regard is the facilitation of the sending of remittances. As pointed out in Chapter Two, remittance money contributes more in poverty alleviation in Africa than foreign aid.

The migrants may benefit from the mutual communications with their families since this may help them ease their pain of separation from home, the pinch of rejection, cultural shock, xenophobic treatment and other negative trends that they may encounter in the foreign land. In this sense, the cell phone provides the migrants with new ways of coping with long periods of separation from family and friends (de Bruijn et al.2009: 15f). Hence, it becomes a tool of empowerment for the migrants as a marginal community. These mutual contacts and support between migrants and their home people serve to affirm Ubuntu solidarity.

Anti-Ubuntu Mobile Cultures

Some cultures that surface with the usage of the mobile phone can be interpreted as diminishing the Ubuntu sense of solidarity. This section exposes the following cultures: the tendency of mobile phone users to pay more attention to the "absent presence" than to those physically near to them, intrusion of public order, divided attention, anti-social youth habits, and perpetuation of traditional gender roles that are harmful to women, as well as gossip and interference of other people's privacy. Other outstanding anti-Ubuntu mobile phone habits include: addiction to the mobile device, feigned alibis and deception tendencies, uncritical consumption of potentially harmful mobile-mediated products and exploitative working cultures. Even in relation to the migration phenomenon mobile phone usage reinforces as well some anti-Ubuntu human relationships.

The section demonstrates as well the fragility of Ubuntu solidarity in contemporary African situation.

When "Absent-presence" Overshadows Neighbour

The mobile phone affects the way people interact today. Even when two persons communicate while face-to-face, their communication will often involve the mobile phone such that it becomes a face-to-face-to-mobile-phone-to-face communication. The mobile phone would be included as a participant in what would otherwise be a face-to-face dyad or small group or even parties. We should as well consider the intrusion of phone calls from third parties during such a face-to-face interaction. During face-to-face talks or in group meetings it has become a normal occurrence that one has to break the dialogue in order to attend a phone call.

There is the general tendency for mobile phone users to pay attention to the 'absent presence' while ignoring the ones physically near them. Thus, one may leave even his wife or her husband and go to a secluded place to attend an incoming call. And upon rejoining the "physical presence", he or she may not be willing to reveal the nature of the conversation just shared with the "absent presence." Mobile phone calls and SMS text messages are often regarded as private matters even among married couples or close friends and prying with another's mobile phone messages is often resented as rudeness. In this sense the "absent-presence" usurps even the position of a spouse.

Intrusion of Public Order

One common complaint about the mobile phone is that it undermines the social order. German sociologist, Hans Paul Barhdt, long before the age of the cell-phone, had considered the telephone as a 'medium of disorganisation' which produces anarchy by enabling everybody to reach everybody else directly, without observing formalised channels of communication (Geser 2005: 23). If Barhdt viewed the fixed telephone as a 'medium of disorganisation', he might probably speak worse of the mobile phone today. Obviously with the mobile phone the 'disorganisation' is far greater since now everybody is enabled to reach everybody else directly, anytime and anywhere, and not only by calling, but also by sending SMS text messages. Viewed against the backdrop of model bureaucracies whereby only vertical (not diagonal) communicative flows are allowed, the perception of such disruptive effects of the phone seem to be pronounced (Geser 2005: 23).

With the mobile phone the disruption of the social order is greater since the mobile phone has a wider penetration and it is more ubiquitous. It is a common experience that the use of the mobile phone tends to develop anti-social behaviours. A recent survey conducted by Intel Company to determine what particularly annoyed the public in mobile phone use (*Heute* 30 June 2009) revealed the following results: 72 percent of the respondents said they were annoyed by motorists who would write SMS while driving, 63 percent said they felt disturbed when someone phoned loudly, and 55 percent said they were disturbed because they were forced to know the content of conversations of other people of which they were not interested. Furthermore, 54 percent of the respondents said they found it rude during an entertainment when the phone of a neighbour rang. Some mobile users may respond in a pavlovian fashion to beeps or buzzes of incoming calls or SMS whereby they would grab at the device promptly to see what is new, often regardless of the distraction such an action may cause on other persons.

In some other studies respondents said that loud telephoning in vehicles of public transport for instance, disturbed them because they could not hear the whole piece of the conversation going on between two mobile communication partners.

But generally the habit of many mobile phone users of talking loudly in public without regard for their neighbour's privacy and welfare reflects a growing spirit of egoism in the African society. A further embodiment and zenith stage of this egoistic spirit is portrayed in malpractices such as corruption, nepotism and tribalism in public offices and in religious circles.

As stated above, there is a "paparazzi-boom" in many societies today on account of the mobile phone. This has not only the benefit of fostering transparency and integrity in society but it often violates the right of other people to privacy. The *New York Times* once reported that an entirely new trend is coming up in the USA in which mobile phone owners hunt on celebrities to snap them and later use their photographs for public gossip. This situation gives prominent personalities a hard time as far as their privacy is concerned.[6]

Serving Two Masters at Time

Among serious social impacts of the mobile phone is the tendency to scatter the attention and diffuse concentration of the users themselves and those around them. Many highway accidents are caused by motorists who use mobile phones while driving. Some recent researches have confirmed that drivers on cell phones kill thousands and snarl traffic. The reason behind is that the reaction time of cell-phone users slows dramatically, and this apart from increasing the risk of accidents, it ties up traffic in general. It is also argued that when young adults use cell phones at the wheel, they are as bad as sleepy septuagenarians.[7]

Another serious impact of the mobile phone is generally experienced in the sphere of education. It is noted for example that, formerly teenagers did not constantly talk to each other on phones with nothing constructive or important to say. But now they tend to waste a lot of time on phone calls, writing SMS text messages, personalizing the mobile phones with ringtones and pictures, and the like. Concern is, therefore, raised among some parents over the long-term effect of societal behaviour especially as regards the children and teenagers of today who have fewer occasions to read and think.

Human beings seem to be losing their ability to set aside hours to simply read without distraction. The situation becomes even more serious these days as cell-phones provide access to the internet such that just at the palm of their hand people can receive breaking news, read newspapers, business reports, and so on. One is tempted to constantly browse, shifting from one website to another. Subsequently, it is feared that people lose the ability to read and think. Many feel that even newspaper readership in many places in the world is deteriorating.

The Youth now "hanging out" Digitally

The mobile phone in some aspects seems only to affirm already existing patterns of youth culture. It is argued for example, that the youth of the mobile age "hang out" with their mobile phones in just the same way as they used to purposelessly and idly hang out on street corners before (Harper 2005: 102). Significantly, with the mobile phone young people tend to solidify their existing parochialism which cherishes the vision of a world populated solely by their own peer groups. Some constantly stick their mobile earphones to their ears and exclude the world around them.

Other areas that portray negative impact of mobiles on the youth are seen in relation to family life. In using mobile phones some young people exhibit a spendthrift that signifies a lack of the sense of community. They seem to treat expenditure as primarily individual rather than collaborative matter. A research finding in some households in England revealed that some young people would use fixed lines to call mobile phones whereas using a mobile phone would be cheaper. As a result, they incur unnecessary telephone costs for their families (Harper 2005: 105).

This youth behaviour which even ignores shared responsibility with regard to household bills emanates from another mobile youth culture of exclusivism. According to the said study, when the youth use their family fixed line to call a friend's mobile phone instead of a fixed line, they want to guarantee that their call is answered only by their friend and not by another member of the friend's family. The growing culture is that teenagers in particular are loath to speak with their friend's families. 'Apparently teenage-parent conversation, whether they be within a family or across families are always difficult' (Harper 2005: 109).

Exclusivism among the youth is also evident in the management of the virtual address book of the mobile phone, since the owner is capable of determining whom to include in it and whom to exclude from it. Young people use this facility to constrain their social worlds to those who have a right to contact them and exclude those who do not have such a right. As a result, they do not make themselves available to be contacted by anyone at any time as the technology was surely developed to provide. Reportedly, teenagers seem to manage this inclusion and exclusion of people in their mobile address book with an extraordinary rigidity. For example, they really avoid picking calls that do not have a caller ID on grounds that it might be someone that they have deleted from their address book, say a friend with whom they have broken up.

Harper, who has noted the emergence of this mobile youth culture, wonders if this behaviour is not redolent of high class Victorian propriety. He maintains that during the Victorian time visitors were required to provide a card first before being accepted into a drawing room, and only on the basis of that card would the host decide whether the caller had rights of access or not (Harper 2005: 110).

Managing a social intercourse so severely as the youth seem to do with their mobile phones will certainly raise concerns in the African society. African societies greatly cherish social interaction. In many African societies friendship between two young people for instance, is not solely an affair of the two of them, rather it becomes an affair of members of their respective families. The same applies to marriages whereby members of extended families of both partners will be wholly involved in the necessary procedures.

Concern over the impact of the mobile phone on the moral life of young people is also great. For instance, according to school reports in Vienna, mobiles contribute to violence among pupils whereby footage of real violence, killing and extreme pornographic acts are discovered in the mobile phones of pupils. Some of the scenes portray beatings of passers-by or classmates. They refer to this as "Happy Slapping". Others are excerpts from films or recordings of real atrocities; all these are filmed with mobile phone and disseminated (*Klasse. Das Elternmagazin* April 2009).

Arguably, the mobile phone *per se* cannot be regarded as the cause of violence or enthusiasm for violence. Violence is a much broader social phenomenon. To address the situation, nevertheless, two strategies are suggested. First, there should be a technical protection of the youth and secondly, education for a critical and self-conscious dealing with inappropriate content of mobile phones should be given (*Klasse. Das Elternmagazin* April 2009).

For Africa such a challenge is also there as the mobile phone continues to proliferate. Responsible handling of the mobile technology by competent authorities for the good of the youth and society at large becomes a great quest.

While on the one hand, the instrumentality of the mobile phone to initiate and sustain relationships and promote self-expression can be perceived as freeing, especially with regard to women, on the other, it opens chances for risky behaviours such as sexual promiscuity and marital infidelity. Studies suggest that cell phones were regarded as encouraging sexual relationships and were thus dubbed as the new Viagra and likewise the abbreviation SMS was interpreted as 'some more sex' (Bell 2005:80. In this context the mobile phone may be interpreted as a factor that contributes towards the spread of HIV/AIDS among young people.

African Women: Digitally confined to the "Kitchen"

The mobile phone exhibits some ambivalence in that, while it seems to liberate women, as noted above, it perpetuates some elements that are inimical to women's lives. Apart from the concerns of women addressed in Chapter Two, the following are other aspects that characterise the life of women in relation to the mobile phone. Mobile phones sometimes reinforce traditional gender power differences characteristic of some African societies. For example, some men ensure that their wives have mobile phones primarily in order to enable them to continue carrying out the daily domestic duties when they are absent from home, even when the men are at home.

According to some women researchers in Africa, some husbands tend to determine how their wives should use their phones, and even whether or not they should be allowed to continue owning one. Mobile phones too, provide a new focal point for social conflict between spouses. Problems of insecurity, insensitivity, mistrust and jealousy are recurrent issues related to mobile phone use as far as gender relations are concerned. Sometimes this results in physical and verbal abuse, particularly by men towards their wives. As a Ugandan woman attests:

These findings suggest that new technologies have become another aspect of oppression of women by men, and a source of inequality between them. These inequalities are not just social: mobile phones can also reinforce economic gender differentials. Handsets and airtime are still expensive, and women may be less able than men to afford their use. However, insufficient official statistics on a range of gender concerns relating to technology mean that these new developments are difficult to analyse.[8]

It is evidently ironical also that the mobile phone, which is widely reputed as a "woman-liberating device", is often perceived to be a lucrative item employed by "sugar-daddies". The rich elderly men use expensive mobiles to lure young school girls into sexual relationships, which quite often result into spoiling the girls' education opportunities and infecting them with HIV viruses.

Mobile Gossip and Intrusion of Private Life

In previous sections "paparazzi-boom" has been described positively as helping to empower whistleblowers and safeguarding social integrity. At the same time, however, the mobile-prompted intrusive trend has a negative impact. Some mobile users often abuse this device by engaging it in gossip, and consequently disrupting social peace and harmony. As depicted in Chapter Two, paparazzi would doggedly pursue celebrities to take candid pictures for sale to magazines and newspapers. Some even use such pictures to blackmail the targeted prominent people.

But the victims are not celebrities alone. Even other people in the society may be similarly affected. In one Tanzanian television broadcast, a woman uses her camera phone to send her girlfriend a snapshot of the latter's husband chatting with another woman. She intends to let her girlfriend know that her husband is cheating on her. But the girlfriend recognises the woman chatting with her husband as none other than her own mother-in-law.

Incidents of mobile users violating other people's right to privacy are numerous. Photos, cartoons or SMS text messages that violate other people's dignity have often been spread through the mobile phone or even shared through the internet.

Mobile Addiction Tendencies

Experience shows that the mobile phone so captivates some people that they can hardly part with it. They carry it with them wherever they go. And some treat it as an "electronic pet," literally constantly petting it as one would do with a cat or a dog (Goggin 2008: 32). Some spend several hours a day using their mobiles; it can be talking, sending text messages or simply giving missed calls to friends and loved ones.

Such a constant preoccupation with the mobile phone certainly costs many mobile users particularly young people, much money and their precious time. But often the habit becomes so overpowering that it amounts to an addiction that causes social disorder. It is said, for example, that many people who are addicted to the mobile phone take a real offence at not getting a missed call or a message answered. It makes them feel deeply upset and sad. In current times mobile phone addiction constitutes a big social problem and psychiatrists express their concern that it is becoming one of the biggest non-drug addictions in the 21st century.[9]

We encounter in this case a trend that militates against human dignity and hence a threat to Ubuntu.

Mobile Alibis and Denialist Attitudes of African Leaders

When using the mobile phone we are familiar with the following automatic responses:

'The number you are calling is not available at present. Please try again later'.

'The number you are trying to reach is busy. Please try again later'.

'The number you are calling is not reachable, please leave a message after the beep'.

These responses are heard when a called number is either switched off or the call is not picked due to a real or presumed absence of the called person. It is true that this automatic mobile facility has the advantage of protecting mobile phone users from a bombardment of phone calls. Unlike fixed telephones, mobile phones have a facility that identifies a calling number and hence enables the user to determine whether to pick a certain call or ignore it. And even when he or she for whatever reason chooses not to pick a call, the automatic response of the phone "saves his or face" by announcing that he or she is not available at the time.

What becomes a matter of concern is the tendency of many mobile users to take advantage of this automatic facility and feign their absence. Ignoring phone calls is for some a growing habit. It so often happens that they are actually present and very much available to attend the incoming calls. The promise of the automatic responses to protect their credibility by announcing their alibi seemingly contributes towards giving them the confidence to ignore other people's calls. The mobile phone responses enable them to get away with their lying. This habit of feigning alibis is indeed a common "vice" committed even by the holiest of persons on earth.

Today deception tendencies in mobile speech are rife, for example, with regard to location or contemporary situational engagement of the mobile phone users. It is discernible that many mobile users often lie to their communication partners about their whereabouts and what they are actually doing at the moment of the communication. A study in Britain has found out that eight out of ten telephone conversations end with a lie from either of the communication partners as an excuse for signing off. The favourite lies are like, 'sorry, the doorbell is ringing,' or 'I left something cooking on the stove' or 'children are making nonsense' (*Heute* 29 April 2009).

There are many other areas in which the mobile phone is employed as a means to facilitate cheating. Conmen and con-women for example have sometimes used the *M-PESA* money transfer facility described above, to fraudulently obtain money from unsuspecting mobile users. In learning institutions too, some unfaithful candidates are said to deploy mobile phones to facilitate their cheating in examinations. To address this problem some schools and universities in Africa today have forbidden candidates to bring mobile phones into examination rooms.[10]

Our interpretation of the mobile phone in this context, therefore, is that it is a device that fosters deceptive tendencies in society. Mobile alibis have often resulted into the collapse of relationships. A tendency of procrastination has been another result and it has led to the postponement or failure to execute important projects that required immediate attention. Left unredeemed, the mobile deceptive tendency may in the long run inculcate a culture of deception whereby lying in mobile phone communications may come to be accepted as part of life management in the digital age.

The reflection, therefore, highlights the imperative of accountability and genuineness in relationships. Ironically, the feigned alibis demonstrated by mobile communications indeed demand a reciprocal emphasis that no genuine human society should be built on lies. Truth should be told at all times in order for any human relationships to genuinely prosper. On the other hand, a relationship that is built on lies is doomed to fail and risks exposure by media (Ugwuanyi 2009: 5). This is manifested by the "watchdog" role of the mobile phone in contemporary society as epitomized by the *paparazzi*. This role which is characterized by demands for transparency, accountability and genuineness sets contemporary relationships under stress since it has created avenues of possible hurts and risks. Apparently the mobile phone directs and exposes human relationships.

Moreover, the mobile alibis are redolent of the alibis of African leaders. The mobile automatic response: 'the number you are calling is not available…' does, in fact, point to the habit of many leaders to absent themselves from duty and to be insensitive to the needs of the poor and needy citizens. It also projects our minds to the denialist attitudes of many African leaders when the question is asked about their responsibility for the African situation of perpetual confinement in a straightjacket of misery. Some African leaders tend to deny responsibility by disproportionately blaming it all on foreign agency. The usual mantra is that colonialism and neo-colonialism are the main factors responsible for Africa's difficulties. For them these factors are convenient alibis for the Continent's enduring bondage to situation of underdevelopment. Some African theologians have referred to this line of thought as "anthropological poverty" (Orobator 2010: 322). It is a mindset that adores the notion that centuries of colonial domination have resulted into a historical psychological conditioning of Africans that has rendered them incapable of envisioning progress.

It is undeniable that colonialism and similar systems have historically played a significant role in damaging Africa's economic basis. But the proponents of anthropological poverty fail to acknowledge the responsibility of current African leaders in subjugating the masses of Africans to enduring bondage to situations of underdevelopment through acts of corruption, irresponsibility and other vices. As Paul Gifford notes, the 'dysfunctional neo-patrimonial political systems through which unaccountable elite maintain themselves in power and wealth' (Gifford 2008: 274) are also to blame for Africa's perpetual misery.

Thus, the mobile age is the right moment for Africa to cross the divide of anthropological poverty and embrace the Ubuntu spirit that will transform the prevailing life-diminishing aspects and promote integral development. Pope Benedict XVI reiterates that "integral development" is that kind of development that promotes the good of every person and the whole person (*Caritatis in veritate*, no.18).

Uncritical Consumption of Mobile-mediated Products

There is also moral concern in the society as regards mobile phone-mediated products. In some parts of Europe people are concerned that high frequency emitters can cause brain damage.[11] Some Christian communities do not allow the installation of mobile masts on their property such as church buildings in fear that the technology carried by the masts could be used to deliver 'revolting and damaging' pornographic material.[12] The fear of pornographic literature being proliferated through mobile phones[13] is consolidated by the possibility now available of downloading internet files directly into the mobile phone, without using a computer. This makes control against harmful literature more difficult than in cyber cafes in which many owners strictly prohibit the downloading of such literature.

In some countries governments take measures that ensure the minimisation of the harm caused by the use of mobile phone. Recently the French Environment Ministry had planned to put in place statutory protection of children against radiation from mobile phones (*Klasse. Das Elternmagazin* April 2009). The measure was envisaged to involve a ban of mobile phone use for children under the age of six. The Ministry's argument was that young people and children are sensitive to radiation because their bodies are still under development.

Moral corruption of young people is another issue of great concern. We have already elaborated on this point above.

Thus, African governments and policy- makers may do well to emulate their counterparts in other parts of the world and put in place measures that ensure responsible handling of the mobile technology and its products for the good of the society. The dire need for telecommunications development in the continent should not warrant such potential mobile phone dangers to go unchallenged.

Utilitarian Mobile Working Cultures

The mobile culture in which we live through which we can now also access our e-mails creates an always-on environment and opens one to perpetual contact. And the expectation that one should be available seems to be increased. In the African context the problem of communication as ground for bad performance at work-place has, to a great extent, got a solution. With the aid of the mobile phone, people can, using small portions of time, undertake a lot of work activities. There is also an increased flexibility with regard to working time and place, since some work activities can be accomplished while away from workplaces and outside business hours. This has an advantage of allowing for more mobility of the workers while simultaneously managing a remote control over their work.

This means, the mobile phone has introduced new working cultures in the society that on one hand can be interpreted as positive since they promote cultures of delivery or performance, which are prerequisites for success and advancement.

Nevertheless, because of the expectation of immediate response prompted by the mobile phone, more and more people feel rushed and pressured in their working lives (Edmondson 2010: 37). And on account of its always-connected nature the mobile phone introduces a work ethic that can be described as barbarous since it reinforces cultures that expect people to be accessible even outside the normal business hours. This blurring of work-life boundaries leads to work intensification and extension assumed by employees. This becomes an occasion for usually unrecognized (and uncompensated) prolonged working hours endured by employees. In other words, the mobile phone tacitly exploits employees by letting them work overtime without due payment. The more a worker via the mobile phone makes himself or herself open and available to the employer and to fellow workers, the more this availability will be exploited (Goggin 2008: 36).

In this respect the mobile phone is by no means an artefact of liberation for the employee, since it serves to perpetuate organisational cultures in which employees have little control and influence; it also leads to exacerbated conflict between work and personal activities (Goggin 2008: 28f).

Equally important is the lack of leisure time for the workers. Leisure is one of the priorities of a civilised society. This is well reflected in the ancient Greek and Latin languages. In the ancient Greek, the word leisure, *skole,* originally meant quiet, peace, to rest and to think without distraction. Later it came to refer to spare time or time to oneself, or time dedicated to personal enhancement without any utilitarian implication. But for the Greek leisure did not imply lack of activity or a time completely free or unobligated, rather it meant a time in which one was free from the necessity of work. Work was therefore termed *askalia,* meaning "not to be at leisure". Likewise in Latin, the word *negotium* was used to refer to "business", "occupation", or "employment". It derives from *ne-gotium,* meaning "not leisure".

The spirit of Ubuntu demands that workers should be liberated from a barbarous work ethic, which makes their jobs the centre of their lives. They should be left to enjoy their leisure time when they happen not to be working (Redcliffe 2005:195).

The mobile-prompted work ethic, moreover, reflects and indeed reinforces the situation of the African woman. In many African households traditional gender roles force women to work like mobile phones; they are an "always-on" lot. A typical daily programme of an average woman may involve: working to earn bread for the family, cooking, washing and other domestic chores. Men might be simply enjoying their leisure time.

An elite woman may liberate herself from such conditions by hiring a house-maid. But ironically, she too may subject the house-maid to the same loathsome routine that women endure at the hands of men, while paying her a meagre wage. Such attitudes are opposed to the Ubuntu spirit.

Mobile Cultures and the Millstone of Migration

We have noted above that mobile communications in relation to migration can be interpreted positively as empowering migrants as well as their loved ones left behind in the sending country. Ambivalence is evident, however, since negative dimensions are embedded in the mobile communications. In the case of transnational mothering described above, for instance, the mobile phone makes it possible for the women to continue carrying out their domestic responsibilities even as they are far away abroad. This attests that the mobile phone reinforces the patriarchal system and its traditional gender roles. Were such communication possibilities unavailable, the patriarchal society would probably rearrange gender roles and let the men who remain at home execute the domestic duties.

Thus, mobile phone use in this respect does not promote emancipative perspectives of the migrant women. And in relation to family solidarity, the existence of transnational family and the thriving of transnational mothering made possible by mobile phone use may tend to naturalise and accept migration and separation of families. In this way the negative impact of migration may go unchallenged.

There is another negative dimension. While on the one hand the mobile phone may provide young people with employment opportunities and thereby deter them from leaving their countries, on the other hand it may function in a reverse order by encouraging further emigrations. This may occur due to the regular communications between migrants and their families back home sustained via the mobile phone. Young people may come to perceive that with the possibility of mobile communications living in far-flung lands does not cut the links with home folks after all. This may be an encouragement for emigration since many African young people have been made to internalise the delusive picture of the world of infinite abundance 'out there'.

At a workshop on African migrants it was observed that the desire to go abroad motivates many young African people to study hard in order to acquire good education and skills that are marketable in the developed world.[14] One positive impact of this migration-oriented ambition for study is that the majority of those young people eventually do not manage to emigrate. As a result, they constitute an important workforce in their countries.

The aspect of remittances is another significant area. It is often one of the most outstanding causes for the weakening solidarity between migrants and their home folks. As the latter are often imbued with the idea of "paradise Europe", they may take advantage of mobile communications to bombard their relatives living abroad with frequent demands for remittances. Unfortunately, they may be ignorant of the difficulties and vicissitudes confronted by the migrants. In fact, many African immigrants in Europe, for example, are either unemployed or hired in low-paying menial jobs for which the host people do not vie. As such, the migrants may not be in a position to satisfy most of the demands and expectations of remittances. On account of such remittance demands the mobile phone is not perceived by all migrants as liberating.

However, according to some African informants living in Europe, many young African migrants, perhaps for fear of mockery from families and friends back home, do not reveal their real life situation they encounter abroad. On the contrary, thanks to the mobile phone, they regularly communicate with the folks back home and send them photos of buildings and posh cars that they claim to be theirs in order to give the impression that now they are living an affluent life. In this way they don't become good messengers to their brothers and sisters about the difficulties and misery experienced by many African immigrants in the developed world. Their life does not turn out to be the "paradise" they expected. The dreams of many are shattered.

There is again the feminine face of migration. Organised bands that deal in women trafficking in Africa abound. Young African women are lured with promises of better employment and lucrative salaries in Europe. The traffickers would arrange all the necessary travel logistics and meet all travel costs on a credit basis requiring that the women pay them back upon securing their employment in Europe. But much to the disappointment of the women, the promised employment turns out to be forced prostitution. The traffickers snatch their passports from them and give them mobile phones in order to keep in touch with them.[15]

Psychological impact of migration as exemplified by the situation of African refugees going to Europe is another area of great concern. These people normally succeed to go to Europe after experiencing conditions of torture. Thus, their first wish in the receiving land is to find a place where they are secured from acts of human persecution and where they may find some rest. But as psychologists specialised in the care of refugees note, refugees are subjected to further shocking experience as they find themselves contained in repatriation camps or subjected to interrogations under the processes of asylum-seeking. What they would rather forget is again minutely scrutinised in the interrogations procedures. In trying to extort the real motive of the migrants coming to Europe, the immigration officers will ask them, for example, whether in their country of origin they were tortured at all, when and how was it carried out, and so on (Preitler 2004: 364). Moreover, the migrants may be subjected to acts of hostility from their hosts, for example, on the basis of race.

From the foregoing, we can see how delicate the problem of migrations is and how Ubuntu solidarity is imperative in ensuring the welfare of the people on the move.

"Absent Presence" and the Culture of Blame

We have observed above with regard to transnational mothering of migrant women that the women may endeavour to provide their children and families with financial wealth and economic stability through the remittances they send home. And with the mobile phone they try to maintain a regular "absent presence" among their family members. Such mobile communications may tend to make the migrant mothers feel satisfied that despite the long distance that stretches between their family and themselves, they, nevertheless, succeed in reasserting their mothering roles. Yet, the favourable gestures of the migrant mothers towards their families often prove to be poor substitute for their physical presence among the family members. Remittances and regular mobile contacts alone do not make up for the feeling of abandonment and alienation experienced by their loved ones back home.

Mobile phone use here reminds the women that as they are far away from home, from their families, they are mostly powerless, although they may own fat bank accounts. This is an important aspect to take into account when considering about Ubuntu solidarity. The quest for material success in the family or society should not be at the expense of family values.

As a result of undermining family togetherness through migration, even when the families eventually come to reunite, things may turn out not to be the same again, since relationships are often strained and difficult to rebuild. During the time of their separation the spouses may have cheated on each other and hence end up blaming each other. Children may blame their mothers for having abandoned them; while mothers may resent their children for not being grateful for the sacrifices they have endured for their sake (Goggin 2008: 113). But husbands may deserve blame too, since their migrant wives had to assume the duty of breadwinners and primary economic providers of the households, in addition to their transnational mothering role. Traditionally it is men who are the breadwinners and primary economic providers of the households.

Thus, the subsequent life of the families may be marred by the culture of blame that eventually may become a "relation-killer" among families. Whenever anything goes wrong in the life of a member of the family, the tendency will be to look around for someone to blame and to impute guilt.

But even governments in the sending countries often have their fair share of blame for the weakening of family unity or even disintegration of the families. Evidently, poverty and other conditions that force people to emigrate abroad may thrive because government systems do not address the problems of corruption and socio-economic and political injustices. On the contrary, seeing that migrants remain in regular contacts with their families per mobile phone, corrupt government leaders may not come to terms with the realities at home that force their citizens into migration. In addition, being economically sustained by the inflow of remittances from millions of their migrant nationals abroad, such government leaders may tend to count migration more as a blessing than otherwise. But migration has two faces. For some it may be a blessing, but for others a curse. One can consider, for instance, the many precarious situations in which migrants often find themselves in such as racist and xenophobic treatment, economic and sexual exploitation and the like.

Fragility of Ubuntu Solidarity in Current Africa

Solidarity is a fragile phenomenon since it involves human connections, cooperation and transfer of resources. This holds true for Ubuntu solidarity as well. The temptation to remain within the confines of kinship is its persistent weakness. Many ethnic clashes that take place in Africa testify to this fact. The Rwandan Genocide in 1994 and the post-election conflicts in Kenya in 2008 were partly fuelled by ethnic differences.

The question of kinship in Africa has also its ramifications in politics. As Chabal notes, kinship can be viewed from the perspective of identity or in terms of the burden of relatives. With reference to kinship as identity, it is stressed that individuals are related to members of their ethnic groups on the basis of tradition and precedence. This view permeates the political sphere such that political behaviour seems to be inflected by ethnic politics which takes priority over other forms of social or professional relationships (Chabal 2009: 45). This is evidenced, for example, in political elections and employment where the slogan "blood is thicker than water" dominates.

The other view of kinship indicates that relatives are an encumbrance to the individual. They are seen to impair one's personal professional or political activities that contribute towards the modernisation of their society (Chabal 2009: 45f). It is true, for example, that on account of the "weight" of relatives some African leaders are forced to indulge in the embezzlement of public funds. In the same rhetoric some African churches which espouse the Gospel of Prosperity discourage their members from entertaining extended family relationships as these are antithetical to personal progress (Martin 2002: 140).

Both views of kinship expose the fragility of Ubuntu solidarity in contemporary African society. The view of kinship as identity tends towards the vice of favouritism, whereas the view of kinship as a mere burden and a hindrance to personal progress runs the risk of embracing individualistic attitudes that may disregard even the poor and needy.

Ubuntu solidarity often fails to transcend national borders. This is evident in the way refugees, displaced persons and migrants are often treated by their hosts. We have the example of South Africa in which the concept of Ubuntu has been well articulated and indeed applied in the people's struggle against apartheid. Yet the Ubuntu paradigm of solidarity does not seem to include people residing beyond the borders of that country. For more than a decade a disgraceful xenophobia targeting black African immigrants has gone on unchecked in that country.

Immigrants from African countries such as Mozambique, Zimbabwe, Zambia, Malawi, Nigeria, Somalia and others, live in South Africa in search of a better life. Yet they are savagely set upon by the local South Africans, beaten up, their property looted, raped and murdered. Notably, undocumented white migrants are spared from this ordeal.

The perpetrators of the crimes are largely those living in poverty, unemployment, have no economic opportunities and are without descent housing. And some commentators have used these factors to rationalise the killings. However, in a country where squalid human conditions exist side by side with great affluence, it is the structural injustice which is to blame. And this injustice cannot be set right by committing another injustice. Nor is poverty an excuse for murder.

The familiar complaint of the South African underclass is that the immigrants take away their jobs, houses and women (*New African* July 2008, 13). A Mozambican man called Mugza, for example, was one of the victims in the atrocities which were committed near Johannesburg in May 2008. He was rounded up by the locals who wrapped him in his only possessions, blankets, and set him alight. While he burned, his killers 'danced, laughed, cheered and jeered' (*New African* July 2008, 12).

South African locals pejoratively call foreigners *makwerekwere* which can be loosely translated as scavengers. But in the civilisation parlance the term *makwerekwere* compares the migrants to *homo caudatus*, i.e. tail-men, "cave men," "primitives," "savages," (Nyamnjoh 2006: 39). *Makwerekwere* are thought to come from far-flug places, the sort of places where 'no South African in his or her right mind would want to penetrate without being fortified with bottles of mineral water, mosquito repellent creams and extra-thick condoms' (Nyamnjoh 2006: 39).

The xenophobic treatment of black African immigrants by South Africans epitomises cases of unrequited Ubuntu solidarity. Ironically, hardly two decades ago, millions of South Africans sought refuge in black African countries during the bad days of apartheid and they were not subjected to similar disgraceful xenophobic acts. For the sake of Ubuntu solidarity many black Africans, not only hosted the South Africans, but also took part in their liberation cause to an extent of shedding their blood.

Concluding Remarks

This chapter has sought to demonstrate that mobile usage in Africa reinforces Ubuntu solidarity. This is evident from the way mobile subscribers share mobile phones among themselves and how mobile communications serve to maintain extended family relationships and social networks. However, it has been noted that other emergent mobile cultures are antithetical to the Ubuntu solidarity since either they diminish human relationships or promote tendencies that violate human dignity.

The correlation between mobile cultures and Ubuntu solidarity has guided us to navigate the question of solidarity among Africans today particularly in relation to ethnic differences and the migration phenomenon. We have come to the conclusion that the trajectory of Ubuntu solidarity on this regard leaves much to be desired. The mobile age is therefore a critical challenge to Africans to cross their divides and foster solidarity.

The next chapter discusses mobile cultures in relation to the concept of social justice.

Notes

[1] According to Acts 17:22-31, after St. Paul had preached in a number of places he arrived in Athens (Greece) where he went to the Areopagus and proclaimed the Gospel in language appropriate to and understandable in those surroundings. The Areopagus represented the cultural centre of the learned people of Athens. Paul preached in the market place there every day, debating with epicurean and stoic philosophers. In *Redemptoris Missio,* No.37 c), Pope John Paul II argues that today the Areopagus can be taken as a symbol of the new sectors in which the Gospel must be proclaimed. He refers to the world of communications as the first Areopagus of the modern age which unifies humanity and turns it into a "global village".

[2] Hosea Mpogole, Hidaya Usanga, Matti Tedre, 'Mobile Phones and Poverty Alleviation: A Survey Study in Rural Tanzania', URL: ict4dblog.files.wordpress.com (accessed 10 August 2010).

[3] Young people in some ethnic communities in Southern Tanzania, for example, resented a custom perpetrated by elders that permitted a man to have sexual relations with his daughter-in-law.

[4] URL: http://digitalorthodoxy.com/index.php?Doo=ContentView&id=286 (accessed 23 February 2009).

[5] Workshop report on African migrants, in Vienna, June 2009.

[6] 'Paparazzi-Boom: Handybesitzer machen Jagd auf Promis' URL: https://www.pressetext.at/news/081021001/paparazzi-boom-handybesitzer-machen-jagd-auf-promis/(accessed 25March 2009).

[7] 'Drivers on Cell Phone Kill thousands, Snarl Traffic', in: *LiveScience,* URL: http://www.livescience.com/technology/050201_cell_danger.html#stats (accessed on 19 October 2009).

[8] Women in South Africa, Domestic Abuse, and Mobile Phones', URL: http://mobileactive.org/taxonomy/term/1239 (accessed 12 March 2009).

[9] See:http://wiki.mediaculture.org.au/index.php/Mobile_Phones_-_Technology_-_Disadvantages (accessed 9 March 2009).

[10] The Catholic University of Eastern Africa in Nairobi, Kenya, is an example of such institutions that had put a ban on mobile phones

and it constituted an irregularity if a candidate was found with a mobile phone in the examination room.

[11]'Residents may soon be receiving mobile calls via God' URL: http://deadlinescotland.wordpress.com/2009/01/07/residents-may-soon-be-receiving-mobile-calls-via-god-451/(accessed 9 March 2009).

[12] 'Church porn protest by phone mast objectors-Mobile Mast Row At Church's Highest Court', URL: http://www.christiantoday.com/article/church.urged.to.reject.mobile.phone.masts.over.porn.concerns/10722.htm (accessed 9 March 2009).

[13] Pornography in USA is said to make more sales than Microsoft, E-Bay, Yahoo, Amazon and Google together See: *Informations-Broschüre, Was ich nicht will, das tue ich, Röm. 7:19*, URL: www.loveismore.de, www.nacktetatsachen.at .

[14] Workshop report on African migrants, in Vienna, June 2009.

[15] Workshop report on trafficking and forced prostitution of African women migrants in Europe, in Vienna, June 2009.

Chapter Four
Mobile Cultures and Social Justice

Media as "Gifts of God"

This chapter aims to address the consequences of the social appropriation of the mobile phone from the perspective of the Christian concept of social justice. Trying to grapple with the impact of the mobile phone on this respect, it would seem important to give a few preliminary remarks. First, the common danger with regard to people's attitude towards emergent media cultures is either falling to one extreme of over optimism or to the other extreme of over pessimism about their shaping effect in society. In fact each medium of social communications has its strengths and weaknesses, subject to uses and abuses.

The Catholic Church in its various official documents[1] that set out basic doctrinal principles and general pastoral guidelines on the media of social communications has a balanced view of the media. It notes that media means of social communications increasingly and profoundly affect the way people live and think in their day-to-day life (*Communio et Progressio*, No.1). However, it regards them as "gifts of God" (*Communio et Progressio*, No. 2) which contribute to people's entertainment, instruction, and can serve to spread and support the Kingdom of God (*Inter Mirifica*, No.1-2) in every culture (*Redemptoris missio*, No. 37). Moreover, on account of their capacity to dismantle barriers that time and space have created between persons and cultures, media means can serve as an instrument of dialogue and information within the Catholic Church, between the Catholic Church and other Christian churches, and with other religions as well as the modern world at large (*Aetatis Novae*, No.10). Again, mass media are dominant sources of definitions and images of social reality for individuals and groups—helping many to make judgments and express values intrinsically imbedded in a given culture.

However, the Church clearly expresses her maternal concern over the harm done to society should there be an evil use of such media technologies. Hence, the Church urges users of technologies not to succumb to a passivity that makes them less vigilant consumers of what is said or shown in the media. On the contrary, moderation and discipline should underline their approach to the mass media (*Catechism of the Catholic Church*, No. 2496).

It is further stressed that mass media should respect and contribute to the integral development of the human person and her or his culture (*Aetatis Novae*, Nos. 7 & 9) and be utilised for the attainment of the common good in the society (*Inter Mirifica*, No. 5).

Chapter Two and Chapter Three of this study have demonstrated how the social appropriation of the mobile phone in Africa is fraught with ambivalence. That is, we experience that both advantages and disadvantages emanate from the ownership or use of the mobile phone and from the mobile-mediated communications. Some of these emergent mobile cultures pose serious questions on the issues of social justice. For example, while the mobile phone is positively appraised as contributing towards the emancipation of women, at the same time it is used by some men to perpetuate some gender roles and stereotypes that eventually enslave women.

This section undertakes to analyse some of the mobile cultures that have been explored in Chapter Two and Chapter Three from the perspective of social justice. We shall approach the question by considering the following aspects of mobile cultures: divided attention in social relationships, growth of deceptive habits, encroachment of economic dependency syndrome, and uncritical consumption of mobile phone mediated products that are harmful to society. Other aspects that indicate user ambivalence in mobile phones and have ramifications in social justice include the interference of mobile users with other people's private lives and their tendency to intrude public order.

Other areas of great concern in social justice are the economic impact of the mobile phone on individual families in Africa and the emergence of new working cultures introduced through mobile phone usage. Then, a case study from Tanzania is presented in which ordinary citizens endeavour to combat graft by doing theology via mobile phone discourses. All these aspects are analysed in this chapter in the light of the Christian understanding of social justice.

The Concept of Social Justice

The second preliminary remark is about the clarification of the concept of social justice from a Christian point of view. This is elaborately presented in the so-called Christian social teaching.[2] In general terms the Christian social teaching refers to the sum total of principles, concepts, ideas, theories, and doctrines that deal with human life as well as society as it has evolved over time from the days of the early church. In more specific terms, however, modern Christian social teaching refers to contemporary church and papal documents and encyclicals that address the social problems of today's world. Its era began with the publication of Pope Leo XIII's Encyclical *Rerum Novarum* in 1891.

In Christian social teaching justice is understood not merely in juridical sense but rather in a more comprehensive sense as a habit whereby a person renders to each one his or her due with constant and perpetual will. Justice, therefore, 'pertains to what each person is entitled to as a human being' (Groody 2007: 97). The Compendium of the Social Doctrine of the Church (CSDC) spells out that justice begins with attention to the needs and rights of each person, but it also extends to working for social structures within larger social networks and institutions that foster life (*Compendium of the Social Doctrine of the Church,* No. 208). As the World Synod of the Catholic Bishops, *Justitia in Mundo,* in 1971 stated: 'Action on behalf of justice and participation in the transformation of the world fully appear to us as a constitutive dimension of the preaching of the Gospel, or, in other words, of the Church's mission for the redemption of the human race and its liberation from every oppressive situation' (*Justitia in Mundo*, No. 6).

The Christian social teaching distinguishes the following three primary dimensions of social justice: commutative or contractual justice, contributive justice and distributive justice.

All these dimensions will help us navigate the path to social justice in dealing with the impact of social appropriation of the mobile phone.

Mobile Cultures and the Demands of Contributive Justice

Contributive justice pertains to what people are expected and able to contribute to their society. It concerns the obligations of a person to others. Chapter Three has discussed how the intrusion of public order and the tendencies of deception are predominant in the use of mobile phones. These mobile cultures can be analysed in relation to human rights and contributive justice. As pointed out, the use of the mobile phone in public places often diminishes people's capacity to keep a separate private life or maintain their peace and order. And again, many mobile phone users tend to lie about their location and their activities. In accordance with the Universal Declaration of Human Rights (Art.19) everyone has the right to seek, receive and impart information and idea through any media and regardless of frontiers. However, this right is not absolute; rather it has to be in conformity with other existing rights. This means, it must uphold human dignity and in no way violate the right of privacy of others or their legitimate interests. This concurs, for example, with Pope John XXIII's Encyclical *Pacem in Terris* which posits that media of social communications that impair reputation of the people and the like should be discarded (*Pacem in Terris*, No 90).

Moreover, such mobile practices revolt against contributive justice which "challenges those who take unfair advantage of a system in the name of claiming their rights without any reference to their responsibilities to a larger, collective body of society (Groody 2007: 100). Hence, from the perspective of contributive justice, mobile phone users are reminded of their duty to look out not only for their own welfare, but also for that of others. And the quest for upholding the common good should not be limited to the context of public use of the mobile phone, but should encompass other aspects of socio-economic life. Thus, contributive justice in the context of the mobile age in Africa can serve as a critical reminder to the leaders that the power entrusted to them by the people should be used for the welfare of the people and not for themselves alone. But it can also be taken as a challenge to African citizens who just sit by and grumble about economic hardships instead of contributing their talents, resources and energy to further the development to their countries.

"Digital Divides" and the Demands of Distributive Justice

Distributive justice specifically pertains to the allocation of resources such as wealth, power and reward to individuals, communities, and cities. It addresses the question whether such resources are being divided equally, by merit, according to status, and so on (Cannon 2009: 36). A glimpse of distributive justice is presented in St. Paul's words: 'Pay all of them their dues, taxes to whom taxes are due, revenue to whom revenue is due, respect to whom respect is due, and honour to whom honour is due'(Rom. 13:7). In the Gospel, John the Baptist urged the upholding of distributive justice as a sign of true conversion in preparation for the immanent Kingdom of God. He urged: 'he who has two coats, let him share with him who has none; and he who has food, let him do likewise' (Lk. 3:11).

Distributive justice requires that the larger society carry out its obligation to individuals and groups. It demands that one's basic rights should be safeguarded and protected. It points out to the fact that individuals as well as groups, being members of a human society, have the right to have their basic needs met. This entails among other things, the provision of the minimum material resources that are necessary for individuals to have a humane and dignified life.

Distributive justice also puts special emphasis on the protection of society's weaker members and advocates a greater solidarity with the poor (Groody 2007: 100). One of the strengths of the early Christian communities was the upholding of distributive justice. The believers sold their possessions and goods and distributed them to all, as any had need (Acts 2: 45). And 'no one said that any of the things which he possessed was his own, but they had everything in common' (Acts 4:32). Indeed many ecclesial communities, like the Small Christian Communities in Africa (SCCs), today strive to emulate the solidarity of these early ecclesial communities. It would be worthwhile for the modern church communities to recognise that the prevalence of distributive justice constituted one of the noble prerogatives of solidarity in the early Christian communities.

The cursory treatment in Chapter Two about the emergence of digital divides and the polarisation between the rich and the poor in Africa has revealed some aspects that call for the interpretation of the demands of distributive justice in the current mobile age. First, as noted, many rural communities cannot enjoy the mobile technology as much as their urban counterparts because they have been denied some basic infrastructures including, good transport system and electric power supply. Thus, the mobile phone has been introduced to communities that are in dire need of essential resources for income generation and for the maintenance of the device itself. As a result, what they gain from their ownership and use of the mobile phone is not comparable to the huge running costs of the mobile phones they have to incur daily. Urban people on the contrary, enjoy the allocation of the best resources of the country, including the best communications systems and electric power supply. This makes them more accessible to sources of income and thus less afflicted by the burden of running their mobile phones. Such a digital divide is probably hardly perceivable in the daily rhythm of life. Distributive justice in this context poses the challenge that a country's natural resources should be used for the benefit of all citizens rather than only a section of them. It is ironical that while the majority of Africans live in rural areas, basic infrastructures, in contrast, are concentrated in urban areas where only a small percentage of citizens live.

Again, as pointed out in Chapter Three, most African mobile phone consumers are poor people who use their devices for maintaining social contacts rather than for incoming generating projects. In order to meet the maintenance costs of their mobile phones they have to sacrifice a lot, sometimes even to an extent of forsaking essential needs like decent food. Distributive justice here poses a critical challenge to African governments and policy makers as well as mobile phone providers to safeguard the basic rights of poor mobile consumers. This includes making the tariffs affordable even to the poor so that they too can enjoy the benefits of mobile technology.

Mobile Work Ethic and Commutative Justice

Commutative justice, also known as reciprocal justice, is the measure of that justice which supposes exchange of things profitable for things profitable. It demands paying good with good. In the

Sermon on the Mount Jesus articulates this justice as he teaches his disciples: 'So whatever you wish that men would do to you, do so to them; for this is the law and the prophets' (Mt. 7:12).

Commutative justice can be brought to bear in the context of the new working cultures that emerge with the proliferation of the mobile phones. As pointed out earlier in Chapter Three, the perpetuity of contact rendered possible by mobile phone use, may reinforce work intensification among employees since they may simply find themselves working beyond office hours and outside their work places. This is true, for example, when employers continue to contact them regarding office matters at their leisure times, sometimes even when they are supposed to enjoy moments of recreation with their families. In the Church too, secretaries in diocesan offices, parishes, seminaries and others often become victims of the new mobile work ethic.

One positive thing with these new working mobile cultures in the context of Africa is that they challenge people to value work as something noble and an important step towards development. This is also resonant with Christian social teaching. For example, in his Encyclical *Laborem Exercens* (On Human Work), issued in 1981, Pope John Paul II counteracted the traditional perception in which work was regarded as a curse after the Fall. Now, according to this Encyclical work not only repairs the consequences of the Fall, but also reflects human participation in God's creation. Work is therefore, to be cherished as a high as well as noble calling. In some developed countries citizens express their disenchantment with a situation in which they receive salary without working (Friesl et al.2009: 42).

But on the other hand, as already emphasised in Chapter Three, the mobile work ethic can be interpreted as barbarous and as a tacit perpetuation of some forms of oppression of workers. It is here that issues of commutative justice come into play. Since it deals with relationships between individuals, groups as well as classes, commutative justice serves to uphold human dignity and social responsibility in issues pertaining to economic transactions, contracts and promises. Pope Leo XIII's Encyclical *Rerum Novarum* (On the Condition of Workers) of 1891, for example, clearly manifests the demands of commutative justice. The Encyclical notes that both the poor and workers on the one hand, and the rich employers on the other, should fulfil their duties, especially those duties that derive from justice. Workers should work faithfully, but employers should not treat their workers as slaves and they should pay them their due wages (*Rerum Novarum*, No. 25).

Admittedly, in the current mobile age, interpretations like this may serve to reveal the condition of exploitation of workers exacerbated by the mobile phone. But practically, with the mobile culture of being always-on, it may be taken for granted that an employee (like any other mobile user) is expected to be reachable at any time and any place. Apparently, employers exploit this situation and make their employees work overtime, without the latter in turn being justified to demand due payment for the work extension they are forced to carry out via such mobile communications.

However, the subjection of workers to the mobile utilitarian culture can be analysed against the backdrop of job insecurity, which characterises the current liquid world. Business enterprises prioritise markets, productivity and effectivity, not workers. In their view only customers are real, while workers are ephemeral. Hence, a company will strive to cultivate the so-called *Life Time Value* (LTV), that is a enduring relationship with a customer until death do them part. Workers, on the other hand, are as disposable as spare parts of a car that can be fitted in and taken out of jobs (Redcliffe 2005:197). Thus, the world of work has become a place of profound insecurity and is dominated by fragile and transitory relationships. As such, not many workers will have the courage to challenge the utilitarian mobile work ethic perpetrated by the employers.

Demands of Social Justice in Mobile Popular Narratives

The majority of Africans stagger under the weight of various burdens of poverty, hunger and underdevelopment chiefly on account of corrupt government systems within their own countries. Nevertheless, most of the average citizens are not resigned in their predicament. On the contrary, they cry foul at what they perceive to be malpractices and engage every means at their disposal to fight against them. It is in this context that the mobile phone proves to be a useful tool since the people voice their disenchantment with the leaders in mobile discourses.

But of particular interest is the fact that these mobile exchanges are carried out by doing theology. What I call theology here is in congruence with what South African theologian, Tinyiko Sam Maluleke, describes below. He contends that much of African theology is not done in writing, but it is expressed in the daily life activities of the people. This means, if only written theology would count, then Africa would be robbed of much of theology. Maluleke points out further:

When we are looking for African theology we should go first to the fields, to the village church, to Christian homes to listen to those spontaneously uttered prayers before people go to bed. We should go to the schools, to the frontiers where traditional religions meet with Christianity. We must listen to the throbbing drumbeats and the clapping of hands accompanying the impromptu singing in the independent churches...Everywhere in Africa things are happening. Christians are talking, singing, preaching, writing, arguing, praying, discussing. Can it be that all this is an empty show? It is impossible. This is an African theology (Maluleke 2005: 485).

The significance of this observation lies in that when the Africans do their theology by dancing, singing, performing and living this means in effect that they dance, sing, and perform their concrete conditions of life. In this way, the actions and voices of the ordinary people which are expressive of theology become at the same time utterances of their social, economic, political and other concerns of their daily lives. In other words, believers offer to God their problems or appeal to His intervention of justice.

The following case study with reference to fighting corruption per mobile phones in Tanzania epitomises such appeals for divine intervention.

Fighting Graft by Mobile Theological Discourses in Tanzania

The following case study from Tanzania which refers to the period between the years 2007 and 2009 serves to pinpoint that some ordinary people in Africa today use the mobile phone to bemoan the difficulties they encounter in everyday living, but more dramatically they do theology at the same time. This is what this section refers to as *mobile theological discourses of the ordinary people*.

Way back in 1980s one commentator had described the situation in Tanzania thus: 'Corruption is rife; virtually nothing gets done without the initial lubrication of bribery' (Hartrich 1983: 92). Today that situation may have worsened. It was revealed at some point that graft was rampant in the country in which some government ministers and other high ranking officials were implicated. A Human Rights Report for Tanzania released by the US Bureau of Democracy, Human Rights and Labour for the year 2008, highlighted that there was little accountability in most government entities in the country and this resulted into 20 per cent of the government's budget in each fiscal year being 'lost to corruption, including theft and fraud, and fake purchase transactions.'[3] Terms like *hongo* (bribery) and *rushwa* (corruption) have usually been the proper expressions of corruption situation in *Swahili* parlance.

But this time around the citizens realised that it was not the ordinary kleptocratic elite's corruption that was prevalent, rather it was grand corruption that was perpetrated by egoistic and unscrupulous leaders that relegated the average Tanzanians into grinding poverty. They dubbed it *ufisadi*, and a perpetrator of grand corruption was named *fisadi* (pl. *mafisadi*). These terms are widely in vogue in Tanzania and Kenya. *Ufisadi* is multifaceted, but as regards the period in question it was most prominently manifested in the signing of deals with foreign companies especially in the mining and energy sector, and the misuse of office by ministers. All these amounted to loss of millions of dollars through corruption.

Amid deteriorating economic conditions the average citizens became poorer and poorer. A typical expression of their poverty level was: *"families survive on a meal a day!"* But as the majority poor languished in grinding poverty the gap between the rich and the poor kept widening. It was then that the common people began to express their concern over the prevailing state of affairs. They voiced their mistrust, protest and dissatisfaction with their political leaders in various ways, including booing at their public addresses.

But a new approach involved the use of mobile phones. The people used this device to decry the rampant corruption in the country and what they perceived as insensitivity of their political leaders to the irruption of the poor. The failure to address the myriad socio-economic problems that plagued the people, made the lives of most of them hang in the balance.

Thus, to express their outcry some people would write SMS text messages in the national language, *Swahili*, and spread them to various parts of the country. One of the widely spread text messages was in the form of a birthday congratulatory message between friends. It stated:

Nakuombea ili furaha yako iongezeke kama bei ya petroli (I pray for you, that your joy may increase like the price of petrol),

Na mashaka yako yapungue kama kura zetu kwa chama. (and may your worries decrease like voters' support for the political party)

Na hekima yako ienee pote kama bidhaa za China (and may your wisdom spread all over like Chinese goods)

Na popote utakapokuwa uwepo wako uthaminiwe kama vile viungo vya albino vinavyopaswa kuthaminiwa na kulindwa (and wherever you may be, may your presence be valued like albinos, who are supposed to be respected and protected).

Apparently, such SMS texts resemble many political jokes that circulate in other parts of the world around election times which sometimes prove to be very instrumental for political parties to win the favour of the voters against their opponents. In the case of Tanzania, the SMS texts such as the one cited above, were exchanged to express an acute situation that prevailed in the country at that time. They reflected actual current problems such as the hiking of fuel prices and high inflation rates. Another concern of the people was over the flooding of Chinese goods in Tanzanian markets, to an extent of overshadowing local industrial manufacturing. Most of the goods, however, were counterfeit and were imported into the country by unfaithful business-people who defied the inspection procedures of the Tanzania Bureau of Standards (TBS). Eventually consumers were served with goods that were potentially harmful to their health.

Then there emerged also in the country a new and horrifying type of violence against the life of persons with albinism. Reportedly, in 2008 hundreds of persons with albinism were killed across Tanzania and numerous others were mutilated in the misguided witchcraft-linked belief that their body parts could be used to create wealth.[4] For example, in the Lake Victoria Zone, especially Mwanza, Shinyanga and Mara regions 'albino organs, particularly genitals, limbs, breasts, fingers and the tongue were reportedly in high demand by people involved in mining and fishing activities' associated with superstition.[5] The SMS text message was an appeal to the general public to garner maximum efforts in order to stamp out these heinous acts.

Other SMS texts were in the form of biblical texts and self-made biblical commentaries that the people used to voice their concerns. These evolved as forms of biblical-oriented liberation discourses exchanged among ordinary citizens in an atmosphere of great freedom and anonymity. In this sense the mobile phone was employed as a tool for theological engagement for liberation.

The following SMS text message was composed in imitation of the form of the Lord's Prayer in order to sarcastically condemn corruption that denied the people of their daily bread:

Enyi viongozi mliotufilisi (You leaders who have made us bankrupt),
Majina yenu ni USANII MTUPU (Your names are PURE FRAUD),
Mtakalo lifanyike nyumbani kwenu tu (Your will be done only at your own homes)
Mtupe leo mabilioni yetu ya EPA (Give us back today the billions of shillings from EPA[6] that you have embezzled),
Wapelekeni MAFISADI mahakamani (Bring all graft offenders to court),
Walipeni walimu na wastaafu hela zao (Pay teachers and retired workers their due payments)
Wasameheni wafungwa wote, kama mlivyowasamehe mafisadi vigogo (Forgive all prisoners as you have forgiven those corrupt big-shots)
Msitutie katika mikataba feki (Don't lead us again into bogus contracts)
Tena mtuondolee mafisadi wote (Purge from our midst all corrupt elements)
Kwa kuwa ufisadi ni fani yenu, na uwongo, na utapeli hata milele. Amina (For corruption is your profession, so also cheating and conning, forever and ever. Amen).

When a corruption scandal became public, some members of the public would initiate a discourse about it and share it per SMS to others such as relatives, friends, co-workers, and finally the message would spread across the country. But as the message would continue to disseminate countrywide the original author would eventually paled into anonymity.

In other SMS text messages the name of a biblical personage would be substituted by that of a government minister or official implicated in a corruption scandal, but its interpretation would be different. For example, following the resignation of government ministers who were implicated in graft, an SMS text was composed and circulated countrywide. The form of the text message was in imitation of Jesus' crucifixion episode, but in an out-of-context way. A minister was portrayed as being crucified on the cross like Jesus Christ. Nevertheless, Jesus' final words on the cross: 'it is finished' are borrowed to refer to the end of the ministerial post of the "crucified minister". And whereas Jesus' innocence is exonerated by the centurion: 'Indeed this was the Son of God', the minister's loss of ministerial post becomes a testimony of his malpractice: 'Indeed this was a *Fisadi*.'

Similarly, a government minister who was forced to resign on account of corruption scandals was portrayed in one SMS text message as regretting his loss of ministerial post and warning incumbent ministers of the possibility of the same fate befalling them. His statements were made to imitate the wording of some Gospel passages:

Kesheni mkiomba kwani hamjui siku wala saa itakapokuja kamati ya uchunguzi (Stay awake and pray, for you do not know the day and the hour when the probe committee will visit you)

Nami naenda mtaani kuwaandalia kijiwe, ili nitakapokuwa nanyi muwepo (I am now going to join the ordinary life, but I will also prepare a place for you so that where I will be you too may come).

Nanyi muonapo tume zaundwa basi mtambue muda wa mavuno wa mafisadi umekaribia (And when you notice that various probe committees are being formed, then know that the time for dealing with corrupt leaders has come).

But the discourses that were exchanged in mobile text messaging were found in their longer versions and elaborations in online newspapers such as *Tanzania Daima, Mwananchi,* and others. The "mobile theologians" would challenge religious leaders—Christian, Muslim and others—to take sides with the poor in their struggle against corruption rather than try to defend or collude with those implicated in corruption scandals. They would call upon bishops and priests, for instance, to emulate some biblical figures such as prophets who in similar capacity as theirs, were on the side of the suffering poor in their cause of liberation and defended them against exploitative socio-political systems. They would criticise the attitude of those religious leaders whose actions and words seemed to preach resignation in the face of such great injustice or tended to maintain impartiality.

Finally, the presentation of a discourse would end with a short prayer like: 'God save Tanzania!' or 'God is on our side!' or 'You corrupt leaders, don't you fear even God?' The texts were normally short, concise and easy to decipher.

The practical efficiency of the mobile phone was clearly realized in these discourses since the message would be disseminated via SMS to millions of people in many parts of the country and even abroad within a very short time. I myself received most of them while out of the country.

Reacting to this situation of rampant graft in the country, the Tanzania Catholic Episcopal Conference focused its Lenten pastoral message in 2009 on the sin of corruption and general moral decadence in the current Tanzanian society. The bishops noted:

A great outcry in our society concerns moral decadence in various echelons of Tanzanian life...Our society has witnessed and has been shaken by unusual acts of graft in which leaders in top positions in the government and its institutions have been implicated. In this Lenten Season, our good and merciful God is ready to forgive us, if we sincerely intend to repent of our sinful ways...we need to build a society that is characterised by righteousness in thought, words and deeds, as St. Paul had lived (*Ujumbe wa Kwaresima* 2009).

Social Justice as Basic Key to True Peace

Some African countries such as Tanzania celebrate an atmosphere of relative peace in the sense that there have been no civil conflicts with armed confrontations as witnessed in other countries. We have to appreciate the efforts of leaders who create conditions for the maintenance of that peace. However, some leaders tend to limit their understanding of peace to the situation of lack of war or ethnic conflicts. Their rhetoric seems to be that as long as there is no war, then the people should be contented and grateful.

But when such kind of peace is trumpeted, often as a justification for them to stay in power, the vast majority of the citizens languish in poverty, hunger, malnutrition, diseases, high rates of criminality, and other forms of untold suffering.

However, African leaders who are famous for being architects of peace, like Julius Nyerere of Tanzania, have indeed been fervent fighters of corruption and other social vices. They are a model for current political leaders to emulate.

It is, therefore, important to underline in this context that social justice is a noble prerogative for obtaining true peace. In fact, a comprehensive understanding of peace is articulated in the social doctrine of the Church. In a nutshell, the social doctrine stresses that integral human development and human solidarity, respect for human dignity of every person, and justice are the basic key to peace (World Peace Day 1 January 1987, No. 7). Hence, the new name for peace is development (*Populorum Progressio*, Nos. 76 & 87), and 'if you want peace, work for justice' (World Day of Peace 1 January 1972). And it is by fighting poverty that the world will most effectively achieve peace.

The First Special Assembly for Africa of the Synod of Bishops of 1994 reiterated this very point when it emphasised that evangelisation should envisage a holistic liberation of human persons, namely setting them free from all scourges that oppress them anthropologically as well as spiritually (*Ecclesia in Africa*, No. 68–70).

Similarly, in his sermon on World Day of Peace 2009, Pope Benedict XVI highlighted the importance of building "participatory institutions" and a "civil society" internationally that enables nations to invest in people, fight crime, strengthen the rule of law and reduce poverty. And in his reflection on World Day of Peace in 2010, the Pope once again argued that peace begins when human beings look at one another as persons, regardless of frontiers in respect to race, nationality, language or religion. When human beings recognize that they have a common Father (God) who loves them all, then it will be possible as well to recognize and respect each other as brothers and sisters. And this is a key to true peace.[7]

Furthermore, the Encyclical *Evangelium Vitae* stresses that:

A society lacks solid foundations when, on the one hand, it asserts values such as the dignity of the person, justice and peace, but then, on the other hand, radically acts to the contrary by allowing or tolerating a variety of ways in which human life is devalued and violated... Only respect for life can be the foundation and guarantee of the most precious and essential goods of society, such as democracy and peace (*Evangelium Vitae*, No. *93*).

All these challenges point out to the fact that the narrative of most poor people in Africa is far from being consonant with the definition of peace, even if armed confrontation is absent. When grinding poverty, hunger, diseases, social insecurity, economic hardships and similar life-diminishing aspects reign, there is no peace in such a society. This understanding should, therefore, serve as a constant reminder to those at the helm of the nation to shrug off their perception that a mere freedom from armed confrontation is synonymous to peace. On the contrary, they should take responsibility and engage themselves in a serious commitment to uplift the people from their misery.

"Domestic Justice" in African Church: Charity does not begin Abroad

Mobile cultures challenge the Church in Africa to exercise "domestic justice" when seeking to promote justice in the society. Admittedly, attitudes that impede the achievement of integral human development do not reside exclusively within the secular realm. On the contrary, "'modes of acting" inimical to integral development can be "found within the Church herself"" (Orobator 2010: 329). Charity begins at home. Thus, while local churches do well to denounce corruption and other malpractices in the African economics and politics, they should in a similar vein adopt an *ad intra* focus. They should evaluate their openness to accept challenge with regard to their attitudes that perpetuate similar vices within the Church. Parallel ecclesiastical obligation on transparency, for example, is called upon on issues pertaining to management of church material resources, in the exercise of authority, equality in mission and option for the poor and the marginalised.

The document from the 1971 Synod of Bishops', *Justitia in mundo*, had this to say with regard to this point:

While the Church is bound to give witness to justice, she recognizes that anyone who ventures to speak to people about justice must be just in their eyes. Hence we must undertake an examination of the modes of acting and of the possessions and life style found within the Church herself.[8]

Similarly, what Pope Paul VI noted in 1975 in his encyclical *Evangelii nuntiandi* is eloquent here as well. He argued that 'modern man listens more willingly to witnesses than to teachers, and if he does listen to teachers, it is because they are witnesses' (*EN* No. 41).

Concluding Remarks

This chapter has attempted to unveil some mobile cultures that either overtly or covertly introduce in the society some new trends that tend to violate various dimensions of social justice in relation to personal privacy, public order, economic disparities and work ethic.

The chapter has also demonstrated that only integral human development will bring lasting peace to African communities. Moreover, citing the case study of Tanzania, the chapter has explicated the benefit of the mobile phone as a tool at the disposal of ordinary people that can be engaged in the theology of liberation within their contemporary context.

The ecclesiological import of this chapter is to highlight the role of Christian communities as agents of social justice in the age of the mobile phone. The Church in her social mission cannot and must not stand aloof as far as the fight for justice is concerned. Rather, it has to engage its maximum efforts to ensure that justice prevails and prospers in society.

Between the Church and the state relationships are ineluctable and one area in which such relationships are salient is the understanding of justice. However, issues of social justice have sometimes put the Church and the state at loggerheads, at times even leading to confrontation. Yet, if the Church is committed to an option for the poor and the oppressed, then it too must face up the challenge of serious confrontation.

Confrontation with politicians is evident, for example, when the Church offers the people civic education during election period. The usual accusation is that by teaching civic education churches meddle with political affairs. Confrontation is often inevitable when the Church sides with the poor in their challenge of the *status quo* by taking responsibility for their lives, by struggling against injustice and standing up for their rights. In fact one prerogative of liberation of the poor is for the poor themselves to understand that they are key agents of change (Dorr 1992: 331). Confrontation is also pertinent as the Church's path towards a true liberation of the oppressed entails calling to conversion the oppressors and challenging the structures of oppression (Groody 2007: 97).

The Church's approach in this mission, nevertheless, is not by taking upon itself a political battle. The Church, on the contrary, envisages social justice through rational argument and reawakening of the spiritual energy, since it is concerned with the inner order, that is the order of the soul, in contrast to the state, which is concerned with the outer order, that is, the order of the commonwealth.

Chapter Five explores the impact of mobile cultures on the life and ministry of a church community.

Notes

[1] The documents include: *Inter Mirifica, Communio et Progressio*, and *Aetatis Novae;* others are *Gaudium et spes, The Catechism of the Catholic Church, Redemptoris missio, and others.*

[2] The concept "Christian social teaching," or also labelled as the "social teaching of the Church" or the "social thought" is usually understood simply as the equivalent of the social doctrine of the Catholic Church. *See:* Karl Rahner (ed.), *Encyclopedia of Theology: A Concise Sacramentum Mundi* (London: Burn and Oates, 1975), 1602.

[3] 'Corruption eats 20 percent of government budget', URL: http://www.ippmedia.com/ipp/guardian/2009/03/03/132696.html (accessed 30 March 2009).

[4] 'Corruption eats 20 percent of government budget', URL http://www.ippmedia.com/ipp/guardian/2009/03/03/132696.html (accessed 30th March, 2009).

[5] 'Superstitious Albino Killings in Tanzania Must Stop', URL http://www.groundreport.com/Opinion/Superstitious-Albino-Killings-in-Tanzania-Must-Sto (accessed 30 March 2009).

[6] EPA is a special Fund established by donor countries for alleviating the country's foreign. Billions of Tanzania shillings from this Fund were embezzled with nobody being held accountable.

[7] "Benedict XVI Offers Key to Peace," in: *Zenit,* Vatican City (1st January, 2010), URL. Zenit.org (accessed on 2 January 2010).

[8] http://catholicsocialservices.org.au/Catholic_Social_Teaching/Justitia_in_Mundo , No. 40 , accessed 15 October 2010.

Chapter Five
Reimagining Church Community in the Mobile Age

The Mobile Phone and the Blurring of Religious Frontiers

The current religious landscape in Africa is a multi-religious context characterised by the booming of churches and mosques as well as religious revivalism. It is an atmosphere marked by an unprecedented scramble for spiritual market in which the major monotheistic and missionary belief systems of the continent, namely, Christianity and Islam, in their myriad forms, largely dominate. African Religion (AR) too, is a significant player in this scenario. Yet it is less competitive since, unlike Christianity and Islam, it is not a missionary religion; it other shortcomings include lack holy texts and creeds, and organized programmes for proselytising. And both Christianity and Islam tend to undermine it as heathen religion and seek to convert its followers.

In such a context a discussion on the role of the mobile phone in shaping the mutual relationships of these various religious groups is helpful. On account of its culture of blurring social borders the mobile phone brings people together in a natural way. This fosters mutual communications among Christians of various denominations as well as between Christians and non-Christians, such as Muslims and members of AR.

Experience shows that the media in Africa is prone to propagating cultures that foster religious polarisation. We often witness how the radio, television, videos, electronic public address systems and print media are often engaged by some faith communities to sow seeds of social disharmony and religious intolerance. For example, Christian-Muslim tensions are exacerbated in some parts of Africa when the media are employed in comparative religious teaching. In this approach, preachers often highlight what they consider to be weak points exhibited in the religion of their opponents, particularly their sacred books, in order to undermine it. Live or recorded religious teachings that are often bristled with mutual contempt, slanders and humiliation, are mediated through the media. This, eventually, leads to an increase in tensions since the faith communities become increasingly polarised (Chesworth 2007: 127).

I contend, therefore, that the mobile phone seems to be more effective in helping religionists of different belief systems transcend their borders than the other electronic media of social communications. For Christian communities this mobile culture is a great potential for dialogue, interreligious coexistence and tolerance.

Virtual Communications vis-à-vis Ecclesial Community

In Chapter Three I have delved into the theoretical development of virtual and face-to-face modes of social communications. As noted, mobile-mediated communications are virtual. And, although they prompt the blurring of social borders, they do not foster social harmony and the warmth of human relationships as much as face-to-face interactions, since some significant social cues are unavailable in them.

This thesis can be of great significance when broadly analysed in relation to ecclesial life and praxis. Indeed a Christian spirituality which prizes the culture of "virtuality" risks undercutting the witness of the Church and undermines physical proximity of the believers. Church life and its liturgies require physical presence to be more effective.

The discussion about virtual and face-to-face communications from an ecclesiological perspective is relevant, since today styles of life abound in which people increasingly shun membership in local ecclesial communities. Adherents to this trend claim that they believe without belonging to a concrete community. This is exemplified by the phenomenon known as do-it-your-self spirituality, in the tendency of Christians to accept Jesus but deny the Church, and in the emergent virtual ecclesial communities that are promoted via media, particularly the Internet. Another area of concern is the seemingly growing number of Christians who prefer to attend worship services from their homes via television rather than physically going to places of worship. Some have referred to this habit as high-tech worship.

It is the pervasive attitude of individualism that partly accounts for the emergence of such religious trends. This owes largely to the life of affluence which gives people a sense of self-sufficiency. The advancement of digital technologies also serves to augment the tendency of Christians to discourage community life. Paradoxically, however, so many people today seem to yearn for some kind of community. As such, if the church community does not welcome them, they resort to other communities, including online communities.

Let us briefly traverse these contemporary spiritual trends that tend to ignore organized religion. It should be clearly understood from the outset, that these belief systems themselves are not influenced or shaped by mobile phone cultures. Nevertheless, they serve to illustrate the impact of the virtual culture of communication that is becoming trendy with the proliferation of the mobile phone.

"Do It Yourself" Spirituality

Today, people especially in the West increasingly draw a clear distinction between "spirituality" and "religion".[1] They advocate spirituality without religion or "do-it-yourself" spirituality as some label it. Its adherents generally set themselves very openly apart from the "established" religions with their fixed creeds and moral codes. And eschewing any kind of "priest" or necessary mediator between oneself and God, they, nevertheless accept "astral guides" and "angels", i.e. helpers and advisors.[2] Chris Tong describes the "do-it-yourself" character of the practitioners of this spirituality thus:

One's "holistic lifestyle" might be comprised of a hatha yoga class on Monday; meditation and astral projection on Tuesday; psychotherapy on Wednesday; communal bread baking and Ayurvedic medicine on Thursday; a day of intimacy with one's spiritual/sexual partner on Friday; a long walk out in nature on Saturday; and a day of just "vegging out" on Sunday. It's completely our choice![3]

Hence, spirituality without religion is flourishing, while going to public liturgy, on the contrary, seems to a wide spectrum of people to turn them off God. Arguably, God does not appeal to them when He gets under a roof (Radcliffe 2008: 1).

Empirical researchers as well as consensus among cultural commentators propose a number of reasons to explain why today spirituality is definitely on the agenda, while religion at the same time is falling out of favour. First of all, quite evident in the current age is the general distrust of the people towards traditional institutions. This is particularly the case among young people. This attitude, however, does not seem to affect religious institutions alone, since the mistrust is also towards other institutions such as political parties, which in some parts of Europe are said to fare worse than religious institutions on this regard.[4] The contention is that spirituality is generally perceived as something life-giving, holistic, enriching, and open-ended, while religion is characterised by the opposite qualities, namely it is deemed to be oppressive, exploitational, and hierarchical, and tends to teach only religion, not spirituality.[5] Allegedly, many people experience ritual as empty, lacking in spontaneity, boring and impersonal (Radcliffe 2008:1).

The general trend thus prefers that religious matters remain in the private sphere. It is also alleged that religion be it Christianity, Islam or any other, either consciously or unconsciously, is prone to instil sentiments of intolerance, sectarianism, and violence either overtly or covertly. And it inspires fears of fundamentalism and the "colonisation of souls" In this connection, mission work with the aim of proselytising is considered a threat to social peace, and should therefore be discouraged. Thus, *mission impossible* seems to be the rightful conclusion (Weber 2008: 306).

Curiously, while efforts are made to keep religions at bay, national and multinational companies, in contrast, are left to freely disseminate their "mission statements". No eyebrow is raised when companies describe the understanding of their mission, their philosophy, and their marketing strategies. The media are full of their advertisement, regardless of what a company advertises; even deadly weapons are accorded a place. This societal bias baffles us. As Weber wonders: Don't we Christians also need a clear "Mission Statement" with which to confess before the entire world that we have been sent by Jesus Christ to the people, how we ourselves understand our mission to be and how we want it carried out? (Weber 2008: 306).

"Yes" to Jesus, "No" to the Church

The slogan 'Jesus, yes, but the Church, no!' is embraced by many people who continue to identify themselves as Christians. The remarkable rise in church desertion currently witnessed in the West is partly blamed on the bad image of some church leaders. The perception of the Church today is about people, such that with the collapse of the image of church leaders comes also the collapse of the image of the Church as an institution.[6] Others attribute the fall in church attendance to the levying of church tax, and in the case of the Catholic Church, to the controversial issues of the exclusion of women from priestly ordination and the Church discipline of mandatory priestly celibacy.[7] It is also contended that some leave the church because they simply want to be free from church doctrines which constantly remind then to do good and shun evil. In England, for instance, church attendance had fallen by 20 percent between 1987 and 1999, while reports of 'spiritual experience' on the other hand had increased by some 60 percent in the same period.[8]

In view of this trend in which people increasingly seek spiritual growth outside the bounds of their local, traditional place of worship, some commentators claim that eventually there will rise many public spiritual directors and that there is the prospect of spiritual direction becoming a business opportunity.[9]

Ironically, it is notable that, although many Christians desert the Church as an institution, their expectation from it, nevertheless, remains high. Even the 'unchurched' Christians would expect, for instance, that the Church should deliver charitable services and maintain a good image. In Vienna, Austria, for example, many poor people who frequent parish offices and church institutions begging for alms confess that they have long left the Church but still depend on it for their living.

Virtual Internet Christian Communities

Today people increasingly join the worldwide web family through the Internet. Such web families are to some extent good. Thanks to the Internet that one's circle of friends can be widened and those who had no chance of winning friends through physical contact can now find them online. Moreover, many marriages today are said to start with contact or friendship per Internet. The web can also contribute to mutual spiritual enrichment among the members. In fact, online pastoral approaches using the Internet, say in pastoral counselling, are much in vogue today (Böhm 2010: 78-85). Likewise, some religious communities deploy the Internet to recruit new members, particularly young people.

Pope Benedict XVI has recently similarly underscored the impact of the Internet in the Church and society. Addressing participants of a congress under the theme *Digital Witnesses, Faces and Languages in the multi-media age* in 2010, he noted that, 'the Internet is by nature open, tendentiously egalitarian and pluralist, but at the same time it also represents a new gulf. Indeed, we talk of the 'digital divide', which separates the included from the excluded, and this must be added to other separations which already divide nations, both from one another and within themselves.'[10]

The Pope uncovered the dangers of conformity and control, of intellectual and moral relativism which this digital medium poses. These are evident, for example, in the diminution of the spirit of criticism, in the way truth may be reduced to simply an interplay of opinions, and in the existence of many forms of degradation and humiliation of individual intimacy that are manifested in the Internet. For this reason, the Pope urged Christians to inhabit the digital universe with a believing heart and help to give a soul to the endless flow of communications on the Internet. With such an attitude, the Internet and the other new forms of media technology may serve as a new way of bringing Christ to the streets.[11]

However, the Internet has the disadvantage of sustaining a global virtual family whose members are largely anonymous. With respect to the vitality of local ecclesial communities, it becomes a matter of great concern when many believers tend to prefer such virtual communities of the Internet to the concrete, tangible ecclesial communities. One may spend hours before the computer communicating with virtual ecclesial members of the blog, while at the same time shunning the physical proximity of local church members.

High-tech Remote Participation in Worship

The revolution in media communications offers possibilities of televised and broadcast Masses and other liturgical functions transmitted in this way. Believers are enabled to participate in worship from home or some other gathering spaces. The televised or broadcast Mass is indeed a source of spiritual comfort and growth to those legitimately impeded, and thus dispensed, from attending Mass due to age, infirmity, distance or some other just cause. Moreover, this is a further source of spiritual nourishment if one after attending the Mass still follows the broadcast or televised Mass. However, some Christians today tend to discourage church-going by substituting Mass attendance with televised or broadcast Mass. In this way they avoid physical proximity and the assertion of the sense of belonging together with the other people of God.

The nature of full liturgical participation, however, requires some kind of physical presence in a single assembly. According to *Sacrosanctum Concilium*, full and active participation by all the people is the primary and indispensable source from which the faithful are to derive the true Christian spirit. Thus, it should be the aim which is to be considered before all else (*Sacrosanctum Concilium*, No. 14). For *Sacrosanctum Concilium*, the promotion of active participation in liturgy means to encourage people to take part by means of acclamations, responses, psalmody, antiphons, songs, actions, gestures, and bodily attitudes, as well as observing moments of reverent silence at the proper times (*Sacrosanctum Concilium*, No.30. Evidently, such participation can only be fully achieved when the believer is physically present at the august Sacrifice rather than following it "virtually" via electronic media.

Some church communities may have a "blessed" problem of an overcrowded church such that some members of the congregation cannot see the altar. In the case of such large assemblies it is permitted to use visual means such as giant screens and video projection to enhance visibility of the liturgical actions and allow the congregations to be attentive to the celebration while simultaneously maintaining the unity of the gathered community. Thus, the emphasis here is that to fulfil the Sunday or holyday obligation, a believer must be part of the concrete assembly not in a form of "absent-presence".

Virtual /Face-to-face Communication and Church as God's Family

The First African Synod opted for the ecclesiological model of the *Church as the family of God* as the guiding idea for evangelisation in Africa. This pastoral option was thought to be particularly appropriate for Africa, since it emphasises the African family-values of 'care for others, solidarity, warmth in human relationships, acceptance, dialogue and trust (*Ecclesia in Africa*, No. 63). These cultural values make people love to share with others, to respect others, to be hospitable to others as well as cherish a sense of togetherness. The Synod regarded these values as key factors in addressing the myriad forms of challenges facing Africa. The challenges include: tribalism, ethnic conflicts, corruption, poverty and others. In this respect the family values promote the upholding of the common good, justice, integral human development, peace, and similar life-affirming aspects.

Today, however, as much of the communication is mobile phone- and computer-mediated, a great deal of ambivalence exists with regard to the applicability of this ecclesiological image. Admittedly, the mobile phone (and e-mails), facilitate communication and sustain contact among family members, colleagues and friends. However, since the mode of communication is virtual, they seem to reinforce a kind of contentment with the virtual presence or "absent presence" of these people. As a result, such virtual communications tend to substitute visits, diminish physical presence and face-to-face communication among family members, friends, co-workers, and the like. In this respect mobile cultures do not advance the elements that foster good family relationship as Africans have known them to be.

Analysed from the perspective of media culture, it may be pointed out that if a medium of social communications is to be relevant to the African context, it ought to help promote the cultural values articulated in the model of the Church as God's family. It is noteworthy that not all new media of social communications are necessarily the best for accomplishing this task. Nor is it true that all old media forms are necessarily the least effective. The Pastoral Instruction on social communications, *Aetatis Novae (New Age)*, may speak eloquently in this context. It urges the Church, for the sake of evangelisation and catechesis, to take steps to preserve and promote folk media and other traditional forms of expression as alternative community media, even in the midst of the multiplicity of newer media forms. The Instruction argues that 'in particular societies these folk media can be more effective than newer media in spreading the Gospel because they make possible greater personal participation and reach deeper levels of human feeling and motivation' (*Aetatis Novae*, No. 16).

The Church in Africa is thus reminded that even with the adoption of the new electronic media forms, traditional forms of expression such as story-telling, drama, folklores, songs, poems, and other live and face-to-face communication forms remain effective methods of evangelisation and catechesis in Africa. After all, African societies still cherish face-to-face communication.

The current Christian landscape in Africa makes this argument in favour of face-to-face communication plausible. In some parts of Africa Christianity is no longer monopolised by the mainline churches rather by Pentecostal churches which continue to proliferate (ter Haar 2001:250). A comparative study of the churches indicates that the retrogression of the mainline churches is partly attributed to the presence of structures in these western-oriented churches that do not foster interpersonal communication. Some scholars claim that in the mainline churches Africans encountered superimposed foreign artificial structures. Some have labelled them as "migrant social structures". They contend that these structures have proved repugnant to the indigenous African systems (Oosthuizen 2000: 278). They maintain that the emphasis on the organisation of the church as an institution is opposed to the African inborn sense of fellowship and mutual caring and sharing. These cultural elements of fellowship are evidently salient features in the typical African family and Religion.

Allegedly, it is this suffocation of the inner need for fellowship that, from a functional point of view, made the mainline churches seem not ideal to Africans. As already hinted earlier, Africans cherish face-to-face fellowship and they want it really practised in their churches. This kind of communication is deemed to advance that support which they normally enjoy within the African extended family system. This makes it imperative within African Christianity today to promote those relevant traditional African approaches which convey meaningful Christian appeal and are purported to meet the African religious yearning and challenges. The Pentecostal churches are said to address this very question since they promote small-scale church communities which reflect the extended family system in the ecclesiastical context (Oosthuizen 2000: 278f). Such small ecclesial communities favour face-to-face fellowship mutual sharing and support typical of an African extended family system.

But it is the same motive of engaging African family values in the Catholic Church's theology and praxis that prompted the Church in AMECEA region[12] to promote the establishment and nurturing of Small Christian Communities (SCCs). SCCs were deemed an essential and new way of being Church. The AMECEA bishops viewed them as 'a means to *localize* and *incarnate* the Church and to make it self-ministering, self-supporting and self-propagating' (Gaillardetz 2008: 123). Successful SCCs foster participation and sharing of the faith and material goods among members centred on biblical teachings. They encourage dialogue and a sense of belonging among members. They promote a civilisation of love expressed through the solidarity which these Christian communities endeavour to establish with the poor and the needy in the society.

When a parish is built with SCCs, there will be generally no spectators since all parishioners become players in the Church ministry. As Bishop Patrick A. Kalilombe avers:

At the root of all this preoccupation with small Christian communities is the conviction that, to be realistic, the formation of a true local church has to start from the bottom, that is by the building up of smaller Christian communities. Because when it comes to real feeling of community and a possibility of on-going community tasks, the community in question must be of such a size, territorial proximity, and sufficient similarity of interests as to draw its members into a feasible entity. Such a small Christian community is the only level at which 'the Church' can concretely live and work. It is at this level, that the church will be really present in the society at large and will be able to act (Kalilombe 1999: 102).

Face-to-face Interaction in Ecclesial Communities

Mobile-mediated communications can be positively appraised for enabling the sustenance of networks and human interconnectedness. Nevertheless, mobile users often indicate that such virtual communications do not substitute the physical contact with their loved ones. On the contrary, such communications express the existing gulf between the communications partners. It is analogical, from ecclesiological point of view, that a concrete local church community gives a believer more sense of belonging and satisfaction, than a merely virtual community of believers like the one formed through the Internet.

This analysis leads us to the discussion about the ecclesiological import of a local church community. Simply stated, what is it that makes it a pre-requisite for a Christian to belong to a local church and to attend a Christian assembly? There are many scripture-based theological reasons that may serve to substantiate the quest for a concrete church community. We can mention a few of them only by passing: church community is God's protection area. It offers protection and security for each individual believer against Satan and his temptation (1Cor. 5, 1-5), against the appeal of a purely secular life (2 Tim. 4:10), against the half-heartedness and our weakness (Heb. 10, 23-25), against false teaching which is opposed to God's word as law (Rom. 16:17), and also against mere semblance and the tendency of being merely nominal Christians. Thus, the Church community can be compared to a herd that offers protection and security to each individual sheep.

Again, Christian believers are called to community life (1Corinthians 1:9; 1Jn 1.3, 6-7). An authentic Christian community transcends boundaries. As the followers of Jesus meet in a gathering to enjoy each other's company in the company of their Master, they, at the same time, commit themselves to mutual assistance, care and encouragement (1Cor. 5, 1-5). Moreover, it is at the assembly of the ecclesial community that the practices of the gifts of the Spirit are determined (1Cor. 5, 1-5), and the members are equipped for service.

Furthermore, it is manifested in the Scripture that it is the practice of the Church for believers to assembly at a place regularly (1Cor. 14, 23-25), for which they ought to encourage one another

(Hebrews 10, 23-25). The community life of the early Christians that was characterised by communal ownership of property, equitable distribution of material resources, devotion to the teachings of the apostles and fellowship, regular prayer and the breaking of bread (Acts 2:42), indeed sets a model for any ecclesial life today.

From the foregoing many ecclesiological and pastoral implications can be pinpointed as we shall survey them now.

Face-to-face Ecclesial Communities and Christian Witness

Bodily proximity, face-to-face interaction and even suffering of believers play a vital role in witnessing Christ to the world. Indeed many believers testify to have been greatly edified and confirmed in their faith by examples of their sisters and brothers in Christ after encountering them face-to-face in worship sessions, meetings, crusades and other occasions. A concrete Christian community is also required for a tangible demonstration of Christian love and compassion. These are important aspects in making Christian belief and evangelisation credible and convincing.

Experiences of church communities around the world have manifested that provision of tangible assistance to church members constitutes an important aspect for forming a sense of belonging among the congregants. A survey among Latino/a Catholics in Chicago indicates over 47 percent of adults said that 'programmes or ministries that help the poor or those in need was the aspect that most attracted them to their parish' (Boguslawski et al. 2008: 119). It was also found out that volunteerism of the parish members outside their own parish, was even stronger among those who were helped by their congregation. The beneficiaries of the help offered by their congregation were also more likely to extend a helping hand to others, for example, by giving them a loan, or helping them to find a job. This research revealed moreover, that some parish members considered the fact of having friends or family in the same parish as one of the most attractive features of their congregations (Boguslawski et al. 2008:118). This means, the presence of such people to whom they are closely related assured them more of social and economic support.

By laying such a great emphasis on face-to-face communication, it does not mean, however, that virtual communication and virtual expression of love do not serve any purpose at all in the Church. In fact, online giving of donations as relief aid to victims of natural catastrophes, say by text messaging per mobile phone has today proved very effective. The soliciting of relief aid for earthquake victims in Haiti in 2010 offers a good example of the efficiency of the online method. And perhaps it also helps overcome the temptation of the donors to flaunt their charity. What I maintain, nonetheless, is that online expression of love and online compassion are less effective in the Christian outreach of faith to the world as compared to face-to-face approach.

Face-to-face Ecclesial Communities versus Dangers of Private Religion

Some scholars argue against the tendency of abandoning religious institutions in favour of private spirituality. They contend that, apart from theological reasons, the presence of significant religious institutions is advantageous to the society at large. Austrian pastoral theologian Paul Zulehner, for example, contends that, a religious institution has the merit of being politically quantifiable, whereas private religion, as studies also testify, is more prone to xenophobia, racism, violent settings and other ambivalences which are hard to discern and check since they develop in one's private sphere of life.[13]

Church Pastors and the Quest for the Apostolate of Presence

The strengths of face-to-face communication as explicated in this section pose a challenge to the pastoral ministry of priests and other agents of evangelization. While the modern media such as the mobile phone may prove very helpful in their ministry, they should, nonetheless, try as much as possible to be physically present at the various activities pertaining to the pastoral care of the people of God. It is very much encouraging when such pastors often take part in the activities of the diverse groups present in the parish, for example, in the meetings of SCCs, pastoral associations of women and youth groups, children's apostolate groups, church choir meetings, and so on. Not that the pastors should always influence the decisions of such groups, but even their mere brief presence during the activities of their flock may elicit a positive pastoral impact.

Mobile Cultures and Border-transcending Churches

The mobile culture of transcending various frontiers can speak eloquently to the Church in Africa since the quest for crossing social borders is more and more felt in the African Continent today on account of its increasingly multicultural and multi-religious topography. Religiously, it is observable for example, that members of one family may belong not only to different religions, but also to different Christian denominations, since even within Christianity churches are in their myriad traditions. The enduring statement of Martin Luther King, Junior, that 11.am on Sunday is the most segregated day of the week (Cruz 2008: 365) holds very true also for Africa in its current Christian landscape.

Churches have many challenges to overcome as far as crossing borders that segregate their members is concerned. One prominent hurdle that some churches have to overcome is the incompatibility of their members on the basis of ethnic or tribal differences. Christians ought to strive to cross this cultural frontier so that it may be possible for members of various ethnic groups to worship together and feel at home in a church community. This is what the Church is called to be and the culmination of such a Church is portrayed by John in the Book of Revelation in which people of all tribes, race and nationality come together to worship the Lord (Rev. 7: 9).

Another divide to cross in the current kaleidoscopic religious situation is the existence of divisions in families and in the society at large owing to denominational differences. It is unfortunate that religious differences contribute greatly to undermine social unity in the continent. Quite often the close affinity and sense of community among members of a certain church denomination tend at the same time to nurse some seeds of harmful denominationalist exclusivism. For example, the fellowship imperative among the 'born-again' Christians is sometimes pushed to such extremes as to cause a complete denial of love even to family members who are not "born-again". This research has uncovered many cases in Tanzania in which non-Pentecostals endure suffering at the hands of their Pentecostal family members simply because they refused to convert to Pentecostalism. In one case a "born-again" daughter left her old and sickly father in the lurch because he was adamant in remaining a Catholic. The father was a widower and the daughter was his only child. Some marriages have also gone on the rocks sometimes at the instigation of pastors because one of the spouses, often the husband, has refused to be a "born-again".[14]

But the reverse is also true. It is a common experience that many "born-again" Christians happen to be mistreated by their own families and relatives on account of their denominational switching. Many young people in Tanzania, for instance, normally convert to Pentecostalism in public schools and colleges.[15] Some parents and relatives may react rigorously to this by denying them care or tuition fees or generally ostracise them.

Since "sheep stealing" among the churches is a widespread phenomenon, it often causes denominational tensions even at funerals. A believer may belong to one Christian denomination for the good part of his or her life, but shift to another in a later stage of life. Some undergo denominational switching at deathbed, often on account of incurable illnesses such as HIV/AIDS, since some church denominations attract them with promises healing and exorcism.

The conversions sometimes take place without the knowledge of their former church pastors and their extended family members. This may lead to interdenominational conflicts. There are many known cases in Tanzania in which family members of one Christian tradition with their respective church members rallying behind them, quarrel with another family of a different Christian tradition over the right to bury the bodies of their deceased relatives. Similar conflicts occur when conversions between Christianity and Islam take place. Some cases have to be solved at the court.

Another area in which the church in Africa ought to promote the transcending of borders is with regard to gender-based issues such as inclusion of women in decision-making processes in the Church, and helping women overcome socio-cultural attitudes that are oppressive to them.

The Gospel of Prosperity and Church-going in Africa

The significance of face-to-face communication among Christian believers is discernible in the churches that preach the so-called the Gospel of Prosperity. In many Christian traditions church-going is usually not associated with the learning of money-making skills and achievement of material betterment of the individual believers. However, matters are different in those neo-Pentecostal and charismatic churches that preach the Gospel of Prosperity. Believers in these churches are taught that they have 'a right to the blessings of health and wealth and that they can obtain theses blessings through positive confessions of faith and the "sowing of seeds" through the faithful payments of tithes and offerings'.[16] Hence, they regard material betterment as a result of faith. And as Kwabena observes, 'wealth, health, success, and ever-soaring profits in business are coveted, cherished and publicly flaunted as signs of God's favour'.[17] As testimony of their prosperity, as a genuine mark of their faith, prosperity pastors carry their bibles along with expensive mobile phones and flaunt their expensive cars and clothes.

And for believers who are overwhelmed by somatic and psychic problems and lack of prosperity or material success in life, the prosperity preachers practice faith healing, exorcism and offer "anointing for vengeance" to help dismantle spiritual traps believed to be set by envious family members and relations.[18] These elements and the promise of material betterment seem to give compelling reasons for the acceptance of this teaching in the African setting. Thus, many Africans populate these pro-prosperity churches and in fact the teaching is the principal growth area of these churches.

The Gospel of Prosperity is a contested teaching and some commentators, such as Kwabena, prefer to call it "the Gospel of Materialism" because of its materialistic orientation. It is criticised for its tendency to use Scripture to support a life of extravagance and flamboyance against the poor, and to make the poor believe that they are always responsible for their own poverty.

The shortcomings aside, it remains relevant to the current discussion that face-to-face relationships and concrete ecclesial gathering are essential even for the economic empowerment of the believers. As the prosperity churches in Africa reveal, a concrete ecclesial community avails its members with the opportunity to learn together their financial skills, to compare notes in their performance and encourage one another with their testimony of faith and material success. And this fosters church-going.

Quest for Solid Church Structures in Africa

Still on the basis of the strength of face-to-face communication, this section undertakes to propose the vital importance of formidable church buildings for the life and ministry of the Church in Africa. In the contemporary Christian landscape in Africa ecclesial assemblies gather for worship in places with extremely diverse conditions, ranging from archaic church buildings constructed by foreign missionaries in the last two centuries to new mega-churches equipped with modern electronic instruments. Many of the proliferating new churches, however, do not place emphasis on enormous church constructions. This, as some scholars note, should not be interpreted simply on account of their poverty which makes them unable to afford enormous constructions. Rather it seems that the church members, driven by inner need for fellowship, feel satisfied to gather in private houses, shacks, in school classrooms or open spaces, provided that their aspect of being church is expressed (Isichei 2004: 195).

Granted, what constitutes church is not a building structure or place of worship, but the communion of the people of God. And in fact, these churches which meet in private homes are reminiscent of the biblical Christian communities that also worshipped in private homes and exercised great fellowship and mutual love as well as tangible support (Acts 2:46; 4:32-35). Thus, physical church structures are not absolutely important for being Church and in many parts of Africa they are today becoming increasingly less formidable.

Viewed from the perspective of Africa, however, it can be countered that, Africa indeed needs formidable church structures. Evidently, church structures function as a meeting place for the worshipping community and a unifying point for the people of God. Moreover, church structures will benefit Africa's future generations. The coming generations, when tested by the winds of secularisation, will at least find in the church structures a focal point of Christian witness of their forefathers and foremothers, that is, we the present generation of believers. In this way church structures will constitute a constant invitation to the will-be straying flock to come back to Christ's sheepfold. *Remember the faith of your ancestors in Christ* will be the inspirational message beaconed from the church buildings.

A glaring example of such a functionality of church structures can be witnessed in Europe today. Admittedly, there is a waning favour with the church institution. Yet the beautiful and magnificent old architecture and Christian art that are displayed in the church structures continue to attract the admiration of many. People visit the churches by droves, be they regular churchgoers or otherwise. And pastors utilize this situation by organising special 'offers' of spirituality to all people.

In Austria, for example, the so-called *lange Nacht der Kirchen* (long night of churches) is one of such 'offers'. These are days on which churches open their doors and invite people to visit them as a way to motivate them to search their own faith and take time to pray—that they may meet God in prayers, conversation or while walking in the churches.

Cardinal Christopher Schönborn, Archbishop of Vienna, while encouraging people to take part in the long night of churches event in 2009 said: 'I wish that on this night we all can experience the Church as a place of joy and from which to obtain spiritual benefit. And I encourage you, through the many forms of prayer given in the programmes to discover the Church anew or again, as a place of prayer'.[19]

It can be argued, therefore, that as far as the African Church is concerned, the gathering of Christian congregations in small thatched huts can be perceived at the moment as very ideal for shaping and furthering ecclesial unity and sense of belonging. However, formidable church buildings need also to be constructed.

The plausibility of this quest is for Africa's main partners in mission, namely, European and American Christians, important to understand. They often discourage the construction of churches and will hardly support such projects. Apparently, they interpret the African Church from the perspective of their own Western Christianity, rather than from the local African context. Their guiding logic seems to be, since with growing trends of secularisation the church institution in the West is increasingly falling out of favour, and hence our own church structures are becoming difficult to maintain, therefore, it is not worth to construct churches in Africa, since in the course of time they will become obsolete too.

Envisioning Church-less African Christianity

The emphasis on face-to-face relationships among church members may help African Christianity survive the onslaught of church-less faith when it overtakes the continent in earnest. This is plausible, since globalising trends will inevitably make the influence of church-less faith flow to Africa. It is evident even today that the continent is wrestling with the problem of its young people uncritically subscribing to whatever the West offers. This ranges from adoption of various cultural life styles—which they learn through the television, Internet, travelling abroad, and other means—to the consumption of Western manufactured goods. The aping and consumption of foreign products are done at the expense of their own cultural and material values.

Hence, the general tendency of cultural alienation of the African renders credence to the fears that the style of church-less Christian faith will, in the course of time, eventually be significantly adopted by many Christians in Africa. The plausibility is augmented by the fact that the Internet and other forms of media technology are increasingly infiltrating Africa with Western influence; their shaping effect is expected to be intensified as well in the life and mission of the Church.

A church-less practice of Christianity is anti-African because it is anti-community. As already explained, such a style of life does not accommodate the warmth of human relationships and inner fellowship that Africans normally enjoy in their everyday living. However, the current Christian landscape in Africa already manifests that those churches that promote face-to-face relationships among their members in terms of worship, mutual care, mutual visits and the rendering of tangible assistance to the needy, are more appealing to the African people. There is certainly a challenge here for those Christians who, despite regularly worshipping together, still maintain a great anonymity among themselves. Such an ecclesial community becomes a quasi virtual ecclesial community that may be easily overtaken by the wave of church-less Christian practice.

Concluding Remarks

This chapter has explored the mobile cultures of crossing divides and virtual communications from ecclesiological perspective in order to navigate the path for church theology and praxis in the mobile age. From the foregoing, it can be proposed that there is a great need for building up vibrant local churches whose members meet regularly in a particular venue and interact with one another on a border-crossing basis.

A church that fosters such relationships becomes a strong community and can more easily promote human dignity and the upholding of the common good. A strong Christian community enables its members to counteract any sort of conflict that may threaten to stifle the integrity of the church community. Some suggest that a section of church community members ought to be trained to acquire the skills of conflict resolution in order to help the ecclesial community deal positively with conflict (Sofield 2000: 123).

In fact, churches need to facilitate the acceptance of differences and emphasise the formation of harmonious relationships in the diversity of cultural backgrounds of their members. Therefore, a parish, for example, by its very nature must be open and welcoming to all. It should create an atmosphere of charity, fraternity and friendship such that all the members feel at home and united, rather than feel isolated and constrained to leave the community.

The mobile culture of transcending borders challenges the church to foster collaborative ministry and dialogue among various church members, namely, the clergy, religious and laity. And active participation of church members such as women, who often tend to be sidelined in decision-making process in the churches, will be encouraged. Ecumenical and interreligious dialogue will also be stressed. And church communities are to be not only the 'voice of the voiceless' in society, but also listening communities.

The mobile phone and other modern media technologies can be positively appraised for being potential tools for evangelisation and should be indeed widely used in the Church to that effect.

Nevertheless, Christian communities should neither shun face-to-face communications, nor stop reaching out to people physically, since these are still very effective pastoral approaches.

The next chapter will deal with the subject of mobile cultures and the pilgrim status of the Church. It will make a theological analysis of migration and how this serves to remind the People of God of their migrant status here on earth.

Notes

[1] 'Unknown gods, declining churches, and the spiritual search of contemporary culture', URL:
http://www.martynmission.cam.ac.uk/CDrane.htm (accessed 24 November 2008).

[2] Chris Tong, 'A Critique of '"Do It Yourself" Spirituality', URL: http://www.firmstand.org/articles/do_it_yourself_spirituality.html (accessed on 8 January 2010).

[3] Chris Tong, 'A Critique of '"Do It Yourself" Spirituality', URL: http://www.firmstand.org/articles/do_it_yourself_spirituality.html (accessed on 8 January 2010).

[4] Paul Zulehner's Press Interview: *Kirchen haben noch eine einzige Chance*, URL: http://www.univie.ac.at/ktf/content/site/pt/aktuelles/zeitworte/article/1475.html (accessed on 20 October 2009).

[5] 'Unknown gods, declining churches, and the spiritual search of contemporary culture', URL:
http://www.martynmission.cam.ac.uk/CDrane.htm (accessed 24 November 2008).

[6] Paul Zulehner's Press Interview: *Kirchen haben noch eine einzige Chance*, URL : http://www.univie.ac.at/ktf/content/site/pt/aktuelles/zeitworte/article/1475.html (accessed on 20 October 2009).

[7] Paul Zulehner argues that the issue of priestly celibacy is only a peripheral theme which has become popularised and church desertion would not stop even if obligatory priestly celibacy were abolished. This is witnessed in the Protestant Churches in Europe in which obligatory celibacy of pastors is not the case and yet the situation of the churches is as precarious as in the Catholic Church. For Zulehner the decisive factors whether a person remains or leaves the church are grounded in the following: whether God for him is interesting, whether the question of life after death makes sense to him, whether the Christian rituals of initiation are important to him, whether those who stand up for the Church are valued in the society. Hence, Zulehner contends that it is the faith of individual Christian that constitutes the main theme: has he or she a strong religious vigour? Does he or she pray? meditate? Translate his or her religious

vigour into a deep religious search for the Gospel truth? Does he/she bring his/her deep religious conviction to the Christian community? Thus, Zulehner concludes that today we are in an age in which it is the faith of the individual Christian that will be relied upon to build the future Church, and no longer the political and church leaders.

Cf. Paul Zulehner, *Kirchen haben noch eine einzige Chance*, URL : http://www.univie.ac.at/ktf/content/site/pt/aktuelles/zeitworte/article/1475.html (accessed on 20 October 2009).

[8]'Unknown gods, declining churches, and the spiritual search of contemporary culture', URL:

http://www.martynmission.cam.ac.uk/CDrane.htm (accessed 24 November 2008).

[9]'Unknown gods, declining churches, and the spiritual search of contemporary culture', URL:

http://www.martynmission.cam.ac.uk/CDrane.htm (accessed 24 November 2008).

[10]'Inhabiting the Digital Universe with a Believing Heart', URL: http://blog.echurchwebsites.org.uk/2010/04/27/pope-benedict-xvi-inhabit-the-digital-universe-with-a-believing-heart-and-help-give-a-soul-to-the-endless-flow-of-communications-on-the-internet/ (accessed 10 June 2010).

[11]'Pope urges Priests to use Communications Media', (Zenit, 29 September 2009), URL: http://www.zenit.org/article-26998?l=english (accessed 10 June 2010).

[12] "AMECEA" stands for Association of Member Episcopal Conferences of Central and Eastern Africa which is formed by Catholic Episcopal conferences of eight countries of the region.

[13]Paul Zulehner: *Kirchen haben noch eine einzige Chance*," URL : http://www.univie.ac.at/ktf/content/site/pt/aktuelles/zeitworte/article/1475.html (accessed on 20 October 2009).

[14]Joseph Mtebe, 'When the Church steals your Wife' in: *The Citizen* 6 August 2010, URL:

http://allafrica.com/stories/201008061095.html (accessed 7 September 2010).

[15]One reason for this is that some teachers take advantage of their classroom to proselytise. Amy Stambach gives an example of American evangelists in Musoma, Tanzania who in teaching English language in public primary schools employed instructional methods

that attracted members to their Church. See, Amy Stambach, *Faith in Schools: Religion, Education, and American Evangelicals in East Africa* (Stanford: Stanford University Press, 2010), 6f. But there is also an element of Prosperity Gospel in these conversions since according to some student informants in Songea, Tanzania, it is widely believed among the students that if one is "saved" then his or her chances of passing examinations are guaranteed.

[16] See: 'Statement on Prosperity Gospel' by the Lausanne Theology Working Group, Africa chapter, at its consultations in Akropong, Ghana, 8-9 October, 2008 and 1-4 September 2009. URL: http://www.christianitytoday.com/ct/2009/decemberweb-only/gc-prosperitystatement.html (accessed 8 January 2010).

[17] J. Kwabena Asamoah-Gyadu, 'Did Jesus Wear Designer Robes?' in: *Christianity Today* (November 2008), URL:http://www.christianitytoday.com/globalconversation/november2009/index.html (accessed 8 January 2010).

[18] J. Kwabena Asamoah-Gyadu, 'Did Jesus Wear Designer Robes?' in: *Christianity Today* (November 2008), URL:http://www.christianitytoday.com/globalconversation/november2009/index.html (accessed 8 January 2010).

[19] "Lange Nacht der Kirchen," URL: http://www.langenachtderkirchen.at/statements/wien/0/articles/2009/04/07/a2636/ (accessed on 8 July 2009) (translation mine).

Chapter Six
Mobile Cultures and Pilgrim Status of the Church

Mobile Cultures and Pastoral Care of Migrants

What I have discussed in Chapter Three with regard to the relationships between mobile phone use and migrants can be brought to bear in theological analysis of the phenomenon of migration. It is important to add here that the current intensification of human migrations in the world is concurrent with a pervasive advancement in mobile technology. In Chapter Three I have pointed out that mobile communications facilitate the sustenance of relationships between migrants and their families or loved ones back home in their country of origin. This makes the migrants feel secure to live and work abroad. This has been attested by Western expatriates living in Africa, a continent they perceive to be insecure, as well as by Africans living in Western countries where they often fall victim to racist and xenophobic acts. In both cases the migrants can always enjoy a virtual companionship of their home folks and seek their solace when confronted with adversities in the foreign land. This affords them with a coping mechanism in their new situation.

In the case of African immigrants in Europe for example, the mobile phone plays a vital role in their struggles to acquire asylum status and the process of integration as a whole. Failure to obtain asylum status is often a big blow to the migrants. As such some would communicate frequently per mobile phone with their pastors back in Africa to ask for their blessings so that things may go well. In such cases some prosperity pastors would even utter prayers of curses upon those "evil people" whose mischievous powers presumably prevent the immigrant from obtaining the coveted asylum status or citizenship.

We have seen, moreover, that the mobile phone challenges the infringement of human mobility as well as transcends culturally constructed borders.

By accomplishing all these tasks in favour of migrants the mobile phone then can be interpreted as a device that endorses the migration phenomenon rather than discouraging it. In other words, by enabling the migrants to ease their pain of living abroad, far away from their loved ones, the mobile phone embraces the mobility of these people instead of demonising it. It apparently proposes that migrating into far-flung places is an acceptable venture. And indeed to embrace the mobility of some persons is to empower them (Radcliffe 2005: 196).

But on the other hand, we notice that the assurance offered by the mobile phone to the migrants at times turns out to be a bogus one, since it may happen that the more they sustain regular contacts with their sending countries, the more they are reminded that they are indeed in a foreign land. Such recognition usually stirs in them a strong homesickness and a longing for reunion with their loved ones back home. Others are pained to realize that devoid of a physical presence they cannot accomplish all things for their sending country and family. An exception to this may occur with regard to those migrants who have fled wars or persecution in their country of origin and may now wish to forget all the bitter past experience they underwent there.

This analysis of the relationship between mobile phone communications and the experience of migrants may lead us to see the imperative for the society to facilitate the integration of immigrants. I advance the argument that the mobile phone here serves to unveil what lies behind the façade of the migration phenomenon. It points to the fragility of migrants. On the part of the Church, this mobile cultural analysis is a critical challenge to engage itself seriously in the pastoral care of migrants.

From a world-wide experience today, the Church is aware that migration offers windows into contemporary forms of oppression (Cruz 2008: 357). Human dignity of the migrants may not be sufficiently respected, or it may be humiliated or even destroyed (*Pontifical Commission for the Pastoral of Migrants and Itinerant Peoples, 1985*). As it is often the case in many receiving countries, civil enforcement authorities may treat immigrants as criminals and adopt tactics for enforcing immigration law that only give rise to migrant smuggling operations and migrant deaths. The larger host society may also contribute to the griefs of immigrants by maintaining misperceptions, xenophobic and racist attitudes towards them.

On account of such a negative impact of migration, the Church makes it its own duty to take care of migrants both physically and spiritually and urges that all aspects that denigrate the human dignity of migrants should be eliminated. In order to address such problems for the sake of migrants the Church sees the need for governments of both sending and receiving countries to work toward a globalisation of solidarity by seeking to harmonise immigration policies that respect the dignity of the migrants.

As the Mexico and U.S bishops' pastoral letter on migrants stated, migrants regardless of their legal status, like all persons, possess inherent human dignity which should be respected.[1] Thus, from the Catholic Social Teaching five principles for migration can be articulated:

Persons have the right to find opportunities in their homeland.

Persons have the right to migrate to support themselves and their families.

Sovereign nations have the right to control their borders.

Refugees and asylum seekers should be afforded protection.

The human dignity and human rights of undocumented migrants should be respected.[2]

The migration phenomenon can have quite an impact on the spiritual life of migrants. It may occur that migrants who once embraced the faith fall into the danger of backsliding. But the reverse is also true, since many who before becoming migrants had rejected the Gospel may now be open to its claims. This provides another motive for the Church to engage itself in the pastoral care of the migrants.

An African immigrant pastor in America notes the following with regard to what the pastoral care of migrants can be envisaged to accomplish:

We want to reach some Africans because they come over here and get lost in the crowd and stay away from church because no one knows them to challenge and encourage them to continue with the faith they had in Africa. We want to provide a cushioning for the social and economic pressures in this country by showing them what they need to do to survive the culture shock here. Our objective is to provide spiritual feeding such as teaching them the word of God and encouraging them to walk with the Lord so they do not lose the spirituality they had in Africa. We also want to reach our fellow Americans with the gospel of Jesus… (Hanciles 2008: 346).

Such a missionary vision portrays a prophetic and kairological understanding of the current ponderous question of human migrations, namely, the view that migrants are a blessing and may turn into missionaries in the receiving countries. The Church wishes that such an understanding should be for all Christian believers the new "eyes" for seeing the migration question. We shall come back to this point at the concluding remarks of this chapter.

Face-to-face Ecclesial Communities and Integration of Migrants

Mobile cultures may be related to migrants in the context of the immigrants' social integration into a host society. Religious organizations such as churches normally play a key role in assisting migrants to integrate. As Pope John Paul II pointed out on World Migrations Day in 1995, 'In the Church, no one is a stranger, and the church is not foreign to anyone, anywhere' (*L'Osservatore Romano* 13 September 1995).

But integration of immigrants is in fact one of the most mind-boggling problems associated with the migration phenomenon. Admittedly both the host society and the migrants themselves may have a part to play in this. While the host society may hinder the integration process by not expressing a welcoming gesture to the immigrants or even subject them to xenophobic and racist acts, the immigrants themselves may as well undermine integration efforts by adopting an attitude of isolation and hostility towards the society of the receiving country. Some immigrants create a parallel society in the receiving country.

In a bid to help migrants integrate church communities may recognise the significance of the social cues available in face-to-face communications which I have dealt with in previous chapters. Undeniably, it is a Christian community that is concrete and harmonious and whose members cherish mutual face-to-face interactions that can in turn create room for welcoming and helping migrants find their place in the society. Virtual ecclesial communities in which an atmosphere of great anonymity reigns, on the contrary, can hardly achieve such a pastoral ministry. This is particularly true of migrants arriving in extremely different cultural environment, like for example African immigrants in Europe or USA.

The assistance rendered to migrants by a local church community may consist of at least two main aspects, namely, religious reassurance and social interaction. With regard to the first aspect, religion in general equips the migrant with spiritual strength. Right from the moment they set out from their country of origin for the adventurous and perilous journeys to the land of the unknown, many migrants who share their experience confess that they commit their lives to divine providence.

Robert Schreiter observes that, religion is for many migrants of the first generation one of the strongest connecting links between their country of origin and their new situation. As such, it is not unusual that migrants in their new environment become more religious than they were in their home country (Schreiter 2008:92). Arguably, however, the new situation the migrants encounter in the receiving country also determines whether the migrants become more or less religious than before. That is, it depends on the cultural worldview and religious practice of the migrants' host societies, whether they are liberal or conservative. It seems that migrants who resort to religion either as a coping mechanism or as a tool in the struggle for more life-giving conditions are likely to become more religious (Cruz 2008: 364). On the other hand, any indication of rejection by the local churches, say on grounds of racism, may make some immigrants abandon their religious faith. This is particularly true of African immigrants in Europe who sometimes encounter acts of hostility from their hosts (ter Haar 2001: 71).

Joining an ecclesial gathering then avails migrants with an opportunity to meet and know members of the congregation and their leaders. Some of these may happen to speak their own language, or understand their customs as well as understand their needs in the new environment as migrants. The church community in its pastoral programmes may also provide advice to the migrants on how to tackle their problems (such as obtaining legal documents) and how to go about other issues pertaining to their survival and integration in the new environment (ter Haar 2001: 74). And since churches offer supportive networks that often privilege upward social mobility or self-improvement of their members, this may benefit migrants as well.

Thus, social contacts which are necessary for the immigrants to survive and even to begin the long climb up the ladder of respectability are forged and sustained through the ecclesial congregation. And for young people, church meeting-points serve a further function of providing possibilities of knowing one another and arranging marriages.

I prescribe face-to-face communication as an important element in this context because religious assurance of immigrants is often facilitated by church liturgy and rituals celebrated in the context of an ecclesial assembly. These worship elements are important in integration because they become moments of establishing identity and membership of the migrants (Schreiter 2008: 92). At any rate, church liturgies and rituals necessitate face-to-face interaction of the ecclesial members.

Endorsement of Migration and Reverse Flow of Mission

As noted in the preceding sections, the mobile phone is quite often a great facilitator for migrants to cope with their new situations and eventually to integrate. When migrants settle in the new society then their contribution becomes more evident. From a missiological point of view, the mobile phone serves to increase a Christian presence in a host country by facilitating the integration of Christian immigrants. Immigrants may contribute positively by producing missionary pastors.

Jehu Hanciles notes this in his study on African missionary pastors in USA. He observes that, the vast majority of African immigrant pastors came to America as migrants, that is, as students, professionals, visitors, refugees, or asylum seekers. But later in the course of their stay there, they became pastors. Hence, they are missionaries because they are migrants, and their sense of missionary calling is framed by the experience of migration.

Hanciles maintains, furthermore, that despite being confronted with various challenges, including racial discrimination in the American society, these migrant pastors play a significant pastoral role. Their missionary goal is far-sighted since their missionary effort is not directed merely to the African immigrant community rather the immigrant community is the initial focus and foundation on which to build a more extensive missionary outreach.

The African immigrants have an advantage in their missionary vision. Contrary to Western missionaries who went to Africa and could never become citizens there, the African immigrant pastors can become full-fledged American citizens. This favourable position presents them with long-term missionary possibilities (Hanciles 2008: 344).

Migrants as Embodiment of the Pilgrim Church

The relevance of the discussion undertaken in the previous section is that it helps us do the theology of migration. Human mobility and border-crossing as epitomized by the phenomenon of migration have a great theological import. First of all, as theologian Gemma Cruz notes, Christianity's master narratives are embedded with stories of journeys undertaken by migrants (Cruz 2008: 368). This is typified by the migration of the chosen people of Israel to the Promised Land, the flight of the child Jesus and his family to Egypt, the itinerant preaching of Jesus himself and his disciples, and the many journeys made by the Apostle Paul and his disciples across the Roman Empire to establish and nurture Christian communities. Without the witness of such countless Christians who crossed the seas and ventured into far-flung unknown territories of the world, Christianity would not become a global religion. Hence, analysed from such a Christian perspective, the phenomenon of migration serves as a heuristic lens for a theology of redemption.

Besides, migration serves to remind the Church of her pilgrim status. Theologian Daniel Groody maintains that to embrace the identity of pilgrim on the part of the Church entails embracing a certain type of mobility in the globalisation context, and seeking to 'transgress all artificial borders that impede the quest for communion with God and with other people (Groody 2008: 352).

A comparison between two types of mobility, namely, tourism and pilgrimage may serve to punctuate the pilgrim status of the Church. In fact, there is a marked contrast between the two modes of mobility in modern era. Tourism is distinguished from pilgrimage in that it is normally carried out for the purpose of business, pleasure and self education through encounter with the exotic. The tourist has money and time to traverse the world, and maintains borders against the natives in order to maintain his or her otherness and manifest his or her freedom. A pilgrim in contrast, detaches himself or herself from quotidian identity and routine in order to embark on a journey that effects a self-transformation, through forgiveness of sins, or enables him or her to respond to the necessity of being in union with God (Groody 2008: 349). Thus, a pilgrim's inner yearning may be manifested through external signs such as acts of self-denial, going long and arduous journeys on foot, special prayers, performing the way of the cross, and so on. In this sense pilgrimage is a kenotic movement. Moreover, pilgrimage is not meant for material profit and it is available even to poor members of the society.

Significant for our purposes here, we need to add another prominent feature that marks off the two kinds of mobility, namely, tourists normally regard with disdain the presence of other tourists at a site. We often hear stories of tourists of a certain nationality evacuating a hotel because of the overwhelming presence of tourists from another nationality. Pilgrims on the contrary, welcome other pilgrims, and treasure the company of other pilgrims since they regard all as potential brothers and sisters on a common journey to God. And, hence, the presence of other pilgrims at a certain site is welcome and cherished since it serves to attest to the authenticity of that site (Groody 2008: 350).

The Vatican Council II chose the metaphor of a *pilgrim people* as one of the images used to define the Church. By using this model for the Church, the Council wanted to stress, among other things, the humanness of the Church, namely, that the Church is a community composed of weak and sinful people. That, like the Old Testament people, the Church is also 'a murmuring people who feel the heat of the sun on their march through the desert of this world' (Fuellenbach 2002: 45). This community of people, therefore, stands constantly in need of God's mercy and forgiveness, and cries out to God for help and relief on its journey, which culminates with the awaited return of the Lord.

I am intrigued by this description, since it vividly portrays the image of African migrants who, at the risk of their lives, try to cross the sea over to fortress Europe. According to the Italian Interior

Ministry's report from January to mid September 2007 a total number 14,200 Africans arrived at the Italian Island of Lampedusa in an attempt to immigrate into Europe. Likewise, in the same period of time in 2008, the number rose to 24,200. This is to say nothing of those who enter Europe at other entry points.[3]

Many of the African migrants perish in the high seas. For the past ten years, for instance, about 10,000 African migrants died at the sea off Sicily, Italy. And for those who survive the ordeal and manage to reach "paradise Europe", it often doesn't turn out to be a happy end. They find themselves standing constantly in need of mercy, crying for relief aid and waiting hopefully to be granted asylum status in the host countries.

Hence, the image of the Church as a pilgrim—a migrant for that matter— on the one hand portrays a corrective and warning against tendencies of triumphalism and comfortable settlement in the world on the part of the People of God. But on the other hand, it challenges Christian communities to be on the side of the marginalised groups in the society, including migrants, the poor, women, and others.

Concluding Remarks

From the foregoing it can be concluded that migration is a symbol that reveals the underlying reality of the Church as pilgrim people. A Christian who recognises his or her pilgrim status grows in faith, since such recognition makes one broader, more global, more welcoming, as well as more Catholic than merely national identity could. But above all, embracing our pilgrim status serves to remind us that we have no lasting city here on earth. As people of faith, we are people on the move and our citizenship is in heaven towards which we journey (Phil. 3:20).

In addition, in the reality of migration, the Church as the People of God encounters its own reality. The mobile phone which embraces migration and serves to integrate migrants in new societies leads us to reflect that as People of God we should not view the reality of migration merely as a problem. Rather, we should accept it as a *kairos*, God-given moment of grace. This *kairos* 'transforms the Church when its members (migrants) embrace their poverty as wayfarers in a passing world. The vicissitudes that migrants encounter in their migrating process are analogous to the struggles of the People of God here below while journeying towards the heavenly rest. In this sense, migration can be seen as part of the ongoing mystery of redemption, contributing to solving the great problems of the human family' (Cruz 2008: 368f).

Hence, as far as Christians in the receiving countries are concerned, the migration phenomenon presents a critical test of their faith. As believers they ought to unlearn the attitudes of the world around them that tends to view immigrants with a hostile attitude and demonise them as criminals. Instead, they should learn to accept these 'guests' at their door with a Christian faith and a biblical hospitality. But by the same token, immigrants should not abuse the hospitality of their hosts such as through criminal acts, unwillingness to integrate, detestation of work, and so on.

As far as Africa is concerned, the problem of migration is a serious one indeed. Many people are forced into migration by ethnic conflicts, wars and extreme poverty conditions. Others become migrants due to factors such as searching for employment opportunities, marriage and so on. Needless to reiterate here the great loss of human resources African experiences due to brain-drain. But reportedly at least 70,000 skilled graduates abandon the continent every year (Calderisi 2007: 5).

But on the other side, it is notable that regardless of the causes of migration, migrants are normally exposed to mistreatment and other manifold challenges. Unfortunately, governments in the sending countries of Africa may not give the problem of migration its due attention. They may be blinded by the fact that migrants continue to keep in touch with their people back home and even send remittances that add revenue to their countries. It is here again, that the mobile phone manifests its ambivalent nature when it facilitates such communications.

Thus, the Church in Africa is called upon to continue dialogue with African governments to address the problems at home that force their people into migration and in this way even prevent further migrations. Such a dialogue should envisage various sorts of assistance to be rendered to their migrant nationals in order to help them overcome challenges facing them abroad and when they visit their countries of origin.

Chapter Seven will explore mobile cultures from biblical and theological perspectives.

Notes

[1] Mexico and U.S bishops' 2003 Pastoral Letter, *Strangers No Longer: Together on the Journey of Hope*, URL: http://www.usccb.org/mrs/stranger.shtml (accessed 28August 2010).

[2] Mexico and U.S bishops' 2003 Pastoral Letter, *Strangers No Longer: Together on the Journey of Hope*, URL: http://www.usccb.org/mrs/stranger.shtml (accessed 28 August 2010).

[3] 'Bootsflüchtlinge aus Afrika', URL: http://www.orf.at/08122633232/?href=http%3A%2F%2Fwww.orf.at%2F08122633232%2F33233txt_story.html (accessed 17 April 2009).

Chapter 7
Biblical and Theological Insights into Mobile Cultures

This chapter attempts to approach mobile cultures from biblical and theological perspectives in order to navigate an appropriate path for the Church and society in mobile Africa. The chapter suggests that the mobile age challenges the Church in Africa to adopt an inner life and praxis that incorporates some positive elements portrayed in mobile cultures. To achieve this, mobile cultures need to be purified and transformed through a biblical and theological infusion, since they are not perfect. As we have noted in Chapter Two and Chapter Three, for instance, the mobile phone is associated with global and local social and economic networks that shape uneven development. Eventually, mobile networks may be sometimes exploitative to some categories of people. We have maintained as well, that mobile networks are not flat even in terms of interpersonal relationships since they are structured by hierarchy that reinforces extractive power relationships.

All these aspects indicate structures of sin that are associated with mobile phones and which need to be purified and transformed. Moreover, when the cultures are appropriated into the Church's life, it is the biblical and Christian doctrinal mysteries that constitute the measure of the Church, not the mobile cultures themselves. We can compare here with the clarification about the precise meaning of the image of the Church as God's family which was opted by African bishops as an appropriate expression of the Church in Africa. By proposing this image the African bishops did not mean that the human family is the measure of the Church as family of God because the human family has its limits and shortcomings. Instead, the Church as God's family is the icon of the Trinity. To elucidate this point African theologian Charles Nyamiti notes that,

We cannot refer to the Church as family of God unless we transcend the biological sense of family and embrace the symbolic sense, namely of the family understood as communion of grace in God's love which brings it about and structures it. Moreover, this image of the family must be joined to that of kinship in Jesus Christ in union with the Holy Spirit. This implies that the Church as God's family is the icon of the Trinity (Nyamiti 2007: 79).

When purified and transformed, mobile cultures will be of greater benefit to the society and the Church in Africa.

Biblical Insights into Mobile Cultures

This section relates the narratives of Africans in their mobile discourses to the narratives of psalmists and the Passion Narrative of Jesus Christ. Moreover, it makes a metaphorical comparison between the significance of mountains in the Bible and the mountains that transmit mobile phone signals. The analysis underscores the importance of the mobile phone in promoting terrestrial and spiritual life in contemporary Africa.

A "Beep" to the Righteous Heavenly Father

Chapter Three has described the mobile phone as suitable medium of popular opinion on account of its adaptability, mobility, flexibility, convenience, connectivity, customisation and context sensitivity. With such qualities the mobile phone has empowered average Africans in terms of freedom of speech. A good example of this advantage has been demonstrated in Chapter Four with regard to mobile discourses of ordinary citizens in the fight against corruption. This section discusses the conditions of the poor people who have been empowered by the mobile phone in the light of some biblical texts.

One of the characteristic features of the mobile discourses against corruption has been an appeal to God by recurrently uttering words like "God save Tanzania" or "God is on our side". Supplicants in *lamentation psalms* portray similar appeals to God that insinuate that they were subjected to comparable miserable situations. Appeal to God for help is regarded as the most important element and the very heart of the complaint psalms (Prinsloo 2003: 369). The appeal is usually in the form of an imperative calling to God for His attention as it is the case in Ps. 130:2 and Ps. 102: 1-2. What is illustrated in these psalms is that the petitioner wants to bring the seriousness of the situation to God's attention as well as persuade God to heed him.

Other lamentation psalms are imprecations in which the supplicant wishes that his enemies be put to shame, be confused, and suffer dishonour (e.g. Pss. 31:17; 35:26; 40:15; 109:29). The petitioner requests God to act decisively against his enemies (Dunn et al. 2003: 369). While the petitioner has such harsh wishes for his enemy, he himself has the assurance that he is righteous before God and that God is on his side to punish the wicked (Ps. 56:9).

Several reasons make the supplicant confident of divine intervention or action on his behalf in his desperate situation. First, it is the characteristics of God that motivate the supplicant. He begs for deliverance from God because he believes that God is righteous (Ps.5:8; 35:24; 71:2), is steadfast in love (Ps.6: 4; 51:1), has power to redeem (Ps. 130:7), and is merciful (Ps.25:6). The second reason why the petitioner calls God to act on behalf of His children is that God has everlasting years as Creator and His presence is eternal (Ps. 102:25-28). The third reason that motivates the petitioner to appeal to God is that if God does not intervene, the unjust people will boast and rejoice that they have prevailed over the righteous. This will be a shame to the petitioner and to God as well (Ps. 35:25).

However, the petitioner's own miserable situation is another justification for God to intervene. He depends on God's help because he is 'poor and needy' (Ps. 86:1) and that his enemies are too strong for him without God's help (Ps. 142: 6b). Moreover, he thinks that his personal qualities too, namely, being devoted to God (Ps. 17: 3-5) and being a "servant" of God (Ps. 143:12), justify him to persuade God to act.

In Psalm 31, for example, the petitioner presents a typical case of marginalisation. His appeal before God is twofold. First, he bemoans the attacks of his enemies upon him. Secondly, he complains that those who inflict suffering on him are not only foreigners, but also members of his own family, friends, neighbours and companions. They all treat him like an outcast. Being abandoned by such people is more disturbing for him since it signifies that the line between friend and foe has become blurred. This epitomises a social rejection and marginalisation whose perpetrators are those who are charged with the duty to protect.[1] The victim of such marginalisation no longer features as a member of the social group that embodies his identity.

That is, instead of being at the centre and made to feel at home in his social group, he or she is forced to operate on the periphery.

Psalmists versus African Victims of Corruption

The narratives of the petitioners in the lamentation psalms have much in common with the narratives of African victims of corruption, that is, the average African citizens in a corrupt system. First, like the supplicant in the psalms, they too are poor and needy. And their condition is attributable to their local mundane situations in which vices such as corruption, impunity and irresponsibility are rampant. Amid the prevalence of such vices, only a handful people enjoy the resources and sense of security in the country. The majority of the citizens are relegated to marginal positions and made to live like foreigners in their own country. Their painful experience of misery, just like the petitioner in Psalm 31, is aggravated by the realization that the perpetrators are not only foreigners, but also their fellow nationals, particularly their leaders who have the duty to protect them.

Secondly, as many average Africans perceive that solutions to problems of corruption become elusive, they too raise their arms towards God in prayer. Many prayer intentions in the Houses of worship express the desire to get good political leaders who are not tainted with corruption. Even in the prayer that was said across Africa in preparation for the Second African Synod some of the petitions expressed this desire. And for some African churches in their current polity prayer and preaching the Word of God are the only measures they recommend as an antidote against corruption. They appeal to God that He should intervene on their behalf and deal with the perpetrators of the vices, but at the same time they discourage their followers from taking part in any form of action that challenges the exploitative economic and political structures.

Some preachers even use the Bible to proof-text their impartiality, claiming, for example, that everyone must submit to governing authorities because all authority comes from God (Rom. 13:1). Some theologians regard this approach as using the Word of God as a "weapon" aimed at wounding the poor and the marginalised (LenkaBula 2008: 302).

Thirdly, very much like some of the supplications in the psalms, the prayers of the faith communities sometimes involve imprecations in which they request God to put corrupt leaders to shame, to confuse them and to let them suffer dishonour. But, on this aspect, the attitude of many African citizens is a far cry from that of the psalmist since many of them can hardly assert their righteousness with regard to corruption. When the psalmist accuses the wicked before God[2], he asserts at the same time that he himself is righteousness. He confidently proclaims before God, 'for I am devoted to you', 'I am a servant of God'. This does not seem to be the disposition of much of the African public with regard to corruption. From what we learn from many parts of the continent the culture of corruption is perpetrated by both leaders and the general public alike.

The point which is emphasised here is not that a corrupt person should not be a whistleblower, nor that a sinner should not correct another sinner. Rather, what I see as a challenge emanating from the psalmist's appeal is that in order to overcome corruption it is not enough to implicate leaders alone. When citizens denounce corruption and other vices, and even persuade God to act decisively on their behalf against corruption offenders, they themselves should similarly express their determination to abolish corruption by not taking part in it. Corruption can be rooted out only with real commitment from both leaders and the society at large.

Perhaps an example will serve to elucidate this point. In the context of political elections in Tanzania, candidates are generally embedded with the mentality that the only sure way to win elections is by corruption. Voters, on the other hand, consider election periods as an opportunity to earn quick money from corrupt candidates. And experience has so far revealed that candidates who never give their voters bribes (described idiomatically as *takrima*, "thanks") will rarely win the elections.

Under such circumstances both the leaders and the general public are responsible for the persistence of the culture of corruption in society. Commenting on this situation, Tanzania's Human Rights Commission and Good Governance Commission Chairman, Judge Amir Manento, had once cautioned that corruption in Tanzania will not be rooted out if the people do not change this mindset (*The Guardian* 4 September 2010).

The spread of counterfeit Chinese goods in Africa is another example of public involvement in the perpetration of the culture of corruption. Tanzanian traders, for instance, order substandard jeans from China and sell them to their fellow citizens at extortionate prices of genuine jeans.

Carmody recounts a similar example with regard to mobile phones in Uganda.

A Ugandan trader will go to China and tell a Chinese cell phone company that they want them to make a phone that they can sell in Uganda for 10,000 shillings (approximately US $5). The Chinese company designs it to look like a Nokia cell phone. A special symbol which is hard to see, is put on the phone to prevent Nokia from suing the company. The phone is put on the market in Uganda and sells for 10,000 shillings. Since it looks like Nokia phone, people buy it thinking they are actually getting such a phone. The phone might last four months. Since it is not from Nokia, the consumer has no recourse to ask for a replacement (2010: 113f).

Thus, the desire of poor African citizens to see that corruption is stamped out of the economic and political systems of their countries bears the rhetoric of any other option for the poor. Corruption does not go simply by wishing it away. It requires the involvement of the poor themselves as key players in their own cause. Lack of participation from the side of the poor in an action that promotes their own cause often renders the option ineffective (Nolan 2009: 53).

The Passion Narrative of Jesus and Post-independence Africa

The mobile outcry against corruption reflects the Passion Narrative of Jesus Christ. The Passion Narrative is a case of an innocent citizen, Jesus of Nazareth, who is persecuted by his regime (Mark 14:1-72; 15:1-47). The Narrative brims with incidents of 'betrayal, denial, mistaken identifications and abandonment' (Schreiter 1997: 60).

However, the cross reveals the emptied self of Jesus and the power of God which is made perfect in weakness (2 Cor 12:9). At the cross Jesus laid down his life as a sacrifice for sins (Heb. 10:12) and as such, though the cross signals in no uncertain terms God's wrathful judgment on sin, it is at the same time the basis upon which God announces forgiveness to all sinners. Jesus' sacrifice 'covers the sins of all people—both perpetrators and victims, oppressors and marginalized, nondisabled and disabled—as well as makes it possible for God to redeem the entire web of sin and its effects' (Yong 2007: 178). Indeed the cross of Jesus reveals God's nonviolent response to sin in the world.

Africans in their diverse contexts can easily perceive the relevance of the Passion Narrative because similar ironies plague their countries during the postcolonial era. Those at the helm of the regime and their accomplices would line up their pockets while the vast majority of the populace that has voted them in power languishes in poverty, often with no hope of redress. The betrayal is made manifest in that political independence in most countries has not been translated into the economic miracle promised by the leaders at the wake of independence and which the people were made to anticipate. But betrayal is likewise evident today when the promises made by politicians to their voters during election campaigns are not kept after they have been voted in power. At the 20th World Economic Forum (WEF) on Africa held in Tanzania in May 2010, Graca Machel, wife of former South African president, Nelson Mandela, had challenged African leaders on this respect. She contended that 'during election campaigns African leaders become so close to their people that they can even share food, kiss children around the streets and dress in simple attires. But soon after they are elected, they neither go to the villages nor share food with them' (*The Guardian* 8 May 2010).

Some politicians who seek to consolidate their grip on power resort to extreme measures to suppress dissent and this often leads to persecutions. God's nonviolent response to human sin as demonstrated at the cross of Jesus is a challenge for leaders not to employ violence to silence discordant voices of the poor citizens who bemoan corruption, kleptocracy and other life-inflicting practices. Instead, they should stoop down and render an altruistic service to the people.

Thus, mobile narratives of the poor should serve as a reminder of God's lavish love that encompasses all people, since He loves and cares for all. When people recognise that they are beneficiary to this divine love they should in turn see themselves as having the mandate to uphold the common good in society.

Mountains for Mobile Technologies versus the Mountain of the Lord

Mountains (geographically elevated parts of the earth) and towers, spires are sought by mobile companies as technically convenient places for placing mobile phone transmitters so that they can send signals far and wide in the cities and villages. In some remote rural areas in Africa mobile communication may be defective due to poor signal. This may require climbing a nearby hill or tree in order to access a good network reception.

This section seeks to identify metaphorically the link between the role of mountains in mobile telecommunications technology and the symbolic value of mountains as applied in the Scripture and Christian spirituality. The purpose is to establish the fact that Scripture offers inspirations and insights into the deployment of the mobile phone as a bearer of God's salvific message to the world.

In various cultures of the world, the notion of mountains as an image and an expression of higher powers, as the habitat of gods and demons, seems to have been a dominant phenomenon. This is manifested in ancient cultures of the world as found in Egypt, Babylon, India and Mexico. Many mythologies reveal their particular "holy mountain" which is perceived to be the cosmic centre where heaven and earth meet. Underlying this conception of mountain among the various world cultures is the experience that all things and beings, the centre of the world and of the soul, have their foundation on the mountain. In a word, 'life comes from the mountains' (Kreppold 1989:40).

In many African cultures too, the concept of mountains as the abode of supernatural powers is widely held. In Tanzania some of those who intend to become traditional healers often initiate themselves into this apprenticeship by disappearing secretly to the mountains for a considerable period of time. When they re-emerge they claim to have obtained new powers for healing people and protecting them from malevolent forces.

In the Old Testament, mountains are portrayed as important sites for God's revelation. The zenith of Abraham's dealings with God, for instance, was marked by his readiness to sacrifice on a height, later referred to as 'on the mountain the Lord will see' (Gen. 22: 1-14). It is at this encounter with God that Abraham receives the definite promise.

Many other important biblical events are described as taking place on the mountains (Ex.3:1-12; Nm. 33:38; Dt. 34:1-8; 1 Kgs.18:15-40). Mountains symbolise God's stability (Ps.30:7), God's power (Ps.121:2) as well as joy and abundance (Isa. 44:23; 55:12; Am. 9:13).

The Prophet Isaiah in his vision of the future importance of the temple hill sees the mountain with the house of the Lord as surpassing all other heights. The vision also exhibits the realisation of the *missio Dei* as it portrays all people streaming to the Lord's mountain (Is. 2: 2-5). The mountain is hallowed as the source of peace and light. Inasmuch as the people will contemplate God in all His goodness, they will all know God without being instructed and there will be no longer room for evil. And the psalmist adds, 'who shall ascend the hill of the LORD? And who shall stand in His holy place? He who has clean hands and a pure heart, who does not lift up his soul to what is false, and does not swear deceitfully. He will receive blessing from the LORD, and vindication from the God of his salvation' (Ps. 24: 3-5). On account of this association of mountains with the divine, spiritual life in Christianity is often described metaphorically as the soul's ascent to God in response to God's descent to human beings in Jesus Christ (Groody 2007: 241).

This comparison between the mountain of the Lord and the mountains that transmit mobile phone signals is meant to express the quest for the Church to engage the mobile phone in evangelisation. When analysed metaphorically, the mountains that are used in mobile technologies should point to the quest for promoting peace, joy and abundance of life for all categories of people in Africa. And they should facilitate the ascent of human souls to God.

Mountains as Symbol of Radical Transformation in Jesus Christ

In the New Testament too, mountains bear an important symbolism. In the Gospel of Matthew, mountains are frequently mentioned in relation to important events in the life and ministry of Jesus. Jesus' teaching which constitutes the Christian manifesto (chapters 5-7) was made on the mountain. In this acclaimed *Sermon on the Mount* Jesus utters radical demands on his would-be disciples to love their enemies, to reject violence, to be ready to make peace. He warns them against the service of Mammon and exhorts them to be generous as regards the distribution of the earth's resources. Comparing these radical demands of Jesus with the mobile discourses of poor people in Africa which we have described previously, we notice that they are the same issues for which the people are yearning.

The relationship between Jesus' ministry and mountains is again demonstrated at Jesus' Transfiguration. Before the eyes of some disciples, Jesus' face shone like the sun, and from the cloud came a voice, 'This is my beloved Son, with whom I am well pleased; listen to him' (Mt. 17: 2-8). The mountain here is a place of transformation that offers the disciples entirely new 'eyes' for seeing Jesus and this transformation should strengthen them in their discipleship to Jesus and in facing trials and suffering.

After his resurrection Jesus sends his disciples forth from a mountain in Galilee (Mt. 28: 16-20). Here, Jesus announces: 'all authority in heaven and on earth has been given to me'. This is in contrast to what transpired at the mountain of his temptation where the devil claimed to have authority over all the kingdoms of the world (Mt. 27: 31). Thus, Jesus falsifies the devil's claim of authority. And with the authority given him by the Father, Jesus gives his disciples a Great Commission to go and make disciples of all nations, to baptize them in the name of the Father and of the Son and of the Holy Spirit, to teach them to observe all that he had commanded the disciples, promising that he will always be with them, to the close of the age (Mt. 28:19-20).

These accounts of the association of Jesus' ministry with mountains may help Christians of the mobile age assess mobile cultures in the light of their faith. First, with regard to the Sermon on the Mount, we can deduce that, if mobile cultures are inspired by Jesus' radical demands, namely, to love one's enemies, to reject violence, to be ready to make peace, to avoid the service of mammon, to be at the service of others, and other similar demands, then, they will benefit the society more. And consequently, a Christian who uses a mobile phone while bearing in mind Jesus' Sermon on the Mount, should be critically challenged to undergo a radical change of heart even in public life. Such a change of heart will entail a personal endeavour to promote the same radical demands of Jesus in society.

In discourses relating to politics and the conditions of the world, many find these radical demands of Jesus as offering solutions to the problems of arms race, ethnical conflicts, poverty, and starvation. Moreover, today quite 'frequently politicians are measured by the Sermon on the Mount and urged to observe it' (Kreppold 1989: 1). At election campaigns for example, voters assess previous performances and promises of candidates on the basis of the same radical demands of Jesus, even if they don't mention them by name.

Set in the African context, it is the implementation of such paramount demands of Jesus that Africans require of their governments. It is precisely due to the failure to meet such demands of justice, peace, compassion, forgiveness, and so on, that the masses of Africans continue to languish in poverty in spite of the presence of abundant natural and human resources in their countries. The same holds true with regard to the sporadic ethnic conflicts and wars that persist in some parts of Africa.

Thus African presidents, government ministers, religious leaders and others should use the mobile phone differently, namely, not merely as a device of social communications, but on top of that as a constant reminder of the need to uphold the common good and to promote integral human development for all citizens.

The salvific role assigned to mountains in the life and ministry of Jesus Christ inspires Christian communities to reflect on the role they can assign to the "mountain" of the mobile technology for the sake of the economy of salvation. Arguably, mobile phones too can be made into messengers of evangelisation. Churches can use them effectively to realize the Lord's great commission in the areas of *kerygma* (proclamation of the Good News),[3] *liturgia* (in public worship), in *martyria* (day-to-day witness of the Christian faith), in *koinonia* (in exercising fellowship among Christians) and in *diakonia* (in rendering various services in the church and community at large).

The enduring challenge emanating from the mountain metaphor is that the mountain of mobile technology should not be an agent of destruction to humans in any aspect of their lives, be it physical, psychological or spiritual. In the spiritual aspect, it should not prevent the People of God from ascending the mountain of the Lord, for instance, through mediating immoral contents. On the contrary, mobile phone antennas placed on the mountains and towers are expected to be bearers of good news and promoters of life-affirming aspects among the mobile consumers, and consequently charting for them a path towards a holistic liberation.

This then constitutes a call on mobile policy makers to relinquish from putting in place policies that denigrate human dignity. It also conscientises mobile consumers not to be willing pawns of mobile phone providers. Instead, they should dialogue with them and spearhead the stripping off of whatever baggage of potential moral corruption and harmful constructs that may accompany the emergent mobile cultures. These may include oppression of children (e.g. through child pornography via mobile phones), bad addiction among the youth and gender-based discrimination against women. In addition, issues like high taxes levied on handsets as well as high air-time tariffs that tend to snatch the poor even of their meagre means of livelihood should be taken into consideration in the dialogue between consumers and their mobile providers.

Quest for "Perpetual Contact" with God

The mobile phone has endowed human beings with the power to converse instantaneously and comfortably across vast distances and maintain a perpetual contact temporally and spatially. Human imagination had formerly reserved this power only for the greatest gods, but today it is in the hands of humans—beings that are far less than angels (Katz et al. 2002:2). Now that this godlike power defies spatial as well as temporal borders, whether one is at the sea, on the mountains, on the sky, one will be accessible and will be able to access others. Evidently, this always-on environment and accessibility augment a situation of ambivalence in the life of a person. On the one hand, the mobile phone seems to enhance a person's security. But on the other, it may jeopardise it, since even enemies may locate him or her easily.

Theologically, however, this always-on environment and accessibility prompted by the mobile phone, should lead the human heart, which is integrally related to the soul's ascent to God, to contemplate human relationships with God. If humans can hardly shake off the searching power of the mobile phone, an artefact made with their own hands, what about the searching power of God?

God is perfect in knowledge (Job 37:16), and is not fooled by outward appearances, since He looks into the heart (1 Samuel 16:7). The psalmist acknowledges this divine searching power as he says: 'O LORD, you have searched me and you know me. You know when I sit and when I rise; you perceive my thoughts from afar....Where can I go from your Spirit? Where can I flee from your presence?' (Psalm 139: 1-12).

It is here that human hypocrisy meets with a rebuttal. The tendency of human beings is to hide the dark side and present the best side to the world, so that people know our virtues but not our vices. And in this way, our good name is preserved. But how about God who digs into us in our active and passive life, and from whom we cannot hide our true nature? This psalm, therefore, reveals that our dark chambers are not hidden before God. This is a warning against hypocrisy which Jesus also condemns (Mt. 23:23).

On the other side, nonetheless, Psalm 139 may lead us to construct a *cell-phone spirituality* which inspires a believer to always seek to remain in perpetual contact with God and cherish it as the true meaning and purpose of life. Believers may ask themselves: if with our mobile phones we cherish perpetuity of communications with our loved ones and the world around us, why don't we in our spiritual life strive as well to maintain an always-on, a perpetual relationship with God our loving Father?

Theological Insights into Mobile Cultures

This section seeks to analyse the virtues of mobile cultures in the light of the Christian doctrines of the Trinity, *Imago Dei*, the Incarnation and the *Visio Dei*. Such a theological infusion will demonstrate that the values promoted through mobile communications, namely, the crossing of borders, dialogue, mutual listening, human interconnectedness, *inter alia*, find their perfection in the Christian mysteries. In the contemporary religious landscape in Africa, such values may prove beneficial to the Church for her to become a prophetic, open, welcoming, dialoguing, and a listening community. But, as already discussed above, when the Church appropriates these values of mobile cultures, they do not become the measure for the Church. The ultimate measure for the Church consists in the divine mysteries of the Trinity, *imago Dei*, the Incarnation, and the *Visio Dei* and many others. Moreover, it is these divine mysteries that serve to transform any structures of sin that are embedded in mobile phone cultures.

What has Christianity to do with the Mobile Phone?

When Tertullian of Carthage (160-c.220), one of the ancestors of Africa, perceived that Christianity was threatened by the contemporary surrounding culture, he recalled upon Christians to identify the dichotomy that exists between the two. He famously posed the question: *What has Jerusalem to do with Athens?* It was a brilliant question: Jerusalem represented the nerve centre of theological and biblical reflection. Athens represented the flowering of Greek culture and of philosophical enquiry which at the time was perceived to be "pagan" and hence, at variance with Christian theology.

Set against a historical continuum, this question is positively appraised inasmuch as it serves as a critical reminder for Christians, not only in Africa, but in the entire universal Church and at all times, to identify Christianity in its interface with contemporary cultures. Since Tertullian's time 'every generation should have asked a similar question, once that question had been modified to reflect the current age' (de Chirico 2008: 129). As Karl Rahner points out, grace always intersects human culture as an essential expression of God's incarnation in the world in Jesus and the Spirit.[4] Tertullian's question is particularly ponderous today since in the contemporary pluralistic milieu the tendency is to absolutise culture at the expense of religious values. Meanwhile, pluralism is fast assuming the character of an ideology with the consequent attitude of timidity or of anxiety on the part of Christians, especially in the West (Newbigin 1989: viii).

Yet as Pope John Paul II pointed out: 'culture is not the measure of the Gospel, but it is Jesus Christ who is the measure of every culture and every human action (Boguslawski et al. 2008: vii). The consideration of human cultures is an important aspect in the ministry of the Church. This is because the Church's whole mission is to proclaim the salvific initiative of God in Christ and hence, it considers as its own 'the joys and the hopes, the griefs and the anxieties of the whole human family of this age' (*GS* No.1).

Christians are often cautioned against adapting blindly to the spirit of the age. On the contrary, they should be able to 'interact in a significant and positive manner with the culture of a given epoch, always avoiding being passively affected by or uncritically subscribing to that same culture' (de Chirico 2008: 129).

In Africa, such an earnest appeal concerns the interface of Christians with African traditional cultures, but now it certainly holds true as well with regard to the emergent media-based cultures shaped by the mobile phone and other electronic media, particularly among the youth. Mobile phone cultures (and cyber culture and similar jargons common in modern technological parlance) are among the contemporary cultures that the Church in Africa has to reckon with.

Arguably, as technology continues to make strides in the field of communication, it becomes imperative to explore the 'nature of the relationship—if any—that exists between the Christian faith and this new media-based culture' (de Chirico 2008: 129). Tertullian's question may, therefore, be modified and adapted to the current digital age in Africa to state: What has Jerusalem to do with the mobile provider *"Tanzatel?"* What has Christianity to do with the emergent mobile cultures in Africa?

Such an evaluation requires a great deal of attention and immediacy, taking into account the fact that the influence that is exerted on the society by the fluidities and flexibilities of mobile cultures is quite remarkable indeed (de Bruijn et al. 2009: 16).

We now turn to the Christian categories that may be applied to purify and transform mobile cultures.

The Holy Trinity as Paradigm of Human Relationships

Christians believe in a God who is in community, relationships, communication and love. The doctrine of God's triune existence 'operates through a plurality of languages, communicating subjects, expressive codes and contents (de Chirico 2008: 129). The Trinitarian communication involves 'the missions of the Second and Third Persons in the world, and God's reconciliation of the cosmos to the divine Being'(Schreiter 1997: 59). The Trinity also reveals unity of the divine Persons. The relational character of Trinitarian Christianity, therefore, 'endorses and demands multiple as well as varied forms of communication' (de Chirico 2008: 129).

The Trinitarian doctrine is indeed a subject of both puzzlement and wonder for Christians. But the thesis of many theologians today, contrary to the former position, is that the Trinitarian doctrine is indeed a practical doctrine with radical implications for Christian life (Veli-Matti 2009: 14). Robert Schreiter notes that the doctrine of the Trinity has recently received renewed interest due to the globalising trends which make the world increasingly pluralistic (Schreiter 1997: 59). Other theologians such as Leonardo Boff too, subscribe to the applicability of this doctrine for developing a socially and politically relevant liberation cause. They maintain, however, that the mystery of the Trinity is not something thought out to explain human problems, but it is the revelation of God as God is, that is, as Father, Son, and Holy Spirit (Veli-Matti 2009: 16).

The Trinitarian doctrine constitutes a paradigm of communications and relationships. It is an inspiration to church communities and society at large to be instruments of love, cordial relationships and communications in the world. This inspiration also mandates that the various media possibilities available in the world, including the mobile phone, should be creatively mobilised to promote God's *shalom* across the entire globe (de Chirico 2008: 130).

The mobile phone is appropriate for this *shalom* mission since it privileges communications that are characterised by border-crossing and social networks. Mobile communications too, serve to point to the fact that for a human society to embody the Trinitarian model of relationships, it must enhance relationships that are based on love. As noted in previous chapters, mobile communications are sometimes imbedded with extractive social and economic structures. Thus, it is the Trinitarian model that should purify and transform mobile communications since it is the paradigm for all human relationships that are based on true love.

As such, theologizing mobile Africa from a Trinitarian perspective is an imperative quest. Plagued as it is by ethnic conflicts, corruption, environmental degradation and other maladies, Africa needs the Trinitarian inspiration to transform all conditions that diminish life, and instead induce changes that promote justice, peace, reconciliation and integral human development.

'Imago Dei' as Paradigm for Crossing Divides in Society

Mobile communications foster connectedness of peoples and the crossing of social borders. These qualities find their perfect expression in the theological category of *imago Dei*. The Christian category has its biblical foundation in the Book of Genesis (Gen 1:26-27; 5:1-3: 9:6; 1Cor. 11:7) and the Letter of James (3:9), in which human beings are described as having been created in the image and likeness of God. This offers the biblical vision of the sacredness of all human life. It teaches us that every person is endowed with inalienable dignity. *Imago Dei* is, therefore, a profound description of human nature. And to define all human beings in terms of this category is to name the personal and relational nature of human existence as well as extol the fact that human life cannot be understood apart from God.

In his reflection on World Day of Peace in 2010, Pope Benedict XVI stated that, the human face is an 'epiphany of God.' Due to the harshness of life and evil this image is often tarnished. Nevertheless, when human beings know that they have a common Father (God) and when they let this Father dwell in their hearts, then it will be possible to recognise and respect each other as brothers and sisters.[5]

Similarly, the International Theological Commission made the following meditation with regard to the *imago Dei*:

Human persons are created in the image of God in order to enjoy personal communion with the Father, Son and Holy Spirit and with one another in them, and in order to exercise, in God's name, responsible stewardship of the created world. In the light of this truth, the world appears not as something merely vast and possibly meaningless, but as a place created for the sake of personal communion (ITC, No.4).

Soong-Chan links the text in Gen.1: 27 that speaks about the endowment of *imago Dei* upon humankind, with the subsequent verse 28, which he refers to as *God's cultural mandate*: 'God blessed them and said to them, "Be fruitful and increase in number; fill the earth and subdue it"'. Soong-Chan sees that this verse shapes our understanding of the cultural mandate commanded by God. He adds that, since human beings are created in the image of God they should be able to mirror God by re-creating His image through culture. The cultural mandate then can be considered as an impetus for such a human reflection of the image of God in culture:

'In Genesis, God gives what we might call the first job description: "Be fruitful and multiply and fill the earth and subdue it". The first phrase, "be fruitful and multiply" means to develop the social world: build families, churches, schools, cities, governments, laws. The second phrase, "subdue the earth", means to harness the natural world: plant crops, build bridges, design computers, compose music. This passage is sometimes called the Cultural Mandate because it tells us that our original purpose was to create cultures, build civilizations—nothing less' (Rah 2009: 133).

Indeed, it is in the creation of culture that the central expression of humanity as well as God's image and spirit at work in humanity are discernible. In the context of his book, Soong-Chan draws from the connection between the *imago Dei* and cultural mandate to launch an appeal that the Church should be freed from what he calls the 'Western, white cultural captivity', so that it can become the multicultural and holistic community that God has called it to be.

The biblical passage in Revelation 7 is cited to support the culmination of the cultural mandate in the image of the Church as a mosaic—a gathering together of all believers, across all races, ethnicities and cultures for the worship of God. This beautiful image is suffocated, nevertheless, if one culture is elevated above another. Such a cultural hegemony is tantamount to affirming that 'one culture and the individuals in that culture are made more in the image of God than others' (Rah 2009: 134).

Apart from such ecclesiological implications, the doctrine of *imago Dei* is an important Christian category in dealing with the poor and the marginalised people in the society since it is a critical challenge to see the personal value of a human being and accordingly grant his or her human rights and justice. Theologian Daniel Groody notes that, this notion of *imago Dei* grounds much of modern Catholic social doctrine and provides an important foundation for questions to do with ecology, humanitarian debates, gender issues as well as eschatological concerns (Groody 2009: 645).

Moreover, the notion of *imago Dei* is quite relevant in the discourse about issues concerning human dignity and human rights because it is not limited to Christian theology but has a universal scope. Its corollaries are in other religious, philosophical and humanitarian traditions, and it bears a close affinity to human rights language as particularly articulated in the 1948 Universal Declaration of Human Rights (Groody 2009: 647). In other words, this theological category is a fitting arena for wrestling with various life-afflicting human divides.

When it comes to the issue of marginalisation of some categories of people in a society, the first divide that ought to be crossed is the failure to recognise their human dignity. Overcoming this frontier implies the assertion that these people are images of God too, despite the social, economic, physical, or whatever other conditions that distinguish them from the rest of us.

However, the rhythm of life seems to operate otherwise. This is evident, for example, in cases of people with physical disability such as albinos in Africa. Some communities subject them to discrimination and even murder them because of the myths surrounding them in the society, which define them as less human or even as a curse from ancestors. Albinos themselves urge the society to cross this problem-person divide, as a member of the Tanzanian Albino Society clearly put it: 'It is very difficult in Tanzania, as in all sub-Saharan countries, to assert our equal dignity. We are human beings just like everyone else, only we need more care.[56]

Then there is the onerous question of African migrants. During the Second African Synod in October 2009, the Apostolic Nuncio in Libya, Giovanni Innocenzo Martinelli, pointed out in his intervention that the mass exodus of Africans in the phenomenon of international migration and internal displacement of people reveals the face of injustice and socio-political ills prevalent in the continent. Similarly, Cardinal Theodore-Adrien Sarr from Senegal, referring to the subsequent death of many Africans at the high seas as they try to cross over to Europe, urged the African Synod to probe the root causes of the migration phenomenon in order to prevent further loss of lives. He argued, furthermore, that preventing the loss of the lives of migrants will also show the world that the life of an African is holy and not cheap as many media channels seem to portray with the scenes of Africans dying at high seas (*Missio Korrespondenz* 2009: 6).

The moral demands of *imago Dei* challenge governments and policy makers in receiving countries to pass laws which respect the human dignity of these people. Their migrant status should not be a licence to subject them to inhuman treatment. As it is often the case, migrants and refugees are labelled in terms of political, legal, and social constructions such as illegal or undocumented aliens, and often feared as taking away jobs from their hosts and portrayed as potential criminals. Such labels and perceptions render them vulnerable to control, manipulation, and exploitation (Groody 2009: 645).

Migrants' sending countries are likewise challenged to be keen in addressing those problems that force their nationals to migrate. The practical implication of *imago Dei*, in line with *Gaudium et spes*, is that people ought to have access to everything necessary for leading a truly human life, including food, clothing, shelter, right to respect, to good reputation, to education, to employment, and other human needs (*GS*, No. 26).

As such, African leaders and policy makers are called upon to construct just policies ordered to the common good and the benefit of the weakest members of the society (Groody 2009: 645). Arguably, the preoccupation of some African governments with the migration question is apparently mainly in terms of how best to benefit from remittances and investment opportunities presented by the migrants.

They may pay little attention to the violation of the human dignity of the migrants amid human trafficking business, sexual exploitation of women in forced prostitution, financial and social exploitation in the host countries, xenophobic and racist acts and other forms of maltreatment.

Thus, *imago Dei*, on the one hand, serves to affirm the value and worth of every human person, and on the other hand, it militates against any tendencies in the society to dominate and oppress the poor, the needy, physically and mentally handicapped people, migrants and refugees, and so on.

The Incarnation and the Crossing of the Divine-Human Divide

The point of departure in the following theological analysis is that the mobile phone in Africa reinforces border-blurring cultures. This is evident not only in terms of interpersonal communications, but also with regard to its pervasive proliferation that has enabled it to reach even the Cinderella regions, or the so-called "communication margins" of Africa. These regions, mostly inhabited by poor rural people, had hitherto not enjoyed the benefits of telecommunications services because their governments had marginalised them. These mobile cultures lead us to reflect on the Incarnation of Jesus Christ.

We read in the Gospel, 'and the Word was made flesh and dwelt among us...' (Jn. 1:1-18). Jesus' Incarnation is God's self-communication to the world. He is the Word of God which is by nature word, dialogue and communication (*Ecclesia in Africa*, No. 71) 'From the beginning it has been a characteristic of God to want to communicate. 'In many and various ways God spoke of old to our fathers by the prophets; but in these last days He has spoken to us by a Son' (Heb.1:1-2). Hence, the *Missio Dei*, that is, God's turning to the world and to human beings, that Yahweh started in the Old Testament, is continued and fulfilled in Jesus Christ through the Incarnation. The notion of the *imago Dei* presented in the Old Testament is realised in the New Testament through the *imago Christi*.

The Incarnate Jesus Christ as the Border-crosser par Excellence

In the Incarnation, Jesus 'was made to cope with a created reality debased by sin. And becoming fully integrated within it, he acted towards its real transformation (de Chirico 2009: 130). Jesus is put forth as the perfect embodiment of God (Heb. 1:3, Col. 1:15) who helps people cross the vast abyss of sin that separated humanity from God, and enables them to migrate back to God (Col. 1: 20). To accomplish this transformation of the created reality, it is Jesus himself who opted first to cross the border over to the dark territory of sinful humanity, a place of complete "otherness" to him (Groody 2009: 649).

However, the theological import of the Incarnation model is not limited to the view of Jesus Christ as one who offers eternal salvation; rather it includes the tangible effects of his ministry. It is a narrative of 'the human Jesus of Nazareth who wearily trod the dusty roads of Palestine where he took compassion on those who were marginalised' (Bosch 1991: 512). The Incarnation manifests how Jesus challenged the marginalising borders set by his society. He did it by sharing table fellowship with outcast public 'sinners' and tax collectors (cf. Mt. 9:10, 11:19; Mk. 2:15-17; Lk. 7:31-35). Moreover, he took sides with the poor and sympathised with the defenceless and the oppressed against their exploiters (cf. Lk. 6:20-26). As to Samaritans who were despised by his society, Jesus showed an open attitude to them (Lk. 10: 10-37, 17:11-19, Jn.4). Jesus' life and ministry were also inclusive of women as opposed to his society which despised them. He freely associated with them and even included some of them in the community of his disciples (Senior et al. 1983: 147). In this community, Jesus gave the women an opportunity to serve him with their own resources (Luke 8:3). This service was their particular form of discipleship (*The Anchor Bible Dictionary* 1992 : 836). Moreover, Jesus called children to himself and urged that they should not be hindered to come to him (Lk. 18:16).

The question of foreigners and migrants was existent during Jesus' days, although the contexts of migrations then may have been different from today's more globalised contexts. It is noteworthy, however, that this problem too raised Jesus' concern as he showed a favourable attitude towards foreigners (Mt. 8:5-13).

The Incarnation is for Christian communities, therefore, a paradigm of border-crossing in their life and ministry. By assuming human conditions Jesus crossed the border that separates the divine and the human, the eternal and the temporal, the invisible and the visible, spirit and matter (Majawa 2005: 19). Hence, the Incarnation proclaims Jesus not only as the *proto* border-crosser, but also as the border-crosser *par excellence,* who challenges all borders that thrust humanity into social and spiritual marginalisation. It sets a critical challenge to Christian communities and societies that shun out migrants, other races, the poor and the handicapped for fear of mingling with their "otherness." The Incarnation is the foundation of restored human dignity, and human history finds its true meaning in it (*EIA,* No. 69).

The Incarnation model is a great boon in the current socio-religious landscape in Africa since it encourages Christian communities to avoid any sort of religious bigotry and excessive particularism within churches themselves and ethnocentrism in the society at large. Admittedly, many of the currently booming churches in Africa, as already noted earlier, tend towards religious extremism. When Christians adopt the Incarnation model, they will instead be challenged to promote harmony, solidarity and reconciliation among all people regardless of their diverse backgrounds.

The Incarnation also serves in a particular way to encourage the preferential option for the poor and the marginalised in the society. It means that a church community 'must combine serious theological reflection with concrete engagement in its social context' (MacPherson 2008: xi). This implies a combination of a theological and spiritual engagement with a political, economic action. Concretely, this entails a practice of solidarity with victims of all kinds of oppression regardless of their differences, be they religious, racial, tribal, ideological, social status, gender, and others.

Therefore, the enduring challenge of the mystery of the Incarnation is that the Church-in-mission cannot claim to proclaim Jesus Christ and carry out effective evangelisation if it addresses only spiritual needs of the people while failing to take into consideration the promotion of their dignity, both individually and collectively in their social, gender related issues, economic, political, cultural and other aspects of life.

The Incarnation and Social Mobility

While we positively appraise mobile phone services for reaching marginalised regions in Africa, we theologically recall that the Incarnation was Jesus' movement from divinity to humanity which was a downward mobility that took him to the most remote and abandoned places of the human condition (Phil. 2:5-11), devoid of life and prosperity. Yet Jesus undertook it all out of pure love and gratuity. Karl Barth notes that, this readiness for downward mobility as manifested by Jesus Christ distinguishes the Christian God from false gods, since the latter are not ready for it (Groody 2009: 649).

The social implication of the message of the Incarnation today is that, while the divine movement tends toward a downward mobility, people in the society tend toward an upward mobility. The paradox is that, while the Incarnation's downward movement is altruistic and sacrificial, the human upward migration is often selfish and works at the expense of the poor, the needy and the weakest in the society. It can be argued, subsequently, that it is this aspiration for upward social mobility, dominated by greed for wealth and power, which mainly accounts for corruption among many African leaders. It is a common experience that most such leaders would enter politics in rags and retire as millionaires, after having appropriated to themselves what was meant for the common good.

The Incarnation and the Quest for Integrative Church Communities

Another point of departure for cell-phone ecclesiological discourse is the adaptability of the mobile phone to local conditions. The mobile phone shapes cultures that are universal or global but, at the same time, it brings the globalising characters to bear in particular local conditions of space and time. In Africa, for example, although the mobile technology may come from Asia or Europe and even if the mobile providers happen to be foreigners, yet the application of the mobile technology would necessitate its adaptation to the local (social, economic, political, and geographical) conditions of the particular African country. This means, the mobile phone has the potential to enter into dialogue with its local customers and accommodate itself in the local environment while at the same time infiltrating it with some globalising trends.

This mobile cultural element leads us to reflect on the enculturation of the Word of God. Analogically, Jesus Christ through the mystery of Incarnation has entered into dialogue with human culture. It is argued that the multiplicity of biblical titles of Jesus Christ such as *Wisdom, Vine, Shepherd* or *Door* can be interpreted as expressions of His openness to all cultures and to individuals of 'varied levels of comprehension and spiritual growth' (Lyman 2009: 424). According to Origen of Alexandria, the Word's accommodation to various forms and through the centuries is the story of God's constant work of redemption.

Christ has consequently bequeathed the Christian faith with the potential to adapt itself to various cultural forms while maintaining its universality. This cultural adaptability of Christianity lends credence to its catholicity (universalistic character), and fosters its dynamism in the world. Thus, the Incarnation event serves to reiterate the quest for the Church to always promote the enculturation of the Christian faith. The Incarnation mystery mandates that ecclesial communities be open communities, which both in their theology and praxis, welcome members of diverse social and cultural backgrounds and make them feel at home as church members.

The "Visio Dei": Overcoming Parochialism and Provincialism

In previous chapters, we have distinguished between face-to-face communication and virtual communication. We have seen in the case of migrants working abroad, for example, how their regular communication per mobile phones with their families back home serves to reinforce their yearning to be with them physically and to see them face-to-face.

Spiritually, this longing for a face-to-face interaction may serve as a metaphor for the yearning of the human soul for the vision of God (*visio Dei*). 'For ... we seek after the city which is to come' (Heb. 13:14) in which we shall see God face to face (1Cor. 13:12) as He is (1Jn. 3:2), since in the heavenly city, His servants shall worship Him and see His face (Rev.22:3-3). This desire for the real vision of God should open the heart of a believer to the critical moral challenge of the Gospel: 'blessed are the pure in heart, for they shall see God' (Mt.5:8).

The vision of God which is the goal of the Christian life has social implications too. It influences social transformation which reinforces love and concern for the poor and needy as well as administration of justice. In Matthew 25: 31-46 Jesus makes the imperative of solidarity with the poor and the needy a dimension of the last judgment. He demonstrates that response to the needs of the hungry, the naked, the sick, prisoners, and strangers is a condition for obtaining the beatific vision of God.

Moreover, the social location of this category of people creates borders at their expense, but Jesus makes an option for them. His verdict of judgment in this Matthean text implies that the extent to which people cross borders in this life determines to what extent they will cross them in the next life. This text is reminiscent of the parable of the rich man and the poor Lazarus which has similar implications (Lk. 16:19-31). Arguably, Matthew 25: 31-46 speaks of the judgment not only of individuals, but also of nations. Hence, the *visio Dei* challenges individuals as well as nations to see life on much expansive spiritual terrain, consistent with God's kingdom imperatives.

Such a vision of life challenges the Church and society in general to transcend the labels of gender, tribe, ethnicity, race, regions or national territoriality as sole markers of identity and instead acquire more inclusive dispositions. As theologian de Gruchy notes:

God calls the Church into existence for the task of proclaiming the reign of God on earth and not to be an exclusive end in itself....No one is excluded, because no one can join due to their own efforts, status or origins. A church that is built upon national, ethnic, class or other exclusive characteristics, loses the right to be called the Church. This, accordingly, implies that the Church's calling to participate in Missio Dei requires the experience of right-relations with God, between men and women and the earth. It also concerns itself with the pursuit for the fullness of life for all (LenkaBula 2008: 301).

This seems to concur with the observations of the Second African Synod. In their deliberations, the Synod participants did not stop at lancing the boil of Africa's problems, rather they suggested remedies too. One of their suggestions with regard to the achievement of reconciliation, justice and peace in Africa, was that concrete action should be taken. They urged that the concrete steps should include heeding the cry of various categories of people in the continent such as the poor, minorities, women deprived of their dignity, those on the periphery of society, poorly paid workers, refugees, migrants and prisoners (Second African Synod, *Instrumentum Laboris*, No. 62). The Synod saw the need to establish forums that are indispensable for promoting authentic justice and durable peace.

Thus, it can be concluded that the *visio Dei* fosters inclusive attitudes in the Church and society and it is opposed to any form of provincialism, be it ideological, political, religious or social (Groody 2009: 663).

Concluding Remarks

This chapter has analysed mobile cultures in the light of the Bible and Christian doctrines of the Trinity, *imago Dei*, the Incarnation, and the *Visio Dei*. In this way the chapter has attempted to establish biblical and theological perspectives for Christian living in the age of the mobile phone. These biblical and Christian categories constitute the measure and inspiration for the Church in the mobile age. We propose to call the aspect of being Church in the mobile age as *Cellphone Ecclesiology*. The mobile cultures serve to point to the divine mysteries since the values of mobile cultures such as dialogue, perpetuity of communication, listening, transcending of frontiers and others are found in their perfection in the biblical and Christian mysteries.

The biblical and theological analysis of the mobile virtues means metaphorically that the mobile phone should be used to spread the message of love, peace, justice, reconciliation, human dignity and integral human development.

Next chapter examines the theological and social implications of the most frequently asked question in mobile communications, "where are you?" in relation to Africa.

Notes

[1] 'Be gracious to me, O LORD, for I am in distress; my eye is wasted from grief, my soul and my body also. For my life is spent with sorrow, and my years with sighing; my strength fails because of my misery, and my bones waste away. I am the scorn of all my adversaries, a horror to my neighbours, an object of dread to my acquaintances... I have passed out of mind like one who is dead; I have become like a broken vessel... But I trust in thee, O LORD, I say, "Thou art my God"'(vv. 1-13).

[2] Irresponsibility of African leaders is one of the salient issues bemoaned by many Africans in their mobile discourses. Interestingly, the word *responsibility* had in its Latin origin a judicial connotation, and it meant to respond (German *antworten*) to an accusation in front of a court. But in its Christian reception the word came to accrue an ethical meaning and an eschatological interpretation with the sense of justifying people before the Judgment Seat of God (Schoberth 2009: 428f).

[3] A good example is a booklet *1000 Text Messages* published in the Philippines (by Espino/Zamudio, Pasay City: 2000) in which Christians have compiled Bible verses in the form of prepared text messages that can be easily exchanged per SMS.

[4] 'Theology of Ministry', URL: http://findarticles.com/p/articles/mi_m1141/is_14_36/ai_59450118 , accessed 15December 2009.

[5] 'Benedict XVI Offers Key to Peace', in: *Zenit,* Vatican City 1 January 2010), URL: Zenit.org, accessed on 2 January 2010.

[6] 'The hunt for Albinos is still on' URL http://observers.france24.com/en/content/20090413-plight-africa-albinos-cameroon-tanzania , accessed 23 May 2009.

Chapter Eight
"Where Are You?" The Mobile Question and Its Implications in Africa

Chapter Three has noted that the question "Where are you?" is one of the most frequently asked questions in mobile communications. It has been pointed out that when persons in a relationship keep asking one another "Where are you?" with the good intention of safeguarding mutual care and security, then this serves to affirm Ubuntu solidarity. But when a person asks about another person's whereabouts simply in order to monitor and control that person then this can prove to be enslaving and hence can diminish Ubuntu solidarity. This chapter studies the theological import of the question "Where are you?" and its implications in contemporary social and Christian life in Africa.

"Where are you?" as God's First Question to Humanity

The question "Where are you?" has a deep theological significance. At the outset it recasts our imagination in the Garden of Eden where God addresses Adam and Eve (Gen.3:8-10). Notably, "Where are you?" is the first question asked by God of human beings at the beginning of the biblical story. It refers us to our origins and to the first things. It remains to be a relevant question today in connection with diverse issues surrounding humanity.

Adam and his wife Eve heard the sound of the LORD God walking in the garden in the cool of the day, and they hid themselves from the presence of the LORD God among the trees of the garden. But the LORD God called to the man, and asked him, "Where are you?" We are presented here with a wonderful image of our Creator. After creating various creatures (Gen. 1-26), and subsequently a man and a woman in His image and likeness (Gen.1:27), God walks in the garden. He wishes to commune with His creation. Unfortunately, He does not find them in the situation of waiting for companionship with Him as expected of them. Hence, God asks them "Where are you?" to challenge them to respond and name by themselves their place of location. It is a spiritual positioning rather than physical location that is at stake here. It is concerned with the relationship with God which Adam and Eve have diminished because of their sin and as a result they hide, since they do not feel safe or secure any longer. Adam's answer is a spiritual as well and it clearly portrays the awareness of both of them that they have divorced themselves from the Creator who desires companionship with them as His creatures.

Theologically God addresses this question "Where are you?" to all human beings through the narrative of Adam and Eve. By this question God is challenging us as well to recall the innocent walking with Him which Adam and Eve were privileged to enjoy before their fall.

"Where are your?" as Challenge to Respect Human Dignity

Since the question "Where are you?" is one of the most dominant questions in mobile telecommunications, it is interesting to rearticulate this question to relate to the contemporary socio-economic, political and religious setting of Africa. The question resonates with the soul-searching question: *quo vadis* Africa? (whither Africa?), that the Second African Synod participants and other commentators have reiterated. It is a relevant question that urges Africa to "stand up" in view of the various challenges it faces.

First of all, the biblical question "Where are you?" provides us with an opportunity to reflect on God's fundamental purpose for humanity which our kaleidoscopic chaos in the mobile world does not easily afford us. As noted above, this question implies relationship. It calls for our assessment of our location in relationship to God and our neighbour. We are one human family, whatever our national, racial, ethnic, economic, and ideological differences. And since, as Genesis teaches us, all of creation was made by God and ultimately belongs to God, it follows that the goods of creation must be used to advance the reign of God and the well-being of all. Consequently, every human being has 'the right to life, to bodily integrity, and to the means which are suitable for the proper development of life: these are primarily food, clothing, shelter, rest, medical care, and, finally, the necessary social services' (*Pacem in Terris*, No. 11). This is opposed to the tendency in the society of a few people controlling the God-given resources at the cost of injustice to other people. In this context then, God's question "Where are you?" is a call to humanity to respect the dignity of all human beings without any partiality. In fact, all our life issues are so connected that the erosion of respect for the life of any individual or group in society necessarily diminishes respect for all life.

This emphasis on the quest for respecting human dignity is helpful for the diagnosis of the current African scenario. The prevailing situation of callousness and social disconnection manifested by some African leaders is reminiscent of the biblical Cain's answer to God: 'Am I my brother's keeper?' This attitude which currently seems to permeate the African social fabric thwarts development. Millions of Africans are condemned to poverty and other miseries on account of this attitude.

Under these prevailing circumstances God's question "Where are you?" may be paraphrased to state, "Where are you Africa?" or "Where are you African leaders?" Concretely the question would mean: see for yourselves the outcome of your deeds! In what position have you placed yourselves and others by the perpetration of corruption, kleptocracy, irresponsibility, neglect of the poor citizens, and so on?

"Where are you?" as a Call to Conversion

The Book of Genesis evidently, presents a matrix of protology and soteriology, it blends together creation and salvation. This is attested by God's promise of salvation to Adam and Eve after their fall: 'I will put enmity between you and the woman, and between your seed and her seed; he shall bruise your head...'(Gen.3:15). This is a message of hope that should encourage sinners towards *metanoia*. Thus, rather than hide with Adam and Eve behind a tree—in a bid to cover the nakedness, they ought to wait in the garden for God to walk towards them. This waiting nevertheless entails repentance and conversion and God will forgive the sinners. This call to conversion applies also in the socio-political sphere. Theologian Peter Phan offers the following compelling argument:

For a Christian, the root solution for the sinful aspects... as well as for any other human problem, is a "conversion," that is, return to God. Since, as Saint Augustine has put it succinctly, sin is aversio a

Deo—a turning away from God—and salvation is conversio ad Deum—a return to God...We must turn away from "money-theism" to monotheism, making the God of Jesus Christ and not Mammon the only true God (Phan 2007: xv).

Some leaders think the correct political logic and convenience is to camouflage their shortcomings, and resort to protectionism and silencing protesting voices. This is quite evident in party-politics in which some political parties marred with corruption, instead of taking corrective measures, deploy various manoeuvres that help them cling to power and maintain their political hegemony in a country. The mobile question "Where are you?" is therefore, a critical reminder that fundamental change comes with repentance and conversion, and not by suppression of dissenting voices and self-protectionism.

"Where are you?" as Mandate for Environmental Stewardship

'Where were you when I formed the earth?' asks God through the psalmist (Ps. 96:5). In Africa there is a great quest for the promotion of environmental stewardship. Irresponsible environmental policies and practices result into environmental degradation and its related hazards. Unfortunately, even some faith communities advocate theologies that eventually may encourage rather than hinder the escalation of this problem. At stake in some emergent churches is the relationship between protology, ecology and eschatology. Due to a literalist interpretation of the Bible there is a tendency to advocate dispensationalist theologies with an emphasis on the separation of Christians from the world, on the coming kingdom of God, and about the proximity of the end-times. This is often coupled with an extremely anthropocentric focus which is at the expense of the rest of the creation. In this context, dispensationalist theology gravitates around the issue of the interaction of humans and the remainder of nature. First, it highlights the relationship between ecology and protology whereby biblical texts such as Genesis 1:28 and others[1] that talk about the status of humans vis-à-vis the rest of creation, are interpreted as promoting dominion of human beings over nature.

Secondly, dispensationalist theology extols the relationship between protology and eschatology whereby proximity of end-times is emphasised with an implication that environmental conservation is superfluous. This theology, in turn, endorses utilitarian and separatist attitudes of humans toward the rest of the creation. Evidently, such theologies are not environmentally-friendly since a human attitude which respects nature merely on account of its utility will pay only 'nominal or no concern at all for ecological justice.'[2]

The biblical texts just cited, on the contrary, emphasise the fact that the rest of the creation should continually elicit a sense of awe from human beings, in accordance with the divine judgement that all what God created was very good (Gen.1:31). It follows that, the attitude of humanity towards the rest of creation should be to perceive it as valuable for its own good, for ethics, aesthetic and religious appeal as well as the common good of the current generation and future generations. This view is opposed to any perception of creation that focuses on domination over it or seeking merely economic gains from it.

The frequent mobile question "Where are you?" if analysed vis-à-vis the protological divine order, calls upon humanity to show respect for the Creator by upholding a stewardship of God's creation. In this call, humanity is challenged to recognise their hierarchical responsibility to care for the rest of nature and that such a care 'makes up an important component of the divine "image" in human beings. It is a component that we can imperfectly, but resolutely, build upon in helping to bring out its perfection in the time-to-come'.[3]

Pope Benedict XVI also points out that if the invisible face of the Creator is recognised as being reflected in the cosmos, then this leads a person to a greater love and respect for creatures, i.e. he himself or she herself, other human beings and the environment. This reflection, thus, underlines the interaction between human ecology and environmental ecology. As the Pope maintains, there exists a reciprocal influence between the face of the person and the "face" of the environment. In this interface, consequently, when human ecology is respected in society, environmental ecology will also draw out benefits. The reverse is also true. Such rhetoric underscores the fact that the duty to protect the environment is derived from the duty to protect the person, considered in himself or herself as well as in relation to others.[4]

Thus, Christian communities should teach believers to recognize that to care for the earth is a duty of faith and a sign of their concern for all people. They are charged with a commitment 'to strive to live simply to meet the needs of the present without compromising the ability of future generations to meet their own needs'.[5]

"Where are you?" and Africa's Enigmatic Christianity

The question "Where are you?" can lead us to reflect on the contemporary enigmatic situation in Africa whereby we concurrently experience the explosion of Christianity and the persistence of corruption. On the one hand, myriad types of churches are booming. They are so diverse that some scholars prefer to speak of African Christianities (Gifford 1998: 325). Crusades in cities and townships, mutual castigation of members of different denominations, and "sheep stealing" are common features of the present Christian topography in most parts of Sub-Saharan Africa. On the other hand, corruption and a host of other social vices flourish as well. Christian scholars often remark on this enigmatic situation when they analyse the resurgence of Christianity in Africa. Lamin Sanneh, for example, notes that Christianity's 'expansion has taken place against the background of massive upheaval, widespread violence, disease epidemics' (Sanneh 2003: 129). This situation prompts more questions than answers.

Another subject of great concern in the current Christian landscape in Africa is the exponential growth of the number of church ministers who assume political roles in high government echelons. This is particularly true of pastors from the Pentecostal or Charismatic Christian traditions. In Tanzania, Kenya and Uganda, to mention but a few examples, there are church ministers who are Members of Parliament or occupy some high government posts. In Tanzania's general elections in 2010 several pastors and bishops from various Christian churches vied for Presidential and Parliamentary seats.[6] They include: Pastor Macmillan Lyimo of Tanzania Assemblies of God (TAG) of Mabibo Dar es Salaam who vied for the presidential seat through an opposition political party *Tanzania Labour*

Party (TLP). Similarly, Anglican Bishop Dr. Gerald Mpango of the Diocese of Western Tanganyika vied for Parliamentary seat through the ruling party *Chama cha Mapinduzi (CCM)*. He reportedly wanted to join politics in order to fight corruption and protect the rights of Tanzanians. Bishop Pius Ikongo of the Tanzania International Fellowship Church in Kilimanjaro also vied for the Parliamentary seat through *CCM*. He claimed to have been sent by God to assume such a political role.

It remains to be asked whether a church minister-turned-politician will really find room to practice his prophetic ministry in systems whereby politicians are often tainted with corruption scandals and protectionism among political party members is high. Some Pentecostal believers I interviewed in Tanzania expressed their pessimism about the susceptibility of such pastors to challenge harmful dysfunctional structures in their political party machinery.

Another pertinent trend in this scenario is that those churches that through pastoral letters or otherwise raise their voices against corruption and other malpractices in a government would often be accused of mixing religion with politics and advised to distance themselves from political affairs. Curiously, no such blame would befall pastors who actually take part in politics as partisans either in the ruling parties or the opposition side. Nor would they be asked by the authorities to desist from their political positions. And experience shows that the "spiritual fathers" of most African politicians are increasingly from those churches that do not "question" their governments. Can the current Christian explosion in Africa then be viewed as a boon to overcome corruption, kleptocracy, and irresponsibility, oppression of the poor, the weak and other scourges of life?

This is a challenging question since the Christian faith in the Paschal Mystery, 'declares itself as the *memoria passionis, mortis et resurrectionis Jesu Christi.*' It is the memory of the passion, death and resurrection of Jesus Christ and at the midpoint of this faith is a specific *memoria passionis*. On this memory is grounded the promise of future freedom for all. These memories are therefore interruptive, illuminative and subversive…'(Lyman 2009: 424).

Political theologian Baptist Metz points out that there are some political implications associated with this memory of Jesus. He maintains that, this memory of Jesus is "dangerous" because it means recalling Jesus' preaching about the kingdom of God as well as remembering his radical solidarity with the dispossessed. It is, precisely, this position that led Jesus to the cross. But at the same time, the memory of Jesus means remembering the future consummation of the kingdom, which promises liberation to the oppressed of this world, and to remember this liberating future, consequently, mandates an interruption of the *status quo*. Moreover, the dangerous memory of Christ threatens the present and 'calls it into question because it remembers a future that is still outstanding (Gaillardetz 2008: 231). Metz proposes here the realm of apocalyptic eschatology the knowledge of which should shock Christians into political action. It would be expected therefore that churches that so passionately preach about apocalyptic eschatology should as well be in the forefront in shocking their followers into political action for the sake of the marginalised in Africa!

Against Compromising the Prophetic Voice

Instead of challenging the *status quo* what is witnessed in many of the sprouting churches in Africa, on the contrary, is that 'the pietistic message of salvation and a better life in the hereafter continues to reign supreme' (LenkaBula 2008: 294). Many seem to preach resignation in the midst of adversity endured by their followers who are encouraged to detach themselves from the practicality of day-to-day life. South African theologian Madipoane Masenya, contends that, such positions to which the churches subscribe, in fact function in the reverse order. They appear to be subjugating tools for political power and economic injustices in favour of those in positions of power as well as serve to consolidate and perpetuate injustices that go unchallenged (LenkaBula 2008: 294). Thus, the silence of the churches spells a socio-economic and political doom on the people they pledge to serve.

This shortcoming in the public role of African churches has engendered many commentators to become less optimistic about the prospect of the current Christian explosion in Africa to contribute significantly towards liberating Africans from their marginalisation. Theologian Paul Gifford who has researched much about African

Christianities is among those who hold such opinion (Gifford 1998: 340-348).

The attitude of impartiality or of being 'willing pawns' of the state as adopted by some African churches is perceived by some as a survival mechanism and a way of finding favour with the governments. We can cite an instance from the largest Pentecostal Church in Tanzania, the Full Gospel Bible Fellowship (FGBF). As evangelist Faustin Munishi narrates, the Archbishop of this church, Zachary Kakobe, was once advised by Bishop Kitonga of the Redeemed Church of Kenya not to challenge an incumbent government. Bishop Kitonga reportedly maintained that due to such an attitude Pentecostal Churches in Kenya have come to win the favour of the Kenyan Government, which in turn involves them in the propagation of its policies among the citizens many of whom are followers of these churches.[7]

Ecclesiologically, the question "Where are you?" can, therefore, be reframed to address Christian churches in Africa, "where are you in relation to the suffering poor in the continent?" The question challenges the impartiality of churches in the face of human suffering. In situations of suffering, as Desmond Tutu once argued, to be impartial and not to take sides, 'is indeed to have taken sides already'. And true Christian worship cannot occur if it is indifferent to the cries of the hungry, of the naked, and the homeless, of the sick, of the oppressed, of the disadvantaged and others (Haw 2009: 482).

Again, it is laudable that Africa today celebrates a rediscovery of Christianity. There are vibrant Christian communities and churches seem to strive to win more and more members to their side. And on Sundays some churches are literally full to the brim. Yet the impact of religion on a society's moral issues is determined not merely by the number of its adherents but, first and foremost, by their integrity (Wijsen et al. 2007: 13). What perhaps remains to be desired in the current African Christian landscape, therefore, is the translation of that religious enthusiasm into acts of integrity in society and the integration of faith with daily life in order to bring a positive impact on the civil society. It is such Christian integrity that will make a Christian civil servant recognise that embezzlement of public funds and other corrupt deals are sins.

When this is achieved, it will help resolve the current African enigmatic situation which leaves many overwhelmed by questions such as: does Christ matter when a Christian pursues a mundanely noble goal or when confronted with a situation which contradicts the Christian Faith? Do Christians who are engaged in politics, business, and similar spheres, regard the Christian code of moral conduct a criterion for their choices as Christians? Does a Christian government minister regard graft as sin? And so on.

Notes

[1] Other examples of biblical texts that relate about the interaction of humans and the rest of the created or natural order include: Genesis 2:15; Exodus 23:12; Leviticus 25:2-5; 26:3-6; Deuteronomy 20:19-20; Hosea 2:18; Psalm 8. According to some biblical scholars, it is misreading of biblical texts on the part of translators and interpreters that results into such endorsement of dominion theologies, but the Hebrew root for the words that are most often translated with 'dominion' or 'rule' or similar words, does not connote force or violence, rather it can be rendered with the expression 'put in charge' with the connotation of 'caring' or 'caring for.' See: 'From 'Dominion to Stewardship?'", in: *Journal of Religion and Society*, Vol. 3 (2008), URL http://moses.Creighton.edu/JRS/2008/2008/-19.ht (accessed 18 June 2009).

[2] From 'Dominion to Stewardship?'", in: *Journal of Religion and Society*, Vol. 3 (2008), URL http://moses.Creighton.edu/JRS/2008/2008/-19.ht (accessed 18 June 2009).

[3] 'From Dominion to Stewardship?' in: *Journal of Religion and Society*, Vol. 3 (2008), URL http://moses.Creighton.edu/JRS/2008/2008/-19.ht (accessed 18 June 2009).

[4] Dominion to Stewardship?" in: *Journal of Religion and Society*, Vol. 3 (2008), URL http://moses.Creighton.edu/JRS/2008/2008/-19.ht (accessed 18 June 2009).

[5] 'Renewing the Earth: An Invitation to Reflection and Action on the Environment in Light of Catholic Social Teaching', URL: www.usccb.org/sdwp/ejp/bishopsstatement.shtml (accessed 10 January 2010).

[6] 'Wachungaji wa kondoo na siasa wapi na wapi?' in: *Habari Leo: Gwiji la Habari Tanzania*, URL: http://www.habarileo.co.tz/uchambuzi/?n=9221 (accessed 10 August 2010).

[7] 'Askofu Kakobe Msiyemjua', URL: http://www.munishi.com/kakobe.htm (accessed 4 September 2010).

Chapter 9
Looking Towards the Future

This study has attempted to explore the impact of the mobile phone on the Church and society in Africa. But before locating the niche of the mobile phone in contemporary Africa, it has made a cursory survey on the various media of social communications that have been employed in the continent before the current pervasive spread of the mobile phone. The study has established that some of these pre-mobile phone media have been tremendously effective in popular expression, in shaping human relationships and fostering dialogue among different faith communities.

The study has then focused its discussion on the mobile phone. It has analysed the impact of the mobile phone in Africa on two levels, namely, from a socio-economic and political point of view, and from a theological perspective. With regard to the former, it has been pointed out that the mobile phone has accomplished an unprecedented pervasiveness in Africa. It has reached even the remotest corners of the continent that traditionally have been known as 'communication margins.' This device is, therefore, perceived to spearhead a telecommunications revolution in Africa. Other perceived benefits of the social appropriation of the mobile phone in Africa have listed as follows: in the economic sector, some governments are said to have increased their revenues through taxes levied on mobile companies. The mobile phone is said to have increased employment opportunities in some countries, and this helps many poor people improve their sources of income. The introduction of mobile banking and money transfer systems has also a positive impact on the economy of ordinary people. In the health sector too, the advantage of the advancement of mobile technology has been seen since mobile phones are now engaged in the facilitation of the delivery of health services. Likewise in politics, the mobile phone helps establish forums of human rights, democracy and good governance, and thus serves to strengthen civil society. This is epitomised by the facilitation of the mobile phone in the fight against corruption, in conducting political elections, the consolidation of security and empowerment of women. In a word, the mobile phone has been described as a technological artefact with multifarious functions that offer manifold possibilities for the holistic liberation of the African people.

Conversely, however, the mobile phone has been portrayed as a technological device that is fraught with ambivalences. In all the aspects that it has been perceived to liberate people in their setting it has at the same time manifested its enslaving effects. For example, with regard to poverty, while the mobile phone is generally hailed as contributing significantly towards poverty alleviation in Africa, an empirical research in the Southern Highlands of Tanzania has revealed, on the contrary, that the domestication of this device among rural communities indeed makes them poorer.

The ambivalences of the mobile phone should challenge African governments, policy makers and mobile providers not to be satisfied merely by the current achievement of bringing the new communication technologies to the people. Rather, they should now help the people overcome the problems embedded in the appropriation of the mobile technologies.

The research has also skirted around the subject of mobile cultures and has interpreted them from the perspective of the Ubuntu philosophy of life. Some mobile cultures have been described as promoting Ubuntu solidarity among Africans, while others as enhancers of anti-Ubuntu aspects. In this analysis the mobile cultures have been read as a corrective hermeneutic to the attitudes and conduct of some leaders and common people in Africa who perpetrate acts that violate human dignity.

And as far as responsibility of leaders and good governance in Africa is concerned, this study has found out that the hue and cry of the people gravitates chiefly around the areas of irresponsibility, corruption, kleptocracy, oppression of women and children, tribalism, ethnical conflicts, religious bigotry and conflicts, and similar tendencies. Africans long for leaders who fully commit themselves to combat such malpractices and who promote the culture of life.

The second perspective of the study has been a theological one. This has been the main focus of the book. I have pointed out that mobile cultures shape new relationships among people since they are solvents of borders and are characterised by dialogue and interconnectedness. All these values promote the dignity of persons and peoples and foster the upholding of the common good. Consequently, they serve to build in Africa the globalisation of solidarity and the civilisation of love.

Ecclesiologically, these virtues of mobile communication have been proposed in this book as markers of the point of departure for the construction of *Cell-phone ecclesiology for Africa*. Such an ecclesiology is deemed to be an important quest in the current African cultural situation. This is because first, unlike African traditional cultural identities that pertain mostly to particular ethnic groups, mobile cultures pervade and cross more categories of people. They are literally solvents of human borders. Secondly, since mobile cultures encompass and define mostly the current youth culture, a *Cell-phone ecclesiology* will be attractive to the African youths and secure their place in the Church. It is worth noting that African churches are mostly populated by young people who tend to shun African cultures and embrace Western cultures. Evidently the mobile phone is currently one of the most salient features of Western influence in Africa.

As a theological work, the book has evaluated mobile cultures in the light of the Bible and Christian doctrines since in constructing *Cell-phone ecclesiology*, it is the divine mysteries that are articulated in the biblical and Christian doctrinal teaching which become the measure and inspiration of Christian communities.

Cell-phone ecclesiology is envisaged to foster ecumenical and interreligious dialogue, dialogue with political leaders and dialogue with various challenges facing the African people. It will cultivate a listening attitude among Church pastors and their flock and militate against all aspects in society that diminish human dignity, and eventually rehabilitate the sense of community among Africans.

Drawing from what has been discussed in this research, I now undertake to underline the following points as a way forward for Africa in tackling the major problems that currently face the continent.

Quest for Ecumenical and Interreligious Dialogue

The contemporary growing plural situation in Africa calls for a broader and more rigorous ecumenical and interreligious approaches. Being home to African Religions (AR), Islam, Christianity and many minority religions, Africa indeed proves to be a fertile ground for a peaceful coexistence of various religious traditions. Yet this multi-religious propensity of Africans is often marred by some religious leaders and institutions that tend to instil sentiments of religious extremism and exaggerated denominationalism. Some parts of Africa are arenas of rehearsal of Muslim-Christian conflicts. Some African Christians as well as Muslims, often behave in ways that tempt one to think that for them only the human dignity of their co-religionists matters. They may love and respect their co-religionists, including those living in far-flung countries, but harbour feelings of antipathy towards those living next door to them simply because they don't belong to their own religion or religious denomination.

It is a common experience that when churches accentuate denominationalist and exclusivist attitudes they often cause spiritual confusion among believers because such dispositions are certainly counterproductive to the Gospel. Ordinary believers are often embarrassed and feel betrayed by their leadership when their churches are torn in conflicts. Questions may be asked such as: 'Are they not all praying to the same God?", and what example are they giving to the flocks they serve?' (Shorter et al. 2001: 86).

Thus, the mobile age in Africa should serve to pinpoint the imperative of promoting ecumenical and interreligious dialogue in Africa. I do not attempt at this juncture to delve into detailed treatment of the subject of dialogue, nor moderate the plethora of challenges encountered in ecumenical and interreligious dialogues. My intention rather, is to draw attention to the need of dialogue or to dialogue about ecumenical and interreligious dialogue in the current African milieu.

Simply put, there is a quest for reinforcing meaningful ways of relating among members of different belief systems and Christian traditions that aim at establishing trust, mutual respect, tolerance, and love. As Notto R. Thalle notes, 'dialogue is people who meet and talk together about their concerns. They knock at each other's doors, are invited into the houses of the others, cross borders, find themselves at the boundary where they listen, observe and speak. And something happens (Thelle N., -- :130) .

When people encounter people of differing religious persuasions doubts, fears, and questions are sure to occur. But as Cardinal Francis Arinze points out, there are a lot of compelling reasons for making dialogue obligatory today. First, the world today experiences the reality of religious plurality which makes it unrealistic to live as if there were only one religion in the world. But secondly, there is more desire for human integration today than ever before in human history since people increasingly frown upon isolationism. Thirdly, dialogues are required since they contribute towards mutual enrichment of religious faith among adherents of different belief systems. Fourthly, dialogue fosters harmony between citizens, and leads to a joint promotion of moral values, development, justice and peace as well as offers solutions to religious extremism. Furthermore, what makes dialogue obligatory is the unity of human nature. The commonality of divine Fatherhood and human nature should be a reason for religionists from different belief systems to want to meet, to listen to one another and try to understand one another (Arinze 1998: 21-33).

Thus, analysed against the perspective of *Cell-phone ecclesiology*, Africa longs for dialogue in all its forms in order to inculcate in its people a culture of unity, love, and mutual respect—socially, religiously, economically and in other spheres of life. And Church leaders, theologians and members of the various churches in Africa are challenged to promote avenues of dialogue within their own denominations, with members of other Christian denominations and with non-Christian religionists such as Muslims and adherents of African Religions.

Need for Meaningful Church-State Dialogue

The Church cannot single-handedly accomplish the demands of human solidarity, social justice, and integral human development, reconciliation, and all other issues pertaining to the dignity of women and men in Africa. This requires that all stakeholders in a nation garner their efforts and advance together towards charting a better future for their people. That makes the cooperation between the Church and state inevitable.

Church-state relationships in many African countries are often strained when churches disapprove of misgovernment and corruption in government circles. Most politicians tend to consider this as an act of churches meddling with political affairs. The same governments that urge churches to build schools, hospitals and provide other social services in order to lift the conditions of their citizens, will nonetheless, not warrant the cooperation of the churches to stamp out the very malpractices, such as corruption, that keep the citizens in perpetual misery.

Such an attitude of downplaying dialogue in affairs that involve the interest of the people is rather unfortunate. But in fact, forums of church-state dialogues are not new in some African states. In Tanzania, during the leadership of the country's first President, Julius K. Nyerere, there existed a Council of Elders which served as an avenue of exchange of ideas between the government and church representation. It comprised of three Catholic bishops, one Anglican bishop and one Lutheran leader. In 1970, for instance, the Council met with Nyerere's Government to resolve a misunderstanding that arose between the Church and the socialist Government. Nyerere had allegedly criticised the Church for not wholeheartedly welcoming his socialist political ideology of *Ujamaa* ("familyhood"), a unique form of African rural socialism. Apparently, at the initial stages of *Ujamaa,* church leaders hesitated to pledge themselves to its cause because they had suspected it of infiltrating some communist leanings into the country. As reaction to such reluctance, politicians took offence with church leaders, branding them as *wanyonyaji* (i.e. exploiters) and *kupe* (i.e. "suckers" of other people's sweat). *Ujamaa* was intended to build a classless Tanzanian society, free from all sorts of exploitation. Hence, any reluctance to support this cause was regarded as an affront to human equality. At the face-to-face meeting with President Nyerere and other Government representatives the church leaders greatly resented such epithets and reminded the Government of the invaluable contribution of various faith communities in Tanzania towards the development of the country (Sivalon 1992: 18).

The mobile age in Africa, therefore, challenges both the Church and African states to create avenues of dialogue between them for the sake of peace, reconciliation, justice and integral development of the people.

Dulles' Model of Dialogue with Christian Politicians

American Catholic bishops were grappling with the question of reception of Holy Communion of some pro-abortion politicians. The bishops had to advise them not to receive Holy Communion. Cardinal Avery Dulles encouraged the U.S bishops to dialogue with dissenting Catholic politicians and with any other persons in public life about their moral responsibilities before advising them to not receive Communion. In the case of defending human life for instance, the Cardinal argued that, the first step should be to make sure that the politicians as well as the American public understand the doctrine of the Church and the reasons for it. For the Cardinal, many politicians, like much of the American public, were apparently, unaware that abortion and euthanasia are serious violations of the inalienable right to life. They seemed to regard them as just "Church" issues, rather than rights governed by the natural law of God, which is binding upon all human beings.[1] In his dialogue proposal Cardinal Dulles noted,

If, after dialogue, the bishop finds the politician incorrigibly opposed to Catholic teaching on this matter, he may have to advise or order the politician not to receive Holy Communion, which is by its very nature a sign of solidarity with the Church. Other steps might also be considered. For instance, the bishop could instruct Catholic parishes and institutions not to invite such politicians to speak on Church premises, not to give them roles in the liturgy and not to honour them with rewards and honorary degrees.[2]

Perhaps such an advice may apply also for the Church in Africa. The Church should thus promote dialogue with African politicians in general. But as for Christian politicians it would probably be of greater benefit to involve a religious infusion in which the formation of conscience of such politicians would be particularly emphasised. This can involve an organised regular Christian education for church members who serve the people in public life, concerning their moral responsibilities. Avenues of dialogue between church leaders and top political leaders such as presidents and ministers, members of parliaments and other civil servants who are members of the Church need to be established.

There is a window of opportunity in this approach, given that African politicians today are probably more inclined to adhering to religion than their counterparts in the early post-independence decades who were often accused of having Marxist leanings. And at any rate, Christian education is imperative since it offers an opportunity for a religious appeal that serves in the formation of conscience. It is such a formation that may really help to change the attitude of the politicians. In the war against corruption, for example, many African Christians believe that there would be much success if at least Christian politicians in a given country could respected the dignity of their fellow human beings whom they relegate to ignoble life of poverty and misery through their acts of corruption and greed. If at least Christian leaders, inspired by mobile ecclesiology, uphold the common good, much of the natural resources in a country will be used for the benefit of the majority of the citizens.

The Vatican Congregation for the Doctrine of the Faith made a similar point when it taught that a well-formed Christian conscience does not permit one to vote for a political programme or an individual law which contradicts the fundamental contents of faith and morals (*Doctrinal Note on Some Questions Regarding the Participation of Catholics in Political Life*, art. 4).

Quest for Listening Leaders

It is needless to reiterate that today we positively appraise the mobile phone for 'revolutionalising' social communications in Africa, and that the secret behind it is that people listen to one another when they use this device. It is important to emphasise, however, that another step towards addressing the problem of the marginalisation of the average Africans is for the African leaders to develop an attitude of listening attentively to their discourses and the popular culture. Listening is a crossing of the divides that separate people. It is an act of transcending borders. Undeniably, without listening there can be no conversation, no dialogue. And many ills in the society are said to be glibly attributed to a failure to listen. This appeal to cultivate an attitude of listening is a challenge to those African leaders who tend to interpret any criticism against their leadership as dissidence or as being ill-motivated. Or those who dismiss voices of discontent with their governments as inauthentic unless brought to them formally in writing.

The quest for listening holds true also for churches. In order to promote dialogue, church leaders, theologians and their Christian communities should cultivate a listening attitude within their own denominations, with members of other Christian denominations and with non-Christian religionists. This means, the entire spectrum and forms of African religious discourses should be taken into account (Maluleke 2005: 490).

Allegedly, three stereotypes of poor listeners are men, churches and leaders. As such, male church leaders are at a triple risk of being caricatured as not listening (Lee 2004: 76). But while such criticisms surface concerning church leaders, there exists in the Church a long history of listening leaders, whose examples can be emulated, not only by church leaders, but also by political leaders. One of such personalities is St. Benedict of Nursia, founder of western monasticism and the Abbot. In his "Rule of St. Benedict" written in the sixth century, the first word is "Listen". He urges: 'Listen carefully, my son, to the master's instructions, and attend to them with the ear of your heart' (Edmondson 2010: 43). In the immediate context in which Benedict is speaking, the injunction refers to the words of the Lord that are for the benefit of a particular community and for ministry. But even today, fifteen centuries after the creation of the Rule, the key values inherent in the Rule are pertinent to ordinary life of the people. The Rule fosters 'listening, hospitality, humility, embracing change, respect for people, learning, prayer and work'.[3] These are qualities of a listening leader, whether this leader serves the people in public life or in church. However, Benedict's Holy Rule suggests that in order for a leader to cross the barriers to listening to the people, he or she has first to learn to listen for 'the sounds of God...Once that barrier is recognized, and down, more listening is bound to be possible' (Edmondson 2010: 43).

A more recent example of a listening leader is the late Pope John Paul II. As bishop of his diocese of Krakow he was said to be a good listener to his flock. He had established many lay-dominated study groups and encouraged each member of the group to speak during meetings and he even listened attentively to young students (Lee 2004: 77).

Listening and mutual dialogue would help ease the tension and solve the conflicts that persist among the various Christian denominations on the one hand, and between Christianity and Islam on the other hand.

Redeeming Ubuntu Solidarity

African leaders should learn to say "we". There is a story of a Christian missionary who during his evangelisation activities among the Igbo of Nigeria had once vividly described to his congregation about the suffering of Jesus Christ. He narrated how Jesus was tortured and beaten. A chief of the tribe then remarked, 'What was the response of his kin group? Did they just leave Him to endure his suffering without coming to his aid?' Apparently, it was incomprehensible that relatives leave one of their own to undergo such horrendous punishment without fighting back. Was he perhaps a bad man? For the Igbo a person who does not possess the support from his kinship people is a vulnerable human being (Kalu 2008: 262).

This perception is shared by many African communities in the Ubuntu philosophy of life discussed in Chapter Three. The sense of belonging together, mutual support and community life are elements that are greatly cherished in Africa. This African philosophy is often summarised in the sentence: 'I am because we are'. As Desmond Tutu explains:

We say a person is a person through other persons. We don't come fully formed into the world. We learn how to think, how to walk, how to speak, how to behave, indeed how to be human from other human beings. We need other human beings in order to be human. We are made for togetherness, we are made for family, for fellowship, to exist in a tender network of interdependence (Haws 2009: 482).

But the major hurdle for many African societies on this regard is to transcend the frontiers of kinship and ethnicity and cultivate a solidarity national unity. Indeed many seem to hallow the philosophy that 'blood is thicker than water'. It becomes counterproductive to the Gospel message when blood remains to be thicker than the waters of baptism. With such a strong and often over-powering centring on family (often one's extended-family) many sins are committed in the name of the family good. The egoistic family-centeredness partly, but significantly, contributes to corruption since the common good is appropriated by a few in the nation.

In several parts of Africa, solidarity is expressed in terms of favourable conditions given (gift) to acquaintances, close relatives, and clients. In this case solidarity represents a carefully delineated and controlled space beyond which gratuity and gift rarely extend. This space is defined by "particularistic and communitarian codes of conduct which have very little in common with the notion of the public good." It has much less in common with the concern for justice, fairness, equity, and common good (Orobator 2010: 328).

Former Mozambican President, Samora Machel once described tribalism as the "'commander-in-chief of anti-African forces'" (Adeyemo 2001:34). But as Chapter Three has manifested, for some Africans Ubuntu has no meaning beyond their national borders. This barrier ought to be crossed during the mobile age. As for the Church, the mobile age affords us to envision an ecclesiology that fosters human interconnectivity and the transcending of borders that hitherto have kept people apart.

All in all, Africans are invited to rediscover a sense of identity that cherishes the common good, solidarity, justice, concern for others, and sense of responsibility. This quest was gravely emphasised by the Second African Synod with regard to African Catholics in public life. Citing the ongoing cause of Beatification of Tanzania's first president, Julius Nyerere, the Synod expressed its hope that saintly politicians and heads of state would emerge in Africa. Such saintly politicians will clean the continent of corruption and other vices that beset African nations as well as promote the upholding of the common good in society ("'Courage! Get on Your Feet, Continent of Africa'" 2010: 20).

The words of Anthony the Great, one of Africa's ancestors speak eloquently to the African situation: 'Our life and death is with our neighbour. We are summoned back to an understanding of personhood that is ultimately relational' (Radcliffe 2005: 135).

And Ghanaian Pentecostal theologian Mensa Otabil notes,

Africans think that we do not deserve much. It started from the past before the white people came with our own forefathers. They did not value the life of others. They made us believe we were nothing. But then the white men came and the colonialism. And we were told we are nothing. The white men left. Then we got independence but our leaders told us we can have nothing. From past to the present we have been reduced in value (Hasu 2007: 235).

May the mobile age in Africa be an age of crossing all harmful divides, an age of changes, and new hope for all categories of people in the continent.

Notes

[1] 'Cardinal Dulles on Communion and Pro-Abortion Politicians', URL:
http://www.zenit.org/article-10488?l=english (accessed 20 November 2008).

[2] 'Cardinal Dulles on Communion and Pro-Abortion Politicians', URL:
http://www.zenit.org/article-10488?l=english (accessed 20 November 2008).

[3] 'Saint Benedict's Rule: Guide for the Ages', URL:
http://www.benedictinewomen.org/downloads/RuleOverview0208.pdf (accessed 5 November 2010).

SELECTED BIBLIOGRAPHY

'A Critique of Do It Yourself Spirituality', URL: http://www.firmstand.org/articles/do_it_yourself_spirituality.html, accessed 8 January 2010.

Adeyemo, T. (2001) 'Africa's Enigma', in: Deryke Belshaw, Robert Calderisi, Chris Sugden (eds), *Faith in Development: Partnership between the World Bank and the Churches of Africa*, Oxford: Regnum Books International.

Aetatis Novae (Pastoral Instruction on Social Communications) URL: http://www.vatican.va/roman_curia/pontifical_councils/pccs/documents/rc_pc_pccs_doc_22021992_aetatis_en.html

Affiong, A. 'Adam Minus Eva', *New African Woman*, No.6, January 2009.

'Africa: Zain introduces Mobile Banking', URL: http://allafrica.com/stories/200902250724.html, accessed 26 February 2009.

Arinze, F. (1998) *Meeting other Believers: the Risks and Rewards of Interreligious Dialogue*, Huntington, Indiana: Our Sunday Visitor.

Asamoah-Gyadu's 'Did Jesus Wear Designer Robes?', in: *Christianity Today*, November 2008), URL: http://www.christianitytoday.com/globalconversation/november2009/response3.html, accessed 10 January, 2010.

'Askofu Kakobe Msiyemjua', URL: http://www.munishi.com/kakobe.htm, accessed 4 September 2010.

Balliet, D. (2010) 'Communication and Cooperation in Social Dilemmas: A Meta-Analytic Review', *The Journal of Conflict*

Resolution: Journal of the Peace Science Society (International), Vol. 54, No.1, February.

Bell, G. (2005) 'The age of the thumb: A Cultural Reading of Mobile Technologies from Asia', in: Peter Glotz, Stefan Bertschi, and Chris Locke (eds), *Thumb Culture, The Meaning of Mobile Phones for Society*, Bielefeld: Transcript Verlag.

Belschaw, D., R. Calderisi and C. Sugden (eds.) (2001) *Faith in Development: Partnership between the World Bank and the Churches of Africa*, Oxford: Regnum Books International.

Benedict XVI (2009) Encyclical Letter *Caritatis in Veritate* (Charity in Truth) Nairobi: Paulines Publications Africa.

Benedict XVI (2005) Encyclical Letter *Deus Caritas Est* (God is Love) Nairobi: Paulines Publications Africa.

'Benedict XVI Offers Key to Peace', in: *Zenit*, 1 January, 2010, URL. Zenit.org, accessed on 2 January 2010.

Boguslawski, S., and R. Martin (2008) *The New Evangelisation: Overcoming the Obstacles*, New York/Mahwah: Paulist Press.

Bosch, D. (1991) *Transforming Mission: Paradigm Shifts in Theology of Mission*, Maryknoll, New York: Orbis Books.

Calderisi, R. (2007) *The Trouble with Africa: why Foreign Aid isn't working*, New Haven and London: Yale University Press.

Cannon, M. (2009) *Social Justice Handbook: Small Steps for a Better World*, Downers Grove, Illinois: InterVarsity Press.

'Cardinal Dulles on Communion and Pro-Abortion Politicians', URL: http://www.zenit.org/article-10488?l=english, accessed 20 November 2008.

Carmody, P. (2010) *Globalization in Africa: Recolonization or Renaissance?* Boulder, London: Lynne Reinner Publishers.

'Cell phones may help "save" Africa', URL: http://news.mongabay.com/2005/0712-rhett_butler.html, accessed 8 February 2009.

'Cell phones mobilised to fight AIDS in Africa', URL: http://www.reuters.com/article/technologyNews/idUSL1269690620070213 (accessed 15 April 2009).

Chesworth, J. (2007) 'Challenges to the Next Christendom: Islam in Africa', in: Frans Wijsen and Robert Schreiter (eds), *Global Christianity Contested Claims*, Amsterdam-New York: Rodopi.

Chitando, E. (2002)'"Down with the devil, Forward with Christ!' A Study of the interface between religious and political discourses in Zimbabwe," in: *African Sociological Review*, Vol.6, No.1, URL: http://www.codesria.org/Links/Publications/asr6_1full/chitando.pdf, accessed 20 December 2009.

'Church porn protest by phone mast objectors - Mobile Mast Row At Church's Highest Court', URL: http://www.christiantoday.com/article/church.urged.to.reject.mobile.phone.masts.over.porn.concerns/10722.htm, accessed 9 March 2009.

Ciorra, A., and James K. (2001) 'The Parish Community and Moral Discernment', in: *Pastoral Life*, Vol.50, No.9, September.

Claver, F. (2008) *The Making of a Local Church*, Maryknoll, New York: Orbis Books.

Communio et Progressio (Pastoral Instruction on the Media), URL: http://www.vatican.va/roman_curia/pontifical_councils/pccs/documents/rc_pc_pccs_doc_23051971_communio_po.html.

Congregation for the Doctrine of the Faith (2003) *Doctrinal Note on Some Questions Regarding the Participation of Catholics in Political Life*, Nairobi: Paulines Publications.

'Corruption eats 20 percent of government budget', URL: http://www.ippmedia.com/ipp/guardian/2009/03/03/132696.html, accessed 30 March 2009.

Cruz G. (2008) 'Between Identity and Security: Theological Implications of Migration in the Context of Migration', in: *Theological Studies*, Vol. 69, No.2, June.

Diakonia: Internationale Zeitschrift für die Praxis der Kirche (2010), 41. Jahrgang, Heft 2, März.

Donner, J. (2005) 'The social and economic implications of mobile telephony in Rwanda: An ownership/access typology', in: Peter Glotz, Stefan Bertschi, Chris Locke (eds), *Thumb Culture: The Meaning of Mobile Phones for Society*, Bielefeld: Transcript Verlag.

Dorr, D. (1992) *Option for the Poor, A Hundred Years of Catholic Social Teaching*, Maryknoll, New York: Orbis Books.

'Drivers on Cell Phone Kill thousands, Snarl Traffic', in: *LiveScience*, URL: http://www.livescience.com/technology/050201_cell_danger.html#stats, accessed on 19 October 2009.

'Dulles on Communion and Pro-Abortion Politicians', URL: http://www.zenit.org/article-10488?l=english, accessed 20 November 2008.

Edmondson, C. (2010) *Leaders Learning to Listen*, Darton: Longman and Todd Ltd.

'Emerging DG Trends that have Alliance Potential', URL: http://www.usaid.gov/our_work/global_partnerships/gda/dem_guide/dem3.html, accessed 12 April 2010.

Espino/Zamudio (2000), *1000 Text Messages*, Pasay City.

European Journal of Theology (2008), XVII, No.2.

Evangelii nuntiandi (Apostolic Exhortation of Pope Paul VI), URL: http://www.vatican.va/holy_father/paul_vi/apost_exhortations/documents/hf_p-vi_exh_19751208_evangelii-nuntiandi_en.html.

Flannery, A. (ed.) (1977), *Vatican Council II, The Conciliar and Post Conciliar Documents, Gaudium et Spes* (Pastoral Constitution on the Church in the Modern World), Dublin: Dominican Publications.
_____,*Vatican Council II, The Conciliar and Post Conciliar Documents, Sacrosanctum Concilium* (Constitution on Sacred Liturgy), Dublin: Dominican Publications.
_____,*Vatican Council II, The Conciliar and Post Conciliar Documents, Inter Mirifica* (Decree on the Means of Social Communications), Dublin: Dominican Publications.

Freedman D. (ed.) (1992) *The Anchor Bible Dictionary*, Volume 4, K-N, New York: Doubleday.

Friesl, C., R. Polak und U. Hamachers-Zuber (eds.), (2009) *Die ÖsterreicherInnen: Wertewandel 1990-2008*, Wien: Czernin Verlag.

'From 'Dominion to Stewardship?'", in: *Journal of Religion and Society,* Vol. 3, 2008, URL: http://moses.Creighton.edu/JRS/2008/2008/-19.ht, accessed 18th June 2009.

Fuellenbach, J. (2002) *Church: Community for the Kingdom*, Maryknoll, New York: Orbis Books.

Gaillardetz, R. (2008) *Ecclesiology for a Global Church: A People Called and Sent*, Maryknoll, New York: Orbis Books.

Geser, H. (2005) 'Is the cell phone undermining the social order?', in: Peter Glotz, Stefan Bertschi, Chris Locke (Eds.), *Thumb Culture. The Meaning of Mobile Phones for Society*, Bielefeld: Transcript Verlag.

Gifford, P. (1998) *African Christianity: Its Public Role*, London: Hurst & Company.

Gifford, P. (2008) 'Trajectories in African Christianity', *International Journal for the Study of the Christian Church*, Vol. 8, No.4, November.

Glanz, M. (2006) *Eine Kulturanalyse der Mobilkommunikation in Österreich am Beispiel Handy-Nutzung im öffentlichen Raum*, unpublished Masters thesis, University of Vienna.

Goggin G. (ed.) (2008) *Mobile Phone Cultures*, London: Routledge.

Göran, Hydén and M. Mmuya (2008) *Power and Policy Slippage in Tanzania: Discussing National Ownership of Development*, Stockholm: SIDA.

Guest, R. (2004) *The Shackled Continent: Africa's Past, Present and Future*, London: Mcmillan.

Gwekwerere, G. (2009) 'Gospel Music as a Mirror of the Political and Socio-Economic Developments in Zimbabwe 1980-2007', in: *Exchange: Journal of Missiological and Ecumenical Research*, Vol. 38, No.4.

Hanciles, J. (2008) *Beyond Christendom, Globalisation, African Migration, and the Transformation of the West*, Maryknoll, New York: Orbis Books.

Harper, R. (2005) 'From teenage life to Victorian morals and back: Technological change and teenage life', in: Glotz, Peter, Stefan Bertschi, Chris Locke (eds), *Thumb Culture: The Meaning of Mobile Phones for Society*, Bielefeld: Transcript Verlag.

Hartrich, E. (1983) *The American Opportunity*, New York: Macmillan.

Hasu, P. (2007) 'Neo-Pentecostalism in Tanzania: Godly miracles, Satanic interventions or human development?', in: Jeremy Gould & Lauri Siitonen (eds), *Anomalies of Aid: A festschrift for Juhani Koponen*, Helsinki: Institute of Development Studies University of Helsinki.

Haws C. (2009) 'Suffering, Hope and Forgiveness: The Ubuntu Theology of Desmond Tutu', in: *Scottish Journal of Theology*, Vol. 62, No. 4.

Healey J., and D. Sybertz (1999) *Towards an African Narrative Theology (Faith & Cultures):* Maryknoll, New York: Orbis Books.

Heute, 29 April 2009.

Heute, 30 June 2009.

Highet, J. (April 2009) 'Inside Nollywood', in: *New African*, No.494.

'HIV/AIDS and Mobile Technology: SMS saving Lives in Africa', URL: http://www.awid.org/eng/Issues-and-Analysis/Library/HIV-AIDS-and-mobile-technology-SMS-saving-lives-in-Africa, accessed 15 April 2009.
http://catholicsocialservices.org.au/Catholic_Social_Teaching/Justitia_in_Mundo, No. 40, accessed 15 October 2010.

http://digitalorthodoxy.com/index.php?Doo=ContentView&id=286, accessed 23 February 2009.

http://wiki.media-culture.org.au/index.php/Mobile_Phones_-_Technology_-_Disadvantages, accessed 9 March 2009.

http://www.news24.com/News24/Africa/Features/0,,2-11-37_1185668,00.html, accessed 26 February 2009.

http://www.newtimesonline.com/content/view/18607/132/, accessed 27 February 2009.

http://www.pwc.com/extweb/pwcpublications.nsf/dfeb71994ed9b
d4d802571490030862f/c79144b731ac02618025746700011320/$
FILE/Budget%202008_9_Summary.pdf, accessed 16 February
2009.

http://www.tanb.org

Informations-Broschüre, Was ich nicht will, das tue ich, Röm. 7:19, URL:
www.loveismore.de, www.nacktetatsachen.at .
International Theological Commission (ITC), *'Communion and Stewardship'*, URL:
http://www.vatican.va/roman_curia/congregations/cfaith/cti_index.htm, No. 4.

'Inhabiting the Digital Universe with a Believing Heart', URL:
http://blog.echurchwebsites.org.uk/2010/04/27/pope-benedict-xvi-inhabit-the-digital-universe-with-a-believing-heart-and-help-give-a-soul-to-the-endless-flow-of-communications-on-the-internet/, accessed 10 June 2010.

'International Women's Day: Women in Mobile and Mobile for Women', URL:
http://mobileactive.org/international-womens-day-women-mobile-and-mobile-women, accessed 12 March 2009.

Isichei, E. (2004) *The Religious Traditions of Africa: A History*, Westport: Praeger Publishers.

Jenkins, P. (2006) *The New Faces of Christianity, Believing the Bible in the Global South,* New York: Oxford University Press.

Jenkins, P. (2007) *The Next Christendom, The Coming of Global Christianity*, New York: Oxford University Press.

John Paul II (1987) 'Message on World Day of Peace', 1 January.

John Paul II, Post-Synodal Apostolic Exhortation, *Ecclesia in Africa*, Nairobi: Paulines Publications-Africa, 1995.

John Paul II (1994), *The Catechism of the Catholic Church*, Nairobi: Paulines Publications Africa.

_____ (1987), Encyclical Letter *Sollicitudo Rei Socialis* (On Social Concern), Nairobi: Paulines Publications Africa,.

Journal of Media and Religion (2009), Vol. 8, No. 2, April-June.

Justitia in Mundo (Document of Synod of Bishops on Justice in the World), URL: http://www.vatican.va/roman_curia/synod/documents/rc_synod_doc_19711130_giustizia_po.html.

Kalu, O. (2008) *African Pentecostalism, An Introduction*, New York: Oxford University Press.

Kärkkäinen, V. (2009) 'The Trajectories of the Contemporary "Trinitarian Renaissance" in Different Contexts', in: *Journal of Reformed Theology*, Vol. 3.

Katz E., James, and M. Aakhus (eds) (2002), *Perpetual Contact: Mobile Communication, Private Talk, Public Performance*, Cambridge: Cambridge University Press.

'Kenya in Crisis', URL: http://news.bbc.co.uk/2/hi/technology/6241603.stm (accessed 16 February 2009).

Khoser, K. (2007) *International Migration: A Very Short Introduction*, New York: Oxford University Press.

Klasse. Das Elternmagazin, April 2009.

Kolade, C. (2001) 'Corruption in Africa: Causes, Effects and Counter-measures', in: Deryke Belschaw, Robert Calderisi, Chris

Sugden (eds), *Faith in Development: Partnership between the World Bank and the Churches of Africa,* Oxford: Regnum.

Kößmeier, N. (2009) 'Afrika—Der schwierige Weg in eine hoffnungsvolle Zukunft', in: *Ordens Korrespondenz, Zeitschrift für Fragen des Ordenslebens,* Jahrgangsverzeichnis des 50. Jahrgangs.

Kreppold, G.(1989) *The Sermon on the Mount: Between Spirituality and Utopia,* Manila: St Pauls Philippines.

Laborem Exercens (Encyclical Letter of Pope John Paul II on Human Work), URL: http://www.vatican.va/edocs/ENG0217/_INDEX.HTM.

'Lange Nacht der Kirchen', URL: http://www.langenachtderkirchen.at/statements/wien/0/articles/2009/04/07/a2636/, accessed 8 July 2009.

Lee, S. (2004) 'Rogue Elements', in: Ian Markham and Kelton Cobb (eds) *Current Conversations in Religion and Theology,* 1 May 2004.

LenkaBula, P. (2008) 'Beyond Anthropocentricity- Botho/Ubuntu and the Quest for Economic and Ecological Justice in Africa' in: *Religion and Theology: A Journal of Contemporary Religious Discourse,* Vol. 15/3-4.

LenkaBula, P. (2008) 'The Shift of Gravity of the Church to Sub-Saharan Africa: Theological and Ecclesiological Implications for Women' in: *International Journal for the Study of the Christian Church,* Vol. 8, No.4, November.

L'Osservatore Romano, 13 September 1995.

Lindhardt, M. (2009) 'More than Just Money: The Faith Gospel and Occult Economies in Contemporary Tanzania', in: *Nova Religio: The Journal of Alternative and Emergent Religions,* Vol. 13, No.1, August.

Lyman, R. (2009) 'Living Faithfully in the midst of Media Violence' in: *Expository Times, International Journal of Biblical Studies, Theology and Ministry*, Vol.120, No. 9, June.

MacPherson N. (2008) *Church at a Crossroads: Being the Church after Christendom* Eugene/ Oregon: WIPF & STOCK.

Magesa, L. (2010) *African Religion in the Dialogue Debate: From Intolerance to Coexistence*, Wien and Zürich: LIT.

Majawa, C. (2005) 'An African Shepherding Ecclesiology in Migrating Process, The Local Church's Commitment to Refugess and the Internally Displaced Persons', unpublished Seminar Paper, University of Eastern Africa, Nairobi (Kenya).

Martin, D. (2002) *Pentecostalism: The World Their Parish*, Oxford: Blackwell Publishers.

Maluleke T. (2005) 'African Theology', in: David F.Ford and Rachel Muers (eds), *The Modern Theologians, An Introduction*, Oxford: Blackwell Publishing.

Meienberg, H. (2008)'Afrika, re-kolonisiert, unter die Räuber gefallen', *Missionsblätter der Benediktiner-Missionare Uznach*, No. 112, 4 September – October.

Message of Pope Paul VI on World Day of Peace, January 1, 1972. Zenit.org, Rome, 27th February, 2009.

Mexico and U.S bishops' 2003 Pastoral Letter, *Strangers No Longer: Together on the Journey of Hope*, URL: http://www.usccb.org/mrs/stranger.shtml, accessed 28August 2010.

Meyrowitz, J. (2003) 'Global Nomads in the Digital Veldt', in: Kristof Nyiri (ed.), *Mobile Democracy, Essays on Society, Self and Politics*, Vienna: Passagen Verlag.

'Migrations' (1985) in: *Pontifical Commission for the Pastoral of Migrants and Itinerant Peoples: Interdisciplinary Studies*, Vol. 1, (Introduction).

'Mission' URL : http://www.diakonia-online.net/d5_leitartikel_2008.pdf, accessed 21 February 2009.

Mitchell, J. (2009) 'Decolonising Religion in African Film', in: *Studies in World Christianity*, Vol.15, Part 2.

'MIVA-Christophorus Aktion 2009', 26th July.

'Mobile phones boom in Tanzania', URL: http://news.bbc.co.uk/2/hi/programmes/click_online/4706437.stm, accessed 11August 2010.

Molony, T. (2009) 'Trading places in Tanzania: Mobility and marginalization at a time of travel-saving technologies', in: Mirjam de Bruijn, Francis Nyamnjoh and Inge Brinkman (eds) *Mobile phones: The New Talking Drums of Everyday Africa*, Leiden: Langaa &African Studies Centre.

Mpogole, Hosea, H. Usanga, M. Tedre, 'Mobile Phones and Poverty Alleviation: A Survey Study in Rural Tanzania', URL: ict4dblog.files.wordpress.com, accessed 10 August 2010.

'Myths hamper AIDS education programmes', URL: http://www.newsfromafrica.org/newsfromafrica/articles/art_801.html, accessed 6 July 2009.

New African (2009), No.486 July.

New African Woman (2009), No.6, January.

Newbigin, L. (1989) *The Gospel in a Pluralist Society*, Grand Rapids, Michigan: Eerdmans.

'Nokia to provide enterprise software for low-end phones', URL:

http://computerworld.co.ke/articles/2009/02/24/nokia-provide-enterprise-software-low-end-phones, accessed 26 February 2009.

Nyamiti, C. (2007) *Studies in African Christian Theology, Vol. 3, Some Contemporary Models of African Ecclesiology: A Critical Assessment in the Light of Biblical and Church Teaching*, Nairobi: The Catholic University of Eastern Africa (CUEA).

Nyamnjoh F. (2006) *Insiders and Outsiders*, London: Zed Books.

Nolan, A. (2009) *Hope in an Age of Despair: And other Talks and Writings,* Maryknoll, New York: Orbis Books.
'Obama declares to Africa: End tyranny, Corruption', URL: http://news.yahoo.com/s/ap/20090711/ap_on_go_pr_wh/obama, accessed 11 July 2009.

Ong, J. (1982) *Orality and Literacy: The Technologizing of the Word*, London: Methuen & Co. Ltd.

Oosthuizen, C. (2000) 'The Task of African Traditional Religion in the Church's Dilemma in South Africa', in: Jakob K. Olupa (ed.) *African Spirituality, Forms, Meanings, and Expressions*, New York: Crossroad Publishing Company.

Orobator, A. (2010) '*Caritas in veritate* and Africa's Burden of (Under) development', in: *Theological Studies*, Vol. 71, No. 2.

Pacem in Terris (Encyclical Letter of Pope John XXIII on establishing Universal Peace in Truth, Justice, Charity and Liberty), URL: http://www.vatican.va/holy_father/john_xxiii/encyclicals/documents/hf_j-xxiii_enc_11041963_pacem_en.html.

'Paparazzo', URL: http://www.thefreedictionary.com/paparazzi, accessed 25 March 2009.
http://www.800padutch.com/amish.shtml, accessed 23 March 2009.

'Paparazzi-Boom: Handybesitzer machen Jagd auf Promis' URL: https://www.pressetext.at/news/081021001/paparazzi-boom-handybesitzer-machen-jagd-auf-promis/, accessed 25March 2009.

Pastoral Letter issued by the Tanzania Episcopal Conference titled: *Kwangu mimi kuishi ni Kristo (Flp 1:21), Ujumbe wa Kwaresima 2009*, 11 February 2009.

Paul VI (1970) 'Regina Coeli Address', May 17, URL: http://www.civilizationoflove.net/19700517_Summary.htm, accessed 3 November 2008.

Paul, S. (2009) *The Ubuntu God, Deconstructing a South African Narrative of Oppression*, Eugene, Oregon: Pickwick Publications.

Phan, P. (2007) 'Foreword', in: Daniel G. Groody, *Globalisation, Spirituality, and Justice: Navigating the Path to Peace*, Maryknoll, New York: Orbis Books.

Pelckmans, L. (2009) 'Phoning anthropologists: The mobile phone's (re-) shaping of anthropological research', in: Mirjam de Bruijn, Francis Nyamnjoh and Inge Brinkman (eds) *Mobile phones: The New Talking Drums of Everyday Africa*, Leiden: Langaa &African Studies Centre.

Pontifical Council for Justice and Peace (2004) *Compendium of the Social Doctrine of the Church*, Nairobi: Paulines Publications Africa.

'Pope urges Priests to use Communications Media', *Zenit*, 29 September 2009, URL: http://www.zenit.org/article-26998?l=english, accessed 10 June 2010.

Populorum Progressio (Encyclical Letter of Pope Paul VI on the Development of Peoples), URL: http://www.vatican.va/holy_father/paul_vi/encyclicals/documents/hf_p-vi_enc_26031967_populorum_en.html.

Preitler, B. (2004) 'Psychologische Betreuung von Flüchtlingen in Österreich', in: Gerda Mehta (ed.), *Die Praxis der Psychologie, Ein Karriereplaner*, Wien: Springer-Verlag.

Prinsloo, W. (2003) 'The Psalms', in: Dunn J. and Rogerson J (eds), *Commentary on the Bible*, Grand Rapids, Michigan/ Cambridge UK: Eerdmans.

'Quo vadis, Afrika? Interventionen der Synodenteilnehmer zu ausgewähten Themen', in: *Missio Korrespondenz*, No. 4, 2009.

Radcliffe, T. (2005) *What is the Point of Being a Christian?* New York: Burns & Oates.

Radcliffe, T. (2008) *Why Go to Church? The drama of the Eucharist*, London: Continuum.

Rah, S. (2009) *The Next Evangelicalism: Releasing the Church from Western Cultural Captivity*, Downers Grove, Illinois: InterVarsity Press.

Rahner, K (ed.) (1975) *Encyclopedia of Theology: A Concise Sacramentum Mundi*, London: Burn and Oates.

Redemptoris Missio (Encyclical Letter of Pope John Paul II on the permanent validity of the Church's missionary mandate), URL: http://www.vatican.va/edocs/ENG0219/_INDEX.HTM

Religion and Theology, A Journal of Contemporary Religious Discourse (2008), Volume 15/3-4.

'Renewing the Earth: An Invitation to Reflection and Action on the Environment in Light of Catholic Social Teaching', URL: www.usccb.org/sdwp/ejp/bishopsstatement.shtml, accessed 10 January 2010.

'Rev. Lowery Inauguration Benediction Transcript', URL: http://blogs.suntimes.com/sweet/2009/01/rev_lowery_inauguration_benedi.html, accessed 12 March 2009.

Rerum Novarum (Encyclical Letter of Pope Leo XIII on the Situation of Workers), URL: http://www.vatican.va/holy_father/leo_xiii/encyclicals/docume nts/hf_l-xiii_enc_15051891_rerum-novarum_sp.html

'Residents may soon be receiving mobile calls via God', URL:http://deadlinescotland.wordpress.com/2009/01/07/resid ents-may-soon-be-receiving-mobile-calls-via-god-451/, accessed 9 March 2009.

Sandercock, L. (1998) *Towards Cosmopolis: Planning for Multicultural Cities,* John Wiley & Sons.

'Saint Benedict's Rule: Guide for the Ages', URL: http://www.benedictinewomen.org/downloads/RuleOverview020 pdf

Sanneh, L. (2003) *Whose Religion Is Christianity? The Gospel beyond the West, Grand Rapids:* Eerdmans Publishing Company.

Schlagheck , M. (ed.) (2000) *Theologie und Psychologie im Dialog über Identität und Fremdheit*, Paderborn: Bonifatius Druck-Buch Verlag.

Schoberth, W. (2009) 'The Concept of Responsibility: Dilemma and Necessity', in: *Studies in Christian Ethics*, Vol. 22, No. 4.

Schreiter, R.(2008) 'Migrantenseelsorge in einer multikulturellen Kirche', in: *Theologie der Gegenwart,* 51. Jahrgang , Heft 2.

Schreiter, R. (1997) *The New Catholicity: Theology between the Global and the Local* Maryknoll, New York: Orbis Books.

Second African Synod (2010) '"Courage! Get on Your Feet, Continent of Africa"' Homily of His Holiness Benedict XVI at the Concluding Mass and Message of the Bishops of Africa to the People of God, Nairobi: Pauline Publications Africa.

Senior, D. and C. Stuhlmueller (1983) *The Biblical Foundations for Mission*, New York: Orbis Books.

Shorter, A. and J. Njiru (2001) *New Religious Movements in Africa*, Nairobi: Paulines Publications Africa.

Sivalon, J. (1992) *Kanisa Katoliki na Siasa ya Tanzania Bara 1953 hadi 1985* (the Catholic Church and politics in Tanzania Mainland), Ndanda-Peramiho: Benedictine Publications, Tanzania.

Sofield L.and C. Juliano (2000) *Collaboration, Uniting our Gifts in Ministry* Notre Dame: Ave Maria Press.

Stambach, A. (2010) *Faith in Schools: Religion, Education, and American Evangelicals in East Africa*, Stanford: Stanford University Press.

'Statement on Prosperity Gospel' by the Lausanne Theology Working Group, Africa chapter, at its consultations in Akropong, Ghana, 8-9 October, 2008 and 1-4 September 2009. URL: http://www.christianitytoday.com/ct/2009/decemberweb-only/gc-prosperitystatement.html, accessed 8 January 2010.

Sundkler B. and C. Steed (2000) *A History of the Church in Africa*, Cambridge: Cambridge University Press.

'Superstitious Albino Killings in Tanzania Must Stop' URL: http://www.groundreport.com/Opinion/Superstitious-Albino-Killings-in-Tanzania-Must-Sto, accessed 30 March 2009.

Ter Haar G. (2001) *African Christians in Europe* , Nairobi: Acton Publishers.

The African Bible, (1999) Nairobi: Pauline Publications Africa.

The African Courier (2008), Vol.11, No. 62, June/July.

The Guardian 8 May 2010.
The Guardian 24 August 2010.

The Guardian on Sunday 1 February 2009.

'The hunt for Albinos is still on' URL http://observers.france24.com/en/content/20090413-plight-africa-albinos-cameroon-tanzania, accessed 23 May 2009.

Thelle, N. (---) 'Interreligious Dialogue: Theory and Experience', in: Viggo Mortensen (Ed.), *Theology and the Religions: A Dialogue* (Grand Rapids/ Cambridge: Eerdmans.

'Theology of Ministry', URL: http://findarticles.com/p/articles/mi_m1141/is_14_36/ai_5945 0118, accessed 15December 2009.

Thomas, B. (2010) 'Beziehungsarbeit im Netz, christliche Internetseelsorge und Onlineberatung ', in: *Diakonia, Internationale Zeitschrift für die Praxis der Kirche,* 41. Jahrgang, Heft 2, März.

Theological Studies (2009), Vol.70, No.3, September.

Uchendu, V. (1965) *The Igbo of Southeast Nigeria,* New York: Holt, Rinehart and Winston.

Ugboajah, F. (1985) (ed.), *Mass communication, Culture and Society in West Africa,* Munich: Saur.

Ugwuanyi C. (2009) 'Relationships: The Role of Media in Building Healthy Relationships', in: *Beauty Within, A Letter to Young Women,* Vol. 4, July-December.

'Unknown gods, declining churches, and the spiritual search of contemporary culture', URL: http://www.martynmission.cam.ac.uk/CDrane.htm, accessed 24 November 2008.

'U.N. Relief Official Condemns Use of Rape in African Wars', URL http://query.nytimes.com/gst/fullpage.html?res=9D01E6DC103BF931A15755C0A9639C8B63, accessed 10 December 2009.

Veller, R. (1993) 'Der Heilige Geist und die Kirchen zur Auseinandersetzung mit Pfingstkirchen und charismatischen Bewegungen in Ostafrika', in: Winfried Brose and Ulrich van der Heyden (eds) *Mit Kreuz und deutscher Flagge 100 Jahre Evangelium im Süden Tanzania zum Wirken der Berliner Mission in Ostafrika*, Münster, Hamburg: Lit.

'Wachungaji wa kondoo na siasa wapi na wapi?' in: *Habari Leo*, URL: http://www.habarileo.co.tz/uchambuzi/?n=9221, accessed 10 August 2010.

Walsh, G. (1996) *Africa in the Media and the Media in Africa: An Annotated Bibliography*, London: Zell.

Weber, F. (2008) 'Missionsland Kirche', in: *Diakonia, Internationale Zeitschrift für die Praxis der Kirche*, Heft 5, Nr.39.

'When the Church steals your Wife' in: *The Citizen* 6 August 2010, URL: http://allafrica.com/stories/201008061095.html, accessed 7 September 2010.

Wijsen, F. and R. Schreiter (eds) (2007) *Global Christianity, Contested Claims*, Rodopi: Amsterdam-New York.

'Women in South Africa, Domestic Abuse, and Mobile Phones', URL: http://mobileactive.org/taxonomy/term/1239, accessed 12 March 2009.

Yong, A. (2007) *Theology and Down Syndrome: Reclaiming Disability in late Modernity*, Waco: Baylor University Press.

Zulehner, P. and J. Brandner (2006) *Gott ist grösser als unser Herz: (1 Joh 3,20), eine Pastoral des Erbarmens*, Ostfildern : Schwabenverlag.

Zulehner's Press Interview: *Kirchen haben noch eine einzige Chance*, URL: http://www.univie.ac.at/ktf/content/site/pt/aktuelles/zeitworte/article/1475.html, accessed 20 October 2009.